W9-CUI-775

Letters from a
WAR
ZONE

Letters from a WAR ZONE

Writings 1976-1989

Andrea Dworkin

E. P. DUTTON NEW YORK

First published in the United States in 1989 by E. P. Dutton,
a division of Penguin Books USA Inc.,
2 Park Avenue, New York, N.Y. 10016.

Published simultaneously in Canada by
Fitzhenry and Whiteside, Limited, Toronto.

Originally published in Great Britain.

Library of Congress Cataloging-in-Publication Data
Dworkin, Andrea.
    Letters from a war zone.
    1. Feminism.   2. Pornography—Social aspects.
3. Women—Social conditions.   4. Sex discrimination
against women.   I. Title.
HQ1154.D847   1989   305.42   89-11895

ISBN: 0- 525-24824-2

10 9 8 7 6 5 4 3 2 1

First American Edition

For further copyright details and a list of previous places of publication, please see pp. 335–337.

Permission has been generously granted to quote from: Robin Morgan,
"Jottings of a Feminist Activist," in *Lady of the Beasts* (New York: Random House, Inc., 1976); copyright © 1976 by Robin Morgan; permission granted by the author.

The preface to *Right-wing Women* (London: The Women's Press, 1981) is
reprinted with the kind permission of the publishers. An abridged version of "Feminism Now" first appeared under the title "There's still a
long way to go" in *The Sunday Times*, June 28, 1987.

For John

"It does not take a long time," said madame, "for an earthquake to swallow a town. Eh well! Tell me how long it takes to prepare the earthquake?"

"A long time, I suppose," said Defarge.

"But when it is ready, it takes place, and grinds to pieces everything before it. In the meantime, it is always preparing, though it is not seen or heard. That is your consolation. Keep it."

Charles Dickens, *A Tale of Two Cities*

Contents

Letters from a
WAR
ZONE

Introduction

I USED TO work as an assistant to the late poet Muriel Rukeyser. I typed okay, but I was no respecter of margins and I didn't like using capital letters, so I wasn't too useful in preparing business letters. I couldn't file because I could never understand why something should be under one heading and not under another, equally apt in my view. When I went to deliver packages, usually manuscripts, for Muriel, or to pick them up, I usually got into a political fight, or ardent discussion, with whoever answered the door. When I went to the library to do research for her, I would get all the material on her chosen subject, survey it all, decide it was *too* boring and she couldn't have had this in mind at all, and go back with nothing. I was the worst assistant in the history of the world. But Muriel kept me on because she believed in me as a writer. No matter how much I fucked up, I had a job, a little change in my pocket, a warm place to go, lunch and dinner, for as long as I could stand it. She had already decided to stand it: she believed in doing whatever was necessary to keep a writer of talent (in her estimation) going. I don't think she ever would have fired me. She had made great sacrifices in her life for both politics and writing, but none, I suspect, had quite the comic quality of her insistent support for me. Out of mercy (and guilt), I eventually quit.

Muriel gave me my first book party, to celebrate the publication of *Woman Hating*; and I thought that was it—I was a writer (sort of like being an archangel) forever. Everything she had tried to tell me was lost on me. She had tried to make me understand that, for a writer, endurance mattered more than anything—not talent, not luck; endurance. One had to keep writing, not to make a brilliant or distinguished or gorgeous first try, but to keep going, to last over hard time. Endurance, she would say, was the difference between writers who mattered and writers who didn't. She had had rough years. I hope someday her story will be told. It is a heroic story. She knew the cost of keeping at writing in the face of poverty, ostracism, and especially trivialization. She knew how much worse it was to be a woman. She knew that one had to survive many desolations and injuries—one would be both bloodied and bowed; but one had to keep writing anyway—through it, despite it, because of it, around it, in it, under it goddam. I was twenty-six, twenty-seven. I had been through a lot in life, but in writing I was an innocent, a kind of ecstatic idiot. For me, writing was pure, magic, the essence of both integrity and power, uncorrupted by anything mean or mundane. Books were luminous, sacred. Writers were heroes of conscience, intensity, sincerity. I had no idea what it meant to endure over time. I had no idea how hard it was to do.

Now, at forty-one, the truth is that I am still a fool for writing. I love it. I believe in it. I do know now how hard it is to keep going. It is perhaps understatement to say that I have never been a prudent writer. In a sense, I am more reckless now than when I started out because I know what everything costs and it doesn't matter. I have paid a lot to write what I believe to be true. On one level, I suffer terribly from the disdain that much of my work has met. On another, deeper level, I don't give a fuck. It is this indifference to pain—which is real—that enables one to keep going. One develops a warrior's discipline or one stops. Pain becomes irrelevant. Being a writer isn't easy or even very civilized. It is not a bourgeois indulgence. It is not a natural outcome of good manners mixed with intelligence and filtered through language. It is primitive and it is passionate. Writers get underneath the agreed-on amenities, the lies a society depends on to maintain the status quo, by becoming ruthless, pursuing the truth in the face of intimidation, not by being compliant or solicitous. No society likes it and no society says thank you. We think that contemporary western democracies are different but we are wrong. The society will mobilize to destroy the writer who opposes or threatens its favorite cruelties: in this case, the dominance of men over women. I have been asked a lot, by interviewers and by women I meet when I travel to speak, what courage is, or how to be courageous. Often, I think that courage is a kind of stupidity, an incapacity, a terrifying insensitivity to pain and fear. Writers need this kind of courage. The macho men romanticize it. I think it is a partial death of the soul.

These are essays and speeches, an occasional interview or book review, written from 1976 to 1987. I wrote them to communicate and to survive: as a writer and as a woman; for me, the two are one. I wrote them because I care about fairness and justice for women. I wrote them because I believe in bearing witness, and I have seen a lot. I wrote them because people are being hurt and the injury has to stop. I wrote them because I believe in writing, in its power to right wrongs, to change how people see and think, to change how and what people know, to change how and why people act. I wrote them out of the conviction, Quaker in its origin, that one must speak truth to power. This is the basic premise for all my work as a feminist: activism or writing. I wrote these pieces because I believe that women must wage a war against silence: against socially coerced silence; against politically preordained silence; against economically choreographed silence; against the silence created by the pain and despair of sexual abuse and second-class status. And I wrote these essays, gave these speeches, because I believe in people: that we can disavow cruelty and embrace the simple compassion of social equality. I don't know why I believe these things; only that I do believe them and act on them.

Every piece in this book is part of my own war against the silence of women. Only four pieces were published in mainstream magazines with decent, not wonderful, circulations: three were published in *Ms.*, the last one in 1983, and one was published in *Mother Jones* a decade ago. Most of the essays and speeches were published in tiny, ephemeral newspapers, most of which are no longer publishing. Three of these pieces were eventually published in the widely distributed anthology *Take Back the Night*. Seven of these pieces have never been published at all; four have been published in English but have never been published in the United States; one, 'Letter from a War Zone', has been published in German and in Norwegian but never in English; and two (one on *Wuthering Heights* and one on *Voyage in the Dark*) were written for this collection. None of these pieces, despite repeated efforts over years, were published in *The Nation*, *The New Republic*, *The Progressive*, *The Village Voice*, *Inquiry*, left-liberal periodicals that pretend to be freewheeling forums for radical debate and all of which have published vicious articles with nasty, purposeful misrepresentations of what I believe or advocate. Some of my pieces were written in the aftermath of such attacks—most were written in the social environment created by them—but I have never been given any right of response. And none of these pieces, despite repeated efforts over years, have been published in the magazines that presume to intellectual independence: for instance, *The Atlantic* or *Harper's*. And I have never been able to publish anything on the op-ed page of *The New York Times*, even though I have been attacked by name and my politics and my work have been denounced editorially so many times over the last decade that I am dizzy from it. And I have never been able to publish in, say, *Esquire* or *Vogue*, two magazines that publish essays on political issues, including pornography, and also pay writers real money. I have been able to travel in the United States and Canada to speak. If the work in this book has had any influence, that is the main reason.

These essays and speeches present a political point of view, an analysis, information, arguments, that are censored out of the Amerikan press by the Amerikan press to protect the pornographers and to punish me for getting way out of line. I am, of course, a politically dissident writer but by virtue of gender I am a second-class politically dissident writer. That means that I can be erased, maligned, ridiculed in violent and abusive language, and kept from speaking in my own voice by people pretending to stand for freedom of speech. It also means that every misogynist stereotype can be invoked to justify the exclusion, the financial punishment, the contempt, the forced exile from published debate. The fact is that these essays and speeches speak for and to vast numbers of women condemned to silence by this same misogyny, this same sadistic self-righteousness, this same callous disregard for human rights and human dignity. I do know, of course, that I am not supposed to keep on writing. One is supposed to disappear as a writer. I have not. I hope that I will not. I know that some other people share the same hope; and I take this opportunity to thank them for the help they have given me over this decade of trying—as I said earlier—to communicate and to survive, as a writer and as a woman; the two are one for me.

Andrea Dworkin
New York City
November 1987

I

TAKE BACK
THE NIGHT

In legend there is relief from the enemy,
sorrow is turned into gladness, mourning
into holiday.
In life, only some of this is possible.
E. M. Broner, *A Weave of Women*

The Lie

1979

The Lie was written as a speech and given at a rally on October 20, 1979, at Bryant Park, behind New York City's formal and beautiful main public library. This park is usually dominated by drug pushers. It, with the library behind it, marks the lower boundary of Times Square, the sexual-abuse capital of industrialized Amerika. 5000 people, overwhelmingly women, had marched on Times Square in a demonstration organized by Women Against Pornography and led by Susan Brownmiller, Gloria Steinem, and Bella Abzug, among others. The March had begun at Columbus Circle at West 59 Street, the uppermost boundary of the Times Square area, and the rally at Bryant Park marked its conclusion. For the first time, Times Square didn't belong to the pimps; it belonged to women—not women hurt and exploited for profit but women proud and triumphant. The March served notice on pornographers that masses of women could rise up and stop the organized trafficking in women and girls that was the usual activity on those very mean streets. Feminists took the ground but didn't hold it.

THERE IS ONE message basic to all kinds of pornography from the sludge that we see all around us, to the artsy-fartsy pornography that the intellectuals call erotica, to the under-the-counter kiddie porn, to the slick, glossy men's "entertainment" magazines. The one message that is carried in all pornography all the time is this: she wants it; she wants to be beaten; she wants to be forced; she wants to be raped; she wants to be brutalized; she wants to be hurt. This is the premise, the first principle, of all pornography. She wants these despicable things done to her. She likes it. She likes to be hit and she likes to be hurt and she likes to be forced.

9

Meanwhile, all across this country, women and young girls are being raped and beaten and forced and brutalized and hurt.

The police believe they wanted it. Most of the people around them believe they wanted it. "And what did you do to provoke him?" the battered wife is asked over and over again when finally she dares to ask for help or for protection. "Did you like it?" the police ask the rape victim. "Admit that something in you wanted it," the psychiatrist urges. "It was the energy you gave out," says the guru. Adult men claim that their own daughters who are eight years old or ten years old or thirteen years old led them on.

The belief is that the female wants to be hurt. The belief is that the female likes to be forced. The proof that she wants it is everywhere: the way she dresses; the way she walks; the way she talks; the way she sits; the way she stands; she was out after dark; she invited a male friend into her house; she said hello to a male neighbor; she opened the door; she looked at a man; a man asked her what time it was and she told him; she sat on her father's lap; she asked her father a question about sex; she got into a car with a man; she got into a car with her best friend's father or her uncle or her teacher; she flirted; she got married; she had sex once with a man and said no the next time; she is not a virgin; she talks with men; she talks with her father; she went to a movie alone; she took a walk alone; she went shopping alone; she smiled; she is home alone, asleep, the man breaks in, and still, the question is asked, "Did you like it? Did you leave the window open just hoping that someone would pop on through? Do you always sleep without any clothes on? Did you have an orgasm?"

Her body is bruised, she is torn and hurt, and still the question persists: did you provoke it? did you like it? is this what you really wanted all along? is this what you were waiting for and hoping for and dreaming of? You keep saying no. Try proving no. Those bruises? Women like to be roughed up a bit. What did you do to lead him on? How did you provoke him? Did you like it?

A boyfriend or a husband or one's parents or even sometimes a female lover will believe that she could have fought him off—if she had really wanted to. She must have really wanted it—if it happened. What was it she wanted? She wanted the force, the hurt, the harm, the pain, the humiliation. Why did she want it? Because she is female and females always provoke it, always want it, always like it.

And how does everyone whose opinion matters know that women want to be forced and hurt and brutalized? Pornography says so. For centuries men have consumed pornography in secret—yes, the lawyers and the legislators and the doctors and the artists and the writers and the scientists and the theologians and the philosophers. And for these same centuries, women have not consumed pornography and women have not been lawyers and legislators and doctors and artists and writers and scientists and theologians and philosophers.

Men believe the pornography, in which the women always want it. Men believe the pornography, in which women resist and say no only so that men will force them and use more and more force and more and more brutality. To this day, men believe the pornography and men do not believe the women who say no.

Some people say that pornography is only fantasy. What part of it is fantasy? Women *are* beaten and raped and forced and whipped and held captive. The violence depicted is true. The acts of violence depicted in pornography are real acts committed against real women and real female children. *The fantasy* is that women want to be abused.

And so we are here today to explain calmly—to shout, to scream, to bellow, to holler—that we women do not want it, not today, not tomorrow, not yesterday. We never will want it and we never have wanted it. The prostitute does not want to be forced and hurt. The homemaker does not want to be forced and hurt. The lesbian does not want to be forced and hurt. The young girl does not want to be forced and hurt.

And because everywhere in this country, daily, thousands of women and young girls are being brutalized—and this is not fantasy—every day women and young girls are being raped and beaten and forced—we will never again accept any depiction of us that has as its first principle, its first premise, that we want to be abused, that we enjoy being hurt, that we like being forced.

That is why we will fight pornography wherever we find it; and we will fight those who justify it and those who make it and those who buy and use it.

And make no mistake: this movement against pornography is a movement against silence—the silence of the real victims. And this movement against pornography is a movement for speech—the speech of those who have been silenced by sexual force, the speech of women and young girls. And we will never, never be silenced again.

The Night and Danger

1979

The Night and Danger was written as a Take Back the Night speech. In New Haven, Connecticut, 2000 women marched. Street prostitutes joined the March and old women in old age homes came out on balconies with lit candles. In Old Dominion, Virginia, blacks and whites, women and men, gays and straights, in the hundreds, joined together in the first political march ever held in Old Dominion, an oligarchal, conservative stronghold, as the name suggests. People marched fourteen miles, as if they didn't want to miss a footpath, under threat of losing their jobs and with the threat of police violence. In Calgary, Canada, women were arrested for demonstrating without a permit, the irony that a March is the safest way (arrests notwithstanding) for women to go out at night lost on the police but not on the women. In Los Angeles, California, the tail end of a double line of 2000 women walking on sidewalks was attacked by men in cars. I don't know how many times I gave this speech, but in giving it I have seen North America and met some of the bravest people around. The Night and Danger has never been published before.

A TAKE BACK THE NIGHT March goes right to our emotional core. We women are especially supposed to be afraid of the night. The night promises harm to women. For a woman to walk on the street at night is not only to risk abuse, but also—according to the values of male domination—to ask for it. The woman who transgresses the boundaries of night is an outlaw who breaks an elementary rule of civilized behavior: a decent woman does not go out—certainly not alone, certainly not *only* with other women—at night. A woman out in the night, not on a leash, is thought to be a slut or an uppity bitch who does not know her place. The policemen of the

13

night—rapists and other prowling men—have the right to enforce the laws of the night: to stalk the female and to punish her. We have all been chased, and many of us have been caught. A woman who knows the rules of civilized society knows that she must hide from the night. But even when the woman, like a good girl, locks herself up and in, night threatens to intrude. Outside are the predators who will crawl in the windows, climb down drainpipes, pick the locks, descend from skylights, to bring the night with them. These predators are romanticized in, for instance, vampire movies. The predators become mist and curl through barely visible cracks. They bring with them sex and death. Their victims recoil, resist sex, resist death, until, overcome by the thrill of it all, they spread their legs and bare their necks and fall in love. Once the victim has fully submitted, the night holds no more terror, because the victim is dead. She is very lovely, very feminine, and very dead. This is the essence of so-called romance, which is rape embellished with meaningful looks.

Night is the time of romance. Men, like their adored vampires, go a-courting. Men, like vampires, hunt. Night licenses so-called romance and romance boils down to rape: forced entry into the domicile which is sometimes the home, always the body and what some call the soul. The female is solitary and/or sleeping. The male drinks from her until he is sated or until she is dead. The traditional flowers of courtship are the traditional flowers of the grave, delivered to the victim before the kill. The cadaver is dressed up and made up and laid down and ritually violated and consecrated to an eternity of being used. All distinctions of will and personality are obliterated and we are supposed to believe that the night, not the rapist, does the obliterating.

Men use the night to erase us. It was Casanova, whom men reckon an authority, who wrote that "when the lamp is taken away, all women are alike."[1] The annihilation of a woman's personality, individuality, will, character, is prerequisite to male sexuality, and so the night is the sacred time of male sexual celebration because it is dark and in the dark it is easier not to see: not to see who she is. Male sexuality, drunk on its intrinsic contempt for all life, but especially for women's lives, can run wild, hunt down random victims, use the dark for cover, find in the dark solace, sanction, and sanctuary.

Night is magical for men. They look for prostitutes and pick-ups at night. They do their so-called lovemaking at night. They get drunk

14

and roam the streets in packs at night. They fuck their wives at night. They have their fraternity parties at night. They commit their so-called seductions at night. They dress up in white sheets and burn crosses at night. The infamous Crystal Night, when German Nazis firebombed and vandalized and broke the windows of Jewish shops and homes throughout Germany—the Crystal Night, named after the broken glass that covered Germany when the night had ended—the Crystal Night, when the Nazis beat up or killed all the Jews they could find, all the Jews who had not locked themselves in securely enough—the Crystal Night that foreshadowed the slaughter to come—is the emblematic night. The values of the day become the obsessions of the night. Any hated group fears the night, because in the night all the despised are treated as women are treated: as prey, targeted to be beaten or murdered or sexually violated. We fear the night because men become more dangerous in the night.

In the United States, with its distinctly racist character, the very fear of the dark is manipulated, often subliminally, into fear of black, of black men in particular, so that the traditional association between rape and black men that is our national heritage is fortified. In this context, the imagery of black night suggests that black is inherently dangerous. In this context, the association of night, black men, and rape becomes an article of faith. Night, the time of sex, becomes also the time of race—racial fear and racial hatred. The black male, in the South hunted at night to be castrated and/or lynched, becomes in the racist United States the carrier of danger, the carrier of rape. The use of a racially despised type of male as a scapegoat, a symbolic figure embodying the sexuality of all men, is a common male-supremacist strategy. Hitler did the same to the Jewish male. In the urban United States, the prostitute population is disproportionately made up of black women, streetwalkers who inhabit the night, prototypical female figures, again scapegoats, symbols carrying the burden of male-defined female sexuality, of woman as commodity. And so, among the women, night is the time of sex and also of race: racial exploitation and sexual exploitation are fused, indivisible. Night and black: sex and race: the black men are blamed for what all men do; the black women are used as all women are used, but they are singularly and intensely punished by law and social mores; and to untangle this cruel knot, so much a part of each and every night, we will have to take back the night so that it cannot be used to destroy us by race or by sex.

Night means, for all women, a choice: danger or confinement. Confinement is most often dangerous too—battered women are confined, a woman raped in marriage is likely to be raped in her own home. But in confinement, we are promised a lessening of danger, and in confinement we try to avoid danger. The herstory of women has been one of confinement: physical limitation, binding, movement forbidden, action punished. Now, again, everywhere we turn, the feet of women are bound. A woman tied up is the literal emblem of our condition, and everywhere we turn, we see our condition celebrated: women in bondage, tied and bound. Actor George Hamilton, one of the new Count Draculae, asserts that "[e]very woman fantasizes about a dark stranger who manacles her. Women don't have fantasies about marching with Vanessa Redgrave."[2] He doesn't seem to realize that we do have fantasies about Vanessa Redgrave marching with us. The erotic celebration of women in bondage is the religion of our time; and sacred literature and devotional films, like the bound foot, are everywhere. The significance of bondage is that it forbids freedom of movement. Hannah Arendt wrote that "[o]f all the specific liberties which may come into our minds when we hear the word 'freedom,' freedom of movement is historically the oldest and also the most elementary. Being able to depart for where we will is the prototypal gesture of being free, as limitation of freedom of movement has from time immemorial been the precondition for enslavement. Freedom of movement is also the indispensable condition for action, and it is in action that men primarily experience freedom in the world."[3] The truth is that men do experience freedom of movement and freedom in action and that women do not. We must recognize that freedom of movement is a precondition for freedom of anything else. It comes before freedom of speech in importance because without it freedom of speech cannot in fact exist. So when we women struggle for freedom, we must begin at the beginning and fight for freedom of movement, which we have not had and do not now have. In reality, we are not allowed out after dark. In some parts of the world, women are not allowed out at all but we, in this exemplary democracy, are permitted to totter around, half crippled, during the day, and for this, of course, we must be grateful. Especially we must be grateful because jobs and safety depend on the expression of gratitude through cheerful conformity, sweet passivity, and submission artfully designed to meet the particular tastes of the males we must please. We must be grateful—unless we are prepared to resist confinement—to resist being locked in and tied up—to resist being bound and gagged and used and kept and kept in and pinned down and conquered and taken and possessed and decked out like toy dolls that have to be wound up to move at all. We must be grateful—unless we are prepared to resist the images of women tied and bound and humiliated and used. We must be grateful unless we are prepared to demand—no, to take—freedom of movement for ourselves because we know it to be a precondition for every other freedom that we must want if we want freedom at all. We must be grateful—unless we are willing to say with the Three Marias of Portugal: "Enough./It is time to cry: Enough. And to form a barricade with our bodies."[4]

I think that we have been grateful for the small favors of men long enough. I think that we are sick to death of being grateful. It is as if we are forced to play Russian roulette; each night, a gun is placed against our temples. Each day, we are strangely grateful to be alive. Each day we forget that one night it will be our turn, the random will no longer be random but specific and personal, it will be me or it will be you or it will be someone that we love perhaps more than we love ourselves. Each day we forget that we barter everything we have and get next to nothing in return. Each day we make do, and each night we become captive or outlaw—likely to be hurt either way. It is time to cry "Enough," but it is not enough to cry "Enough." We must use our bodies to say "Enough"—we must form a barricade with our bodies, but the barricade must move as the ocean moves and be formidable as the ocean is formidable. We must use our collective strength and passion and endurance to take back this night and every night so that life will be worth living and so that human dignity will be a reality. What we do here tonight is that simple, that difficult, and that important.

Notes

1. Giacomo Casanova, *History of My Life*, trans. Willard R. Trask (New York: Harcourt Brace Jovanovich, 1971), Vol. 11, p. 15.

2. Jean Cox Penn and Jill Barber, "The New Draculas Become the Kinkiest Sex Symbols Ever," *Us*, Vol. III, No. 7, p. 27.

3. Hannah Arendt, *Men in Dark Times* (New York: Harcourt, Brace & World, Inc., 1968), p. 9.

4. Maria Isabel Barreno, Maria Teresa Horta, and Maria Velho da Costa, *The Three Marias: New Portuguese Letters*, trans. Helen R. Lane (New York: Bantam Books, 1976), p. 275.

Pornography and Grief
1978

Pornography and Grief was written as a speech for a Take Back the Night March that was part of the first feminist conference on pornography in the United States in San Francisco, November 1978. Organized by the now defunct Women Against Violence in Pornography and Media (WAVPM), over 5000 women from thirty states participated and we shut down San Francisco's pornography district for one night. The ground was taken but not held.

I SEARCHED FOR something to say here today quite different from what I am going to say. I wanted to come here militant and proud and angry as hell. But more and more, I find that anger is a pale shadow next to the grief I feel. If a woman has any sense of her own intrinsic worth, seeing pornography in small bits and pieces can bring her to a useful rage. Studying pornography in quantity and depth, as I have been doing for more months than I care to remember, will turn that same woman into a mourner.

The pornography itself is vile. To characterize it any other way would be to lie. No plague of male intellectualisms and sophistries can change or hide that simple fact. Georges Bataille, a philosopher of pornography (which he calls "eroticism"), puts it clearly: "In essence, the domain of eroticism is the domain of violence, of violation."[1] Mr Bataille, unlike so many of his peers, is good enough to make explicit that the whole idea is to violate the female. Using the language of grand euphemism so popular with male intellectuals who write on the subject of pornography, Bataille informs us that "[t]he passive, female side is essentially the one that is dissolved as a separate entity."[2] To be "dissolved"—by any means necessary—is the role of

19

women in pornography. The great male scientists and philosophers of sexuality, including Kinsey, Havelock Ellis, Wilhelm Reich, and Freud, uphold this view of our purpose and destiny. The great male writers use language more or less beautifully to create us in self-serving fragments, half-"dissolved" as it were, and then proceed to "dissolve" us all the way, by any means necessary. The biographers of the great male artists celebrate the real life atrocities those men have committed against us, as if those atrocities are central to the making of art. And in history, as men have lived it, they have "dissolved" us—by any means necessary. The slicing of our skins and the rattling of our bones are the energizing sources of male-defined art and science, as they are the essential content of pornography. The visceral experience of a hatred of women that literally knows no bounds has put me beyond anger and beyond tears; I can only speak to you from grief.

We all expected the world to be different than it is, didn't we? No matter what material or emotional deprivation we have experienced as children or as adults, no matter what we understood from history or from the testimonies of living persons about how people suffer and why, we all believed, however privately, in human possibility. Some of us believed in art, or literature, or music, or religion, or revolution, or in children, or in the redeeming potential of eroticism or affection. No matter what we knew of cruelty, we all believed in kindness; and no matter what we knew of hatred, we all believed in friendship or love. Not one of us could have imagined or would have believed the simple facts of life as we have come to know them: the rapacity of male greed for dominance; the malignancy of male supremacy; the virulent contempt for women that is the very foundation of the culture in which we live. The Women's Movement has forced us all to face the facts, but no matter how brave and clear-sighted we are, no matter how far we are willing to go or are forced to go in viewing reality without romance or illusion, we are simply overwhelmed by the male hatred of our kind, its morbidity, its compulsiveness, its obsessiveness, its celebration of itself in every detail of life and culture. We think that we have grasped this hatred once and for all, seen it in its spectacular cruelty, learned its every secret, got used to it or risen above it or organized against it so as to be protected from its worst excesses. We think that we know all there is to know about what men do to women, even if we cannot imagine why they do what they do, when something happens that simply drives us mad, out of our minds, so that we are again imprisoned like caged animals in the numbing reality of male control, male revenge against no one knows what, male hatred of our very being.

One can know everything and still not imagine snuff films. One can know everything and still be shocked and terrified when a man who attempted to make snuff films is released, despite the testimony of the women undercover agents whom he wanted to torture, murder, and, of course, film. One can know everything and still be stunned and paralyzed when one meets a child who is being continuously raped by her father or some close male relative. One can know everything and still be reduced to sputtering like an idiot when a woman is prosecuted for attempting to abort herself with knitting needles, or when a woman is imprisoned for killing a man who has raped or tortured her, or is raping or torturing her. One can know everything and still want to kill and be dead simultaneously when one sees a celebratory picture of a woman being ground up in a meat grinder on the cover of a national magazine, no matter how putrid the magazine. One can know everything and still somewhere inside refuse to believe that the personal, social, culturally sanctioned violence against women is unlimited, unpredictable, pervasive, constant, ruthless, and happily and unselfconsciously sadistic. One can know everything and still be unable to accept the fact that sex and murder are fused in the male consciousness, so that the one without the imminent possibility of the other is unthinkable and impossible. One can know everything and still, at bottom, refuse to accept that the annihilation of women is the source of meaning and identity for men. One can know everything and still want desperately to know nothing because to face what we know is to question whether life is worth anything at all.

The pornographers, modern and ancient, visual and literary, vulgar and aristocratic, put forth one consistent proposition: erotic pleasure for men is derived from and predicated on the savage destruction of women. As the world's most honored pornographer, the Marquis de Sade (called by male scholars "The Divine Marquis"), wrote in one of his more restrained and civil moments: "There's not a woman on earth who'd ever have had cause to complain of my services if I'd been sure of being able to kill her afterward."[3] The eroticization of murder is the essence of pornography, as it is the essence of life. The torturer may be a policeman tearing the fingernails off a victim in a prison cell or a so-called normal man engaged in the project of attempting to fuck a woman to death. The fact is that the process of killing—and both rape and battery are steps in that process—is the prime sexual act for men in reality and/or in imagination. Women as a class must remain in bondage, subject to the sexual will of men, because the knowledge of an imperial right to kill, whether exercised to the fullest extent or just part way, is necessary to fuel sexual appetite and behavior. Without women as potential or actual victims, men are, in the current sanitized jargon, "sexually dysfunctional." This same motif also operates among male homosexuals, where force and/or convention designate some males as female or feminized. The plethora of leather and chains among male homosexuals, and the newly fashionable defenses of organized rings of boy prostitution by supposedly radical gay men, are testimony to the fixedness of the male compulsion to dominate and destroy that is the source of sexual pleasure for men.

The most terrible thing about pornography is that it tells male truth. The most insidious thing about pornography is that it tells male truth as if it were universal truth. Those depictions of women in chains being tortured are supposed to represent our deepest erotic aspirations. And some of us believe it, don't we? The most important thing about pornography is that the values in it are the common values of men. This is the crucial fact that both the male Right and the male Left, in their differing but mutually reinforcing ways, want to keep hidden from women. The male Right wants to hide the pornography, and the male Left wants to hide its meaning. Both want access to pornography so that men can be encouraged and energized by it. The Right wants secret access; the Left wants public access. But whether we see the pornography or not, the values expressed in it are the values expressed in the acts of rape and wife-beating, in the legal system, in religion, in art and in literature, in systematic economic discrimination against women, in the moribund academies, and by the good and wise and kind and enlightened in all of these fields and areas. Pornography is not a genre of expression separate and different from the rest of life; it is a genre of expression fully in harmony with any culture in which it flourishes. This is so whether it is legal or illegal. And, in either case, pornography functions to perpetuate male supremacy and crimes of violence against women because it conditions, trains, educates, and inspires men to despise women, to use women, to hurt women. Pornography exists because men despise women, and men despise women in part because pornography exists.

For myself, pornography has defeated me in a way that, at least so far, life has not. Whatever struggles and difficulties I have had in my life, I have always wanted to find a way to go on even if I did not know how, to live through one more day, to learn one more thing, to take one more walk, to read one more book, to write one more paragraph, to see one more friend, to love one more time. When I read or see pornography, I want everything to stop. Why, I ask, why are they so damned cruel and so damned proud of it? Sometimes, a detail drives me mad. There is a series of photographs: a woman slicing her breasts with a knife, smearing her own blood on her own body, sticking a sword up her vagina. *And she is smiling.* And it is the smile that drives me mad. There is a record album plastered all over a huge display window. The picture on the album is a profile view of a woman's thighs. Her crotch is suggested because we know it is there; it is not shown. The title of the album is "Plug Me to Death." And it is the use of the first person that drives me mad. "Plug Me to Death." The arrogance. The cold-blooded arrogance. And how can it go on like this, senseless, entirely brutal, inane, day after day and year after year, these images and ideas and values pouring out, packaged, bought and sold, promoted, enduring on and on, and no one stops it, and our darling boy intellectuals defend it, and elegant radical lawyers argue for it, and men of every sort cannot and will not live without it. And life, which means everything to me, becomes meaningless, because these celebrations of cruelty destroy my very capacity to feel and to care and to hope. I hate the pornographers most of all for depriving me of hope.

The psychic violence in pornography is unbearable in and of itself. It acts on one like a bludgeon until one's sensibility is pummelled flat and one's heart goes dead. One becomes numb. Everything stops, and one looks at the pages or pictures and knows: this is what men want, and this is what men have had, and this is what men will not give up.

As lesbian-feminist Karla Jay pointed out in an article called "Pot, Porn, and the Politics of Pleasure," men will give up grapes and lettuce and orange juice and Portuguese wine and tuna fish, but men will not give up pornography. And yes, one wants to take it from them, to burn it, to rip it up, bomb it, raze their theaters and publishing houses to the ground. One can be part of a revolutionary movement or one can mourn. Perhaps I have found the real source of my grief: we have not yet become a revolutionary movement.

Tonight we are going to walk together, all of us, to take back the night, as women have in cities all over the world, because in every sense none of us can walk alone. Every woman walking alone is a target. Every woman walking alone is hunted, harassed, time after time harmed by psychic or physical violence. Only by walking together can we walk at all with any sense of safety, dignity, or freedom. Tonight, walking together, we will proclaim to the rapists and pornographers and woman-batterers that their days are numbered and our time has come. And tomorrow, what will we do tomorrow? Because, sisters, the truth is that we have to take back the night every night, or the night will never be ours. And once we have conquered the dark, we have to reach for the light, to take the day and make it ours. This is our choice, and this is our necessity. It is a revolutionary choice, and it is a revolutionary necessity. For us, the two are indivisible, as we must be indivisible in our fight for freedom. Many of us have walked many miles already—brave, hard miles—but we have not gone far enough. Tonight, with every breath and every step, we must commit ourselves to going the distance: to transforming this earth on which we walk from prison and tomb into our rightful and joyous home. This we must do and this we will do, for our own sakes and for the sake of every woman who has ever lived.

Notes

1. Georges Bataille, *Death and Sensuality* (New York: Ballantine Books, Inc., 1969), p. 10.

2. Bataille, *Death and Sensuality*, p. 11.

3. Donatien-Alphonse-François de Sade, *Juliette*, trans. Austryn Wainhouse (New York: Grove Press, Inc., 1976), p. 404.

II

W O R D S

Live as domestic a life as possible. Have
your child with you all the time.... Lie
down an hour after each meal. Have but
two hours' intellectual life a day. And never
touch pen, brush or pencil as long as you
live.

Dr S. Weir Mitchell's
prescription for Charlotte
Perkins Gilman

The Power of Words

1978

In the spring of 1978, the Massachusetts Daily Collegian, *the school newspaper of the University of Massachusetts at Amherst, became a battleground for women's rights. Women journalists reporting on so-called women's issues, including, as I remember, the DES health emergency, were censored: their stories were suppressed or cut to pieces. They were lectured sanctimoniously about free speech and the high calling of objective journalism by boy editors even as they were being denied access to print. The women fought back. Julie Melrose, women's editor, was threatened and an atmosphere of violence was palpable. The male editors especially aroused anger against the women by calling them lesbians.* The Power of Words *is about the hate campaign these male editors waged. Instead of being intimidated, the women occupied the offices of the newspaper and appropriated its equipment to put out an insurgent newspaper (in which* The Power of Words *was published). They set up a blockade, physically resisting efforts to remove them. They held the offices for twelve days. The Chancellor of the University set up a commission to investigate their charges. His commission recommended separate women's pages and autonomy. The Chancellor refused to implement the recommendations. A few years ago, a man was made women's editor. The claim was that no qualified woman existed.* The Power of Words *was given as a speech at a rally to support the occupiers when they were still inside. Robin Morgan and Janice Raymond also spoke; and Simone de Beauvoir sent a message of solidarity. Feminists do fight for freedom of speech when it is a real fight for real freedom of real speech.*

IN BERLIN, IN the late 1920s, Joseph Goebbels, soon to be Nazi Minister of Propaganda under Hitler, organized an anti-Semitic propaganda campaign that took the form of cartoons. These cartoons all ridiculed one individual, a Jewish police official. In one cartoon this man, broadly caricatured with a huge, crooked nose and derisively nicknamed "Isidor," is sitting on a pavement. He is leaning against a lamppost. A rope is around his neck. Flags emblazoned with swastikas fly from the rooftops. The caption reads: "For him too, Ash Wednesday will come." "Isidor" became a mocking synonym for Jew; the cartoons became a vehicle for attributing repulsive characteristics and behaviors to Jews as a group. The police official sued Goebbels to stop publication of the libelous, malicious material. Goebbels, making full use of democratic protections ensuring free speech, was acquitted. On appeal, his acquittal was upheld because the court equated the word Jew with Protestant or Catholic. If there was no insult involved in calling a Protestant a Protestant, how could there be injury in calling a Jew a Jew?

In a world with no history of persecuting Jews because they are Jews, the decision would have made sense. But in this world, the one we still live in, all words do not have equal weight. Some words can be used to provoke the deepest hatred, the most resilient impulses toward slaughter. Jew is one such word. Goebbels used it cynically, with cunning, to provoke a genocide of nearly unparalleled monstrosity.

Another word that can be manipulated to induce both fear and violence is the word lesbian. In a time of burgeoning feminism, it is this word that spreaders of hate spit, whisper, and shout with varying degrees of contempt, ridicule, and threat.

We cannot afford to make the mistake made by the pre-Nazi German court: we cannot afford to overlook the real power and the real meaning of words or the real uses to which words are put.

It is no secret that fear and hatred of homosexuals permeate our society. But the contempt for lesbians is distinct. It is directly rooted in the abhorrence of the self-defined woman, the self-determining woman, the woman who is not controlled by male need, imperative, or manipulation. Contempt for lesbians is most often a political repudiation of women who organize in their own behalf to achieve public presence, significant power, visible integrity.

Enemies of women, those who are determined to deny us freedom and dignity, use the word lesbian to provoke a hatred of women who do not conform. This hatred rumbles everywhere. This hatred is sustained and expressed by virtually every institution. When male power is challenged, this hatred can be intensified and inflamed so that it is volatile, palpable. The threat is that this hatred will explode into violence. The threat is omnipresent because violence against women is culturally applauded. And so the word lesbian, hurled or whispered as accusation, is used to focus male hostility on women who dare to rebel, and it is also used to frighten and bully women who have not yet rebelled.

When a word is used to provoke hatred, it does not matter what the word actually means. What matters is only what the haters insist it means—the meaning they give it, the common prejudices they exploit. In the case of the word lesbian, the haters use it to impute a gross, deviant masculinity to the uppity woman who insists on taking her place in the world. To women raised to be beautiful, compliant, and desirable (all in male terms), the word lesbian connotes a foul, repellent abnormality. It brings up women's deep dread of exile, isolation, and punishment. For women controlled by men, it means damnation.

It is horrifying, but not surprising, that the males on the *Collegian*—these boys who before your very eyes are becoming men—have used the word lesbian in the malicious way I have just described. With contempt and ridicule, they have been waging a furtive, ruthless propaganda campaign against the feminist occupiers. They are using the word lesbian to rouse the most virulent woman-hating on this campus. They are using the word lesbian to direct male hostility and aggression against the feminist occupiers. They are using the word lesbian to dismiss every just charge the feminist occupiers have made against them. They are using the word lesbian to justify their own rigid opposition to the simple and eminently reasonable demands these women have made. They are using the word lesbian to hide the true history of their own woman-hating malice in running that corrupt, pretentious, utterly hypocritical newspaper. They are using the word lesbian to cover over the threats of violence made before the occupation against the head of the Women's Department—threats of violence made by her male colleagues. They are using the word lesbian to cover up their consistent, belligerent refusal to publish crucial women's news. And, painfully but inevitably, they are using the word lesbian to divide

29

women from women, to keep women staffers in line, to discourage them from associating with feminists or thinking for themselves. Intimidated by the malicious use of the word lesbian, women are afraid of guilt by association. Hearing the derision *and* the threats, good girls, smart girls, do what is expected of them.

Feminists are occupying the offices of the *Collegian* because words matter. Words can be used to educate, to clarify, to inform, to illuminate. Words can also be used to intimidate, to threaten, to insult, to coerce, to incite hatred, to encourage ignorance. Words can make us better or worse people, more compassionate or more prejudiced, more generous or more cruel. Words matter because words significantly determine what we know and what we do. Words change us or keep us the same. Women, deprived of words, are deprived of life. Women, deprived of a forum for words, are deprived of the power necessary to ensure both survival and well-being.

When all news pertaining to women is omitted from a newspaper, or distorted beyond recognition, a crime is being committed against women. It is a bitter irony that this crime is euphemistically called "objective journalism." It is another bitter irony that when women attempt to stop the crime, they are accused of impeding something called "free speech." It is interesting that the phrase "objective journalism" always means the exclusion of hard-hitting women's news and it is curious how the valiant defenders of so-called free speech threaten violence to shut women up. Marxists call these perplexing phenomena "contradictions." Feminists call them facts.

I say to you that the men who control the *Collegian* have used words to foster ignorance and to encourage bigotry; to keep women invisible, misinformed, and silent; to threaten and bully; to ridicule and demean. It is shameful to continue to tolerate their flagrant contempt for women, for lesbians; for words, for news, for simple fairness and equity. It is honorable and right to take from them the power they have so abused. I hope that you will strip them of it altogether. In the words of the great Emmeline Pankhurst, "I incite this meeting to rebellion."

A Woman Writer and Pornography
1980

A part of this essay was published as an Afterword to both the British and German editions of Pornography: Men Possessing Women. *In the United States, the whole essay was published in a small literary review. I wonder if even a thousand people had the opportunity to read it. It took me a year to find that small outlet. Looking back on this essay now, I can only say that I considerably understated the effects pornography has had on me; no doubt I was afraid of being ridiculed. I know some of the most brilliant, and certainly the strongest, women of my time, and there is nothing unique in pornography's effect on me.*

WRITING IS NOT a happy profession. The writer lives and works in solitude, no matter how many people surround her. Her most intensely lived hours are spent with herself. The pleasures and pains of writing are talked around or about but not shared. Her friends do not know what she does or how she does it. Like everyone else, they see only the results. The problems of her work are unique. The solution to one sentence is not the solution to any other sentence. No one else knows where she is going until she herself has gotten there. When others are contemplating the results, she is on her next project, all alone again. Her colleagues and competitors for the most part are dead. The work itself involves using the mind in an intense and punishing way. The solitude demanded by the work is extreme in and of itself. Others rarely live so alone, so self-created. She is not a male writer, which means that she cleans her own toilet and does her own laundry. If she is ruthless and singleminded, she does only her own portion of the housework, not his or theirs. The rewards of her work are in her work. There are no weekly wages, no health benefits, no promotions, no cost of living raises, no job descriptions. When she does actually earn money, it will be in a lump sum that must presumably last forever. If she becomes a "celebrity" or even "famous," she may gain easier access to print or to money but lose that honest sense of privacy without which even solitude is meaningless. As more and more people know her writing, they think they know her. Her writing goes out into the world brazen and intractable as she faces the blank page in what at best is a room of her own. Her mind and imagination grind on, facing life, facing knowledge, facing creation, while the world around her spits on or chatters about what she has already done and nearly forgotten. Writing is absolutely extreme, at once irredeemably individual and irredeemably social. No writer can explain how she does what she does so that another can replicate the process and come up with the same results; at the same time, only through reading brave and original writers can one learn how to write.

When I go into a bookstore, especially a women's bookstore, I try to stand the lives behind the books in a line: add up the years it took to write all those books, the days and hours spent, the minds used and used, the material resources gone through, the mental trouble, the difficulty of the lives, the sorrow, the great battles behind the books even before the battle for publication could begin. And also the pleasure. The pleasure of the writing, of moving from here to there, of going deeper, of seeing and knowing, of showing. Despite the sexual hysteria of our time, a woman writer's pleasure is not to be measured in orgasms but in writing. It is a pleasure that cannot be shared. The reader's pleasure is different and cheaper.

Each book in a writer's life is another circle of hell: and people choose hell because they love pleasure. A writer's hell is a writer's pleasure not because writers are simple-minded masochists but because writers, whatever their ideologies or protestations, are worldly: mired in time and meaning; not just entranced by the display of the material world or, in contemporary jargon, "the games people play," but infatuated and obsessed with the muck of real life. Writers are arrogant and greedy and ambitious in that experience is not enough, sensation is not enough, knowledge is not enough: one must remake it all, have it all one more time but in another way, a way that cannot be translated or described, only done and experienced. Writing is not one step removed from life; it is as intense and consuming as anything life has to offer. But love happens, earthquakes happen: one must decide to write. It is not an accident. It is willed and it sets one apart. Especially if one is a woman, one is set apart. It is in the privacy and the greed and the punishment of the writing itself that one is set apart.

In writing my new book, I experienced the most intense isolation I have known as a writer. I lived in a world of pictures—women's bodies displayed, women hunched and spread and hanged and pulled and tied and cut—and in a world of books—gang rape, pair rape, man on woman rape, lesbian rape, animal on woman rape, evisceration, torture, penetration, excrement, urine, and bad prose. I worked on the book for three years. After the first year a friend entered my room and remarked that she was more at ease in the local porn stores. A half a year later, the friend with whom I lived asked me quietly and sincerely to refrain from showing him any material I might be working on and also, please, to keep it out of any room other than my own. I have good and kind friends. Their nerves could not withstand even the glimpses they got. I was immersed in it.

Under the best of circumstances, I do not have pleasant dreams. I work while I sleep. Life goes on, awake or asleep. I spent eight months studying the Marquis de Sade. I spent eight months dreaming Sadean dreams. Let the men joke: these were not "erotic" dreams; dreams of torture are dreams of hate, in this case the hate being used against female bodies, the instruments of hate (metal or flesh) being used to maim. Only one woman understood me. She had worked as an editor on the collected volumes of Sade's work at Grove Press. After completing the editing of the first volume, she attended an editorial meeting where plans were being made to do a second volume. She explained that she couldn't stand the nightmares. "We should start making movies of your nightmares," the chief editor told her. They did.

But the nightmares were the least of it. The reading itself made me physically sick. I became nauseous—if I were male, I might dare to say full of fear and trembling and sick unto death. The President's Commission on Pornography and Obscenity (1970) reported this as a frequent effect of pornography on women and then concluded that pornography had no harmful consequences. Personally I consider nausea a harmful consequence, not trivial when the life involved is one's own. I became frightened and anxious and easily irritable. But the worst was that I retreated into silence. I felt that I could not make myself understood, that no one would know or care, and that I could not risk being considered ridiculous. The endless struggle of the woman writer to be taken seriously, to be respected, begins long before any work is in print. It begins in the silence and solitude of her own mind when that mind must diagram and dissect sexual horror.

My work on Sade came to an end, but not before I nearly collapsed from fatigue: physical fatigue because I hated to sleep; physical fatigue because I was often physically sick from the material; mental fatigue because I took on the whole male intellectual tradition that has lionized Sade; but also moral fatigue, the fatigue that comes from confronting the very worst sexual aspirations of men articulated by Sade in graphic detail, the fatigue engendered by sexual cruelty.

The photographs I had to study changed my whole relationship to the physical world in which I live. For me, a telephone became a dildo, the telephone wire an instrument of bondage; a hair dryer became a dildo—those hair dryers euphemistically named "pistols"; scissors were no longer associated with cutting paper but were poised at the vagina's opening. I saw so many photographs of common household objects being used as sexual weapons against women that I despaired of ever returning to my once simple ideas of function. I developed a new visual vocabulary, one that few women have at all, one that male consumers of pornography carry with them all the time: any mundane object can be turned into an eroticized object—an object that can be used to hurt women in a sexual context with a sexual purpose and a sexual meaning. This increased my isolation significantly, since my friends thought I was making bad jokes when I recoiled at certain unselfconscious manipulations of a hair dryer, for instance. A male friend handed me a telephone in an extremely abrupt way. "Don't you ever push that thing at me again," I said in real alarm, knowing whereof I spoke. He, hating pornography, did not.

I had to study the photographs to write about them. I stared at them to analyze them. It took me a long time to see what was in them because I never expected to see what was there, and expectation is essential to accurate perception. I had to learn. A doorway is a doorway. One walks through it. A doorway takes on a different significance when one sees woman after woman hanging from doorways. A lighting fixture is for light until one sees woman after woman hung from lighting fixtures. The commonplace world does not just become sinister; it becomes disgusting, repellent. Pliers are for loosening bolts until one sees them cutting into women's breasts. Saran Wrap is for preserving food until one sees a person mummified in it.

Again, the nausea, the isolation, the despair. But also, increasingly, a rage that had nowhere to go, and a sense of boredom through it all at the mindless and endless repetition in the photographs. No matter how many times women had been hung from light fixtures or doorways, there were always more magazines with more of the same. A friend once said to me about heroin: "The worst thing about it is the endless repetition." One can say the same about pornography, except that it goes beyond anything that one can repeatedly do to oneself: pornography is what men do to women. And the mundane world in which men live is full of doorways and light fixtures and telephones, which may be why the most pervasive abuse of women takes place in the home.

But the worst effect on me was a generalized misanthropy: I could no longer trust anyone's enthusiasms, intellectual, sexual, esthetic, political. Underneath, who were they and would the woman hanging in the doorway matter to them? I felt as if I had walked out on to a sandbar not knowing it to be a sandbar, thinking it merely the shore. Time passed and the sea crept up all around, and I did not see it because I had learned to hate the shore. If I swam and swam and swam to save myself, what would I find if I reached the shore? Would there be anyone there? Or would it be desolation? A smartass remark about pornography was desolation. A trivialization of pornography was desolation. An enthusiasm for pornography was desolation. A detachment from pornography was desolation. An indifference to pornography was desolation. Men made clever small talk. Women did not know. It took everything I had sometimes to dare to talk to a friend about what I had seen. I had been a hopeful radical. Now I am not. Pornography has infected me. Once I was a child and I dreamed of freedom. Now I am an adult and I see what my dreams have come to: pornography. So, while I cannot help my sleeping nightmares, I have given up many waking dreams. As a worldly writer—mired in time and meaning, infatuated and obsessed with the muck of real life—I decided that I wanted women to see what I saw. This may be the most ruthless choice I have ever made. But in the privacy of writing, it was the only choice that gave me the pleasure of writing, that greedy, arrogant pleasure: it was the only choice that enabled me to triumph over my subject by showing it, remaking it, turning it into something that we define and use rather than letting it remain something that defines and uses us. Writing is not a happy profession. It is viciously individual: I, the author, insist that I stand in for us, women. In so doing, I insist on the ultimate social meaning of writing: in facing the nightmare, I want another generation of women to be able to reclaim the dreams of freedom that pornography has taken from me.

Susannah Cibber

1978

I read Mary Nash's wonderful book, The Provoked Wife, *the biography of actress Susannah Cibber, just by accident, because I read a lot without much plan. I loved the book and wanted other women to know about it so I wrote a review of it. I was never able to find a publisher for the review and the book has been out of bookstores for years. Another lost woman lost again in another lost book. No wonder being a found object sounds good to some women.*

The Provoked Wife by Mary Nash
(Boston: Little, Brown and Company, 1977)

RIGHT NOW, I am doing research for a book on pornography. I am reading in history, philosophy, developmental psychology, law, literature, and theater. The work is onerous and often terribly depressing. The worst is reading the great sexual prophets— Havelock Ellis, so-called feminist; Kinsey, so-called sexual liberal; D. H. Lawrence, so-called sexual visionary; and so on, ad nauseam. Without exception, these pioneers of "freedom" are apologists for or advocates of rape and brutality. Their hatred of women permeates their theories, investigations, discoveries. But one vein of research has given me that deep pleasure of seeing women truly revealed: reading biographies and autobiographies of fine actresses, most of them long forgotten, those women who project female presence on a stage even as they portray female suffering, degradation, and the pathetic drama of being the conquered. No book has moved me more deeply than Mary Nash's sensitive and beautifully written life of Susannah Cibber, a superb eighteenth-century actress whose life has been buried in obscurity, even as the legend of her major leading man, David Garrick, has continued to grow over the centuries. She was the great actress of her time. In her acting, she embodied a rare and translucent integrity. And no contemporary woman can read her story without also recognizing that she was a great woman, a survivor as well as an endurer, one who in her private dignity transcended the victimizing circumstances of her personal life.

In Cibber's time, wives and children were chattel property, and it was the custom to make as much profit from them as possible. Children were leased or sold into labor. Cibber's father, recognizing her talent as a singer, forced her onto the stage. Her brother, Thomas Arne, a gifted composer, exploited her talent to establish his own fame. But she excelled him in her singular capacity to discipline her talent, and soon she was recognized in her own right. Her father, as was the custom, forced her into marriage with Theophilus Cibber, an actor and ambitious hustler whose profligacy—rightly called vice—had slowly killed his first wife, also an actress until her husband turned her into an embattled, captive, abandoned wife. Susannah's mother, in an unparalleled act of strength, managed to arrange that the husband-to-be sign an agreement vouchsafing Susannah's earnings to Susannah. This agreement was not honored for many years—one attempt on Susannah's part to get a theater manager to pay her directly led to intense violence on her husband's part—but later in life, Susannah was able to use this agreement to protect her own earnings.

To meet his ever-increasing financial needs, Theophilus forced Susannah to "entertain" an admirer, William Sloper, a wealthy, married man. But Mr Sloper's admiration for Cibber was genuine; he was not looking for a whore. The two became deep friends and, with Theo's encouragement, perhaps his insistence, the friendship developed into a sexual relationship. The three lived at first together, Theo delivering Cibber to Sloper's bedroom. Sloper paid Theo's debts and bills, and Theo remained tyrant, controller.

When Cibber and Sloper tried to escape Theo's malicious protectorate by offering him financial support forever in exchange for independence, Theo, as so many men before and since, found power over a woman even more dear to him than money. He wreaked vengeance on the two: he prosecuted Sloper for seducing his wife, published a transcript of the trial, and Cibber was marked as an adultress and pariah for the rest of her life. Theo's vengeance did not stop there: he kidnapped Cibber, prosecuted Sloper a second time. Afraid of a violent husband who was determined to reclaim her—body and property, if not soul—Cibber was forced to leave England to hide. She was also forced out of her profession.

After three years of isolation, helped especially by Handel, Cibber returned to the stage in Ireland, out of the reach of English law. Eventually she returned to England, her integrity and power as an actress dwarfing the malice of her cruel and pathetic husband. She and Sloper lived together until she died. She bore three children, one of Theo, two with Sloper. Only one (with Sloper) lived into adulthood. One of Cibber's triumphs was that this child, a daughter, made a safe and happy marriage and was accepted back into society.

Like George Eliot, nearly a hundred years later, Cibber worked, she was magnificent, she was famous, and she was shunned. Unlike Eliot, she was exiled for the most part within England, as if contact with the notorious adultress would contaminate those purer persons who are, after all, the very essence of virtue. Even her closest colleague, David Garrick, the actor who owed so much of his ability to realize a character on stage to her artistry and presence, was reluctant to visit her where she lived with Sloper.

In the English theater at that time, it was common practice for actors to manage theater companies. Patents, difficult to obtain and expensive, had to be bought from the government, or the companies were outlaws. Cibber wanted to manage a licensed company with Garrick and another colleague. Rather than share management with a woman, and possibly with this woman in particular, Garrick cunningly held Cibber at bay, while he made and executed other plans, which excluded her. The actress continued to work with him; the woman forgave.

For the last several years of her life, Cibber was in great pain from a stomach ailment, perhaps ulcers or colitis. She degenerated visibly over a long period of time. Garrick continued to ascribe her illness to "temperament," even when she was near death. The evidence, as Nash makes clear, is that Cibber worked despite the debilitation of her illness. She stretched to the outer limits of her physical capacity. When Garrick learned she was dead, he said, "then half of Tragedy is dead." London's two major theaters, bitter rivals, both closed that night to honor and mourn her. She is buried in an anteroom of Westminster Abbey, not in the Abbey itself with Garrick and the other sublime figures of British theater. When Sloper died, his legal family destroyed every remnant of her existence. Today's inhabitants of the Cibber-Sloper house, who are conversant with the history of the restored eighteenth-century dwelling and the Sloper family, know only that "old Sloper" had a mistress, some actress.

We have Garrick's legend, but Nash has given us something finer—Cibber's story. To a profession that has consistently degraded women, Cibber brought integrity. Now, when actresses are compelled to act out for us our most abject humiliations, Cibber's resurrection in this book reminds us that one must not and need not give in.

Whose Press? Whose Freedom?
1983

The editor who published this essay invented the title. I didn't see it before it was published. I didn't anticipate it either. The title suggests that I am dealing with contemporary journalism and conjures up the pornography debate, intentionally I think. But this essay is about male power, misogyny, and literature. The two books reviewed here are intelligent, original books about how men use power to suppress women's deepest, most creative, and most significant speech. Both books should be read if they can be found. People have told me that I was terribly hard on these books. I didn't mean to be. They are about what is killing me—how women's writing is demeaned and how women are kept from publishing. My intemperance and impatience are from pain and also from an acute, detailed knowledge of how this hatred of women's writing is both institutionalized and indulged. So I am not happy with what these books leave out and I keep saying that they have not said enough. But nothing is enough. So let me now thank these writers for these books. I learned from both of them.

How to Suppress Women's Writing by Joanna Russ
(Austin, Texas: University of Texas, 1983)

Intruders on the Rights of Men by Lynne Spender
(Boston: Routledge & Kegan Paul, 1983)

THESE ARE TWO energetic and passionate books. Each analyzes and describes some part of the politics of survival for women writers. Neither conveys the sheer awfulness of the nightmare itself: the nightmare that extends over the course of a life day in and day out; the wearing away of body, mind, and heart from poverty, invisibility, neglect, endemic contempt and humiliation. That is the story of

41

women's writing. When I was younger, I read writers' biographies fast and loved the bravery of enduring any hardship. Now I know that the years are slow, hard, and hungry—there is despair and bitterness—and no volume read in two hours can convey what survival itself was or took. These books both fail to show what survival as a woman writer of talent really costs, what the writing itself costs: and so both shortchange the intense brilliance of much of the women's writing we have.

Russ is a speedy, witty writer, full of fast perceptions and glistening facts. One can slip and slide all over her prose and it is fun: unless or until you start getting pissed off. You want to know more and deeper stuff about the writers she invokes, something about the texture of their lives, more about the books they wrote, some mood and some substance relating to the writers or the work that is considered and sustained in quality, something of the concrete world surrounding them. Perhaps it is a matter of taste, but maybe it is not. One gets tired of hearing women writers referred to but not known or conveyed. This is a political point.

Nevertheless, Russ has some brilliant insights into how women's writing is suppressed. She explicates the basic hypocrisy of liberal democracy with amazing accuracy:

> In a nominally egalitarian society the ideal situation (socially speaking) is one in which the members of the "wrong" groups have the freedom to engage in literature (or equally significant activities) and yet do not do so, thus proving that they can't. But, alas, give them the least real freedom and they *will* do it. The trick thus becomes to make the freedom as nominal a freedom as possible and then—since some of the so-and-so's will do it anyway—develop various strategies for ignoring, condemning, or belittling the artistic works that result. If properly done, these strategies result in a social situation in which the "wrong" people are (supposedly) free to commit literature, art, or whatever, but very few do, and those who do (it seems) do it badly, so we can all go home to lunch. (pp. 4–5)

Many of the writers Russ refers to, however, did not live in a nominally egalitarian society. They lived, for instance, in England in the eighteenth and nineteenth centuries. They lived difficult, often desperate lives, constrained, almost in domestic captivity. They were middle-class in their society's terms, which does not translate into anything Amerikans on the face of it understand. They were poor;

42

they were poorly educated or self-educated; mostly they died young; they had virtually no social existence outside the patronage of husbands or fathers. Russ invokes the misogyny surrounding their work then, but ignores the ways in which their works continue to be marginal now. This is a real loss. The marginality of works acknowledged as "great books" is a fascinating political phenomenon. The urgency of getting those books to the center of culture has to be articulated by those who recognize the prodigal substance of those books. As Russ so rightly says, *Wuthering Heights* is misread as a romance—Heathcliff's sadism is, in fact, exemplary. *Wuthering Heights* brilliantly delineates the social construction of that sadism, its hierarchical deployment among men to hurt and control them and then the impact of that male humiliation on women; it also provides a paradigm for racism in the raising of the young Heathcliff. The book should be of vital interest to political scientists and theorists as well as to aspiring writers and all readers who want abundantly beautiful prose. Similarly with *Jane Eyre*: the book should be, but is not, central to discourse on female equality in every field of thought and action. It would also be useful to understand how George Eliot can be recognized as the supreme genius of the English novel and still be largely unread. (We do read Tolstoy, her only peer, in translation.) Russ avoids Eliot, perhaps because the magnitude of her achievement suggests that "great writer" is a real category, small and exclusive, with real meaning.

The strategies of suppression that Russ isolates travel nicely through time. It is doubted that a woman really wrote whatever it is (that is a dated strategy: the contemporary version is that the writer is not a *real* woman in the *Cosmo* sense, hot and free). It is acknowledged that a woman wrote the book, but it is maintained that she should not have—it masculinizes her, makes her unfit for a woman's life, and so on. The content is judged by the gender of the author. The book is falsely categorized: it falls between genres so it is misread or dismissed; a man connected to the woman publishes her work under his name; the woman herself is categorized in some way that slanders her talent or her work. Or, it is simply discounted, according to the principle: *"What I don't understand doesn't exist."* Our social invisibility, Russ writes, "is not a 'failure of human communication.' It is a socially arranged bias persisted in long after the information about women's experience is available (sometimes even publicly insisted upon)." (p. 48) Russ develops each of these ideas with sophistication and wit.

There are two spectacular insights in her book. About *Villette* she writes: "If *Villette* is the feminist classic I take it to be, that is not because of any explicit feminist declarations made by the book but because of the novel's constant, passionate insistence that things are *like this* and not *like that*..." (p. 105) She has articulated here that which distinguishes feminist thinking and perception from the more corrupt and disingenuous male approaches to life and art.

She also discerns in the whole idea of regionalism as a literary subspecies a strategic way of trivializing and dismissing women. Willa Cather and Kate Chopin are regionalists (one might include Eudora Welty and Flannery O'Connor) but Sherwood Anderson (!), Thomas Wolfe, and William Faulkner are not. Of course, Faulkner is; and he is a great novelist too, in my view. *Regionalist* is used to suggest a small, narrow writer, a woman; it is not used, even though accurate, to describe Mr Faulkner.

I have three serious arguments with Russ's book. First, she claims that "[a]t the high level of culture with which this book is concerned, active bigotry is probably fairly rare. *It is also hardly ever necessary*, since the social context is so far from neutral." (p. 18) I think bigotry on the high level is active, purposeful, malicious, and as common and slimy as the bigotry in other social sewers. The misogynist spleen pollutes criticism and makes life hell for a woman writer. The misogynist spleen suffuses the publishing industry—how women writers are talked about and to, treated, paid, actually published, sexually harassed, persistently denigrated, and sometimes raped. I take the bigotry of high culture to be active.

Second, Russ scrutinizes rightly the wrongheadedness of those who trivialize or dismiss books written by the "wrong" people, but she seems to think that all books by "wrong" people are created equal and I don't. She says with some disbelief that some women actually thought Dorothy Sayers was a minor novelist until they read *Gaudy Night*. I read *Gaudy Night*, which I liked enormously, and still think Sayers is a minor novelist. I think great books, as distinguished from all other books, do exist. It is true, as Russ eloquently insists, that many of them have been left out of the literary canon because of racial, sexual, or class prejudice. It is also true—which Russ

ignores—that books by the "right" people are often overestimated
and their value inflated. I think this matters, because I do think great
books exist and they do matter to me as such. I think that writing a
great book, as opposed to any other kind, is a supreme accomplishment; I think reading one is a gorgeous and awesome experience.

Finally: I intensely disliked Russ's "Afterword," in which she
presents a pastiche of fragments from the writings of some women of
color. Despite the apologia that precedes the "Afterword," suggesting
that it is better to do something badly than not at all, I experienced
Russ's homage to women writers of color as demeaning and
condescending (to me as a reader as well as to them as writers). Fine
writers are worth more. Neglect is not corrected unless the quality of
respect given to a writer and her work is what it should be. I think
some of these writers are fine and some are not very good; a few I
don't know; some wonderful writers are omitted. This hodgepodge
suggests, among other things, that distinctions of excellence do not
matter, whereas to me they do, and I am insulted as a writer on behalf
of the excellent writers here who are treated in such a glib and
trivializing way. I simply abhor the lack of seriousness in this
approach to these writers.

Lynne Spender's book, *Intruders on the Rights of Men*, is about
publishing: how men keep women out of literature altogether or
allow us in on the most marginal terms. "In literate societies," she
writes, "there is a close association between *the printed word* and the
exercise of *power*." (ix) This is something Amerikans have trouble
understanding. One of the awful consequences of free speech/First
Amendment fetishism is that political people, including feminists,
have entirely forgotten that access to media is not a democratically
distributed right, but rather something gotten by birth or money.
Wrong sex, wrong race, wrong family, and you haven't got it.
Spender's political clarity on the relationship between being able to
make speech public, and power in the material sense of the word,
enables her to shed a lot of light on the inability of women to change
our status vis-à-vis speech in books. She tends to define equality in a
simple-minded way: equal numbers of women to men and
participation on the same terms as men. Nevertheless, she challenges
the so-called neutrality of culture as such; she understands that there
is a politics to illiteracy that *matters*; she never loses sight of the fact

45

that power allows or disallows speech, and that male power has marginalized and stigmatized women's speech. She underestimates how much female silence male power affirmatively creates.

Her discussion of the power of the publishers is inadequate. It is conceptually the bare bones. She does not discern the wide latitude that individual men in publishing have for sexual abuse and economic exploitation of women on whim. She does not analyze the structure of power within the industry—the kinds of power men have over women editors and how that affects which women writers those women editors dare to publish. She does not discuss money: how it works, who gets it, how much, why. She does not recognize the impact of the humongous corporations now owning publishing houses. She does not deal with publishing contracts, those adorable one-way agreements in which the author promises to deliver a book and the publisher does not promise to publish it. *But*: she *does* discuss, too briefly, sexual harassment in publishing—an unexposed but thriving part of the industry, because if women writers, especially feminists, will not expose it (for fear of starving), who will? The book is very interesting but much too superficial. It gives one some ideas but not enough analysis of how power really functions: its dynamics; the way it gets played out; the consequences of it creatively and economically for women writers. Spender is an advocate of women's independent publishing, which is the only suggested solution; but she does not explore the difficulties and dangers—political and economic—of small, usually sectarian presses.

Both *Intruders on the Rights of Men* and *How to Suppress Women's Writing* are genuinely worth reading, but they will not bring the reader closer to what it means for a woman to write and publish; nor will either book get the writer herself through another day.

Preface to the Paperback Edition of *Our Blood*

1981

Our Blood is out of print again in both the United States and Britain.

Our Blood is a book that grew out of a situation. The situation was that I could not get my work published. So I took to public speaking—not the extemporaneous exposition of thoughts or the outpouring of feelings, but crafted prose that would inform, persuade, disturb, cause recognition, sanction rage. I told myself that if publishers would not publish my work, I would bypass them altogether. I decided to write directly to people and for my own voice. I started writing this way because I had no other choice: I saw no other way to survive as a writer. I was convinced that it was the publishing establishment—timid and powerless women editors, the superstructure of men who make the real decisions, misogynistic reviewers—that stood between me and a public particularly of women that I knew was there. The publishing establishment was a formidable blockade, and my plan was to swim around it.

In April 1974 my first book-length work of feminist theory, *Woman Hating*, was published. Before its publication I had had trouble. I had been offered magazine assignments that were disgusting. I had been offered a great deal of money to write articles that an editor had already outlined to me in detail. They were to be about women or sex or drugs. They were stupid and full of lies. For instance, I was offered $1500 to write an article on the use of barbiturates and amphetamines by suburban women. I was to say that this use of drugs constituted a hedonistic rebellion against the dull conventions of sterile housewifery, that women used these drugs to turn on and swing and have a wonderful new life-style. I told the editor that I suspected women used amphetamines to get through miserable days and barbiturates to get through miserable nights. I suggested, amiably I thought, that I ask the women who use the drugs why they use them. I was told flat-out that the article *would say* what fun it was. I turned down the assignment. This sounds like great rebellious fun—telling establishment types to go fuck themselves with their fistful of dollars— but when one is very poor, as I was, it is not fun. It is instead profoundly distressing. Six years later I finally made half that amount for a magazine piece, the highest I have ever been paid for an article. I had had my chance to play ball and I had refused. I was too naive to know that hack writing is the only paying game in town. I believed in "literature," "principles," "politics," and "the power of fine writing to change lives." When I refused to do that article and others, I did so with considerable indignation. The indignation marked me as a wild woman, a bitch, a reputation reinforced during editorial fights over the content of *Woman Hating*, a reputation that has haunted and hurt me: not hurt my feelings, but hurt my ability to make a living. I am in fact not a "lady," not a "lady writer," not a "sweet young thing." What woman is? My ethics, my politics, and my style merged to make me an untouchable. Girls are supposed to be invitingly touchable, on the surface or just under.

I thought that the publication of *Woman Hating* would establish me as a writer of recognized talent and that then I would be able to publish serious work in ostensibly serious magazines. I was wrong. The publication of *Woman Hating*, about which I was jubilant, was the beginning of a decline that continued until 1981 when *Pornography: Men Possessing Women* was published. The publisher of *Woman Hating* did not like the book: I am considerably understating here. I was not supposed to say, for example, "Women are raped." I was supposed to say, "Green-eyed women with one leg longer than the other, hair between the teeth, French poodles, and a taste for sautéed vegetables are raped occasionally on Fridays by persons." It was rough. I believed I had a right to say what I wanted. My desires were not particularly whimsical: my sources were history, facts, experience. I had been brought up in an almost exclusively male tradition of literature, and that tradition, whatever its faults, did not teach coyness or fear: the writers I admired were blunt and not particularly polite. I did not understand that—even as a writer—I was supposed to be delicate, fragile, intuitive, personal, introspective. I wanted to claim the public world of action, not the private world of feelings. My ambition was perceived as megalomaniacal—in the wrong sphere, demented by prior definition. Yes, I was naive. I had not learned my proper place. I knew what I was rebelling against in life, but I did not know that literature had the same sorry boundaries, the same absurd rules, the same cruel proscriptions.* It was easy enough to deal with me: I was a bitch. And my book was sabotaged. The publisher simply refused to fill orders for it. Booksellers wanted the book but could not get it. Reviewers ignored the book, consigned me to invisibility, poverty, and failure. The first speech in *Our Blood* ("Feminism, Art, and My Mother Sylvia") was written before the publication of *Woman Hating* and reflects the deep optimism I felt at that time. By October, the time of the second speech in *Our Blood* ("Renouncing Sexual 'Equality'"), I knew that I was in for a hard time, but I still did not know how hard it was going to be.

"Renouncing Sexual 'Equality'" was written for the National Organization for Women Conference on Sexuality that took place in New York City on October 12, 1974. I spoke at the end of a three-hour speakout on sex: women talking about their sexual experiences, feelings, values. There were 1100 women in the audience; no men were present. When I was done, the 1100 women rose to their feet. Women were crying and shaking and shouting. The applause lasted nearly ten minutes. It was one of the most astonishing experiences of

* I had been warned early on about what it meant to be a girl, but I hadn't listened. "You write like a man," an editor wrote me on reading a draft of a few early chapters of *Woman Hating.* "When you learn to write like a woman, we will consider publishing you." This admonition reminded me of a guidance counselor in high school who asked me as graduation approached what I planned to be when I grew up. A writer, I said. He lowered his eyes, then looked at me soberly. He knew I wanted to go to a superb college; he knew I was ambitious. "What you have to do," he said, "is go to a state college—there is no reason for you to go somewhere else—and become a teacher so that you'll have something to fall back on when your husband dies." This story is not apocryphal. It happened to me and to countless others. I had thought both the guidance counselor and the editor stupid, individually stupid. I was wrong. They were not individually stupid.

my life. Many of the talks I gave received standing ovations, and this was not the first, but I had never spoken to such a big audience, and what I said contradicted rather strongly much of what had been said before I spoke. So the response was amazing and it overwhelmed me. The coverage of the speech also overwhelmed me. One New York weekly published two vilifications. One was by a woman who had at least been present. She suggested that men might die from blue-balls if I were ever taken seriously. The other was by a man who had not been present; he had overheard women talking in the lobby. He was "enraged." He could not bear the possibility that "a woman might consider masochistic her consent to the means of my release." That was the "danger Dworkin's ideology represents." Well, yes; but both writers viciously distorted what I had actually said. Many women, including some quite famous writers, sent letters deploring the lack of fairness and honesty in the two articles. None of those letters were published. Instead, letters from men who had not been present were published; one of them compared my speech to Hitler's Final Solution. I had used the words "limp" and "penis" one after the other: "limp penis." Such usage outraged; it offended so deeply that it warranted a comparison with an accomplished genocide. Nothing I had said about women was mentioned, not even in passing. The speech was about women. The weekly in question has since never published an article of mine or reviewed a book of mine or covered a speech of mine (even though some of my speeches were big events in New York City).* The kind of fury in those two articles simply saturated the publishing establishment, and my work was stonewalled. Audiences around the country, most of them women and men, continued to rise to their feet; but the journals that one might expect to take note of a political writer like myself, or a phenomenon like those speeches, refused to acknowledge my existence. There were two noteworthy if occasional exceptions: *Ms.* and *Mother Jones.*

---

* After *Our Blood* was published, I went to this same weekly to beg—yes, beg—for some attention to the book, which was dying. The male writer whose "release" had been threatened by "Renouncing Sexual 'Equality'" asked to meet me. He told me, over and over, how very beautiful *Our Blood* was. "You know—um—um," I said, "that—um, um—That Speech is in *Our Blood*—you know, the one you wrote about." "So beautiful," he said, "so beautiful." The editor-in-chief of the weekly wrote me that *Our Blood* was so fine, so moving. But *Our Blood* did not get any help, not even a mention, in those pages.

In the years following the publication of *Woman Hating,* it began to be regarded as a feminist classic. The honor in this will only be apparent to those who value Mary Wollstonecraft's *A Vindication of the Rights of Women* or Elizabeth Cady Stanton's *The Woman's Bible.* It was a great honor. Feminists alone were responsible for the survival of *Woman Hating.* Feminists occupied the offices of *Woman Hating*'s publisher to demand that the book be published in paper. Phyllis Chesler contacted feminist writers of reputation all over the country to ask for written statements of support for the book. Those writers responded with astonishing generosity. Feminist newspapers reported the suppression of the book. Feminists who worked in bookstores scavenged distributors' warehouses for copies of the book and wrote over and over to the publisher to demand the book. Women's studies programs began using it. Women passed the book from hand to hand, bought second and third and fourth copies to give friends whenever they could find it. Even though the publisher of *Woman Hating* had told me it was "mediocre," the pressure finally resulted in a paperback edition in 1976: 2500 leftover unbound copies were bound in paper and distributed, sort of. Problems with distribution continued, and bookstores, which reported selling the book steadily when it was in stock, had to wait months for orders to be filled. *Woman Hating* is now in its fifth tiny paperback printing. The book is not another piece of lost women's literature only because feminists would not give it up. In a way this story is heartening, because it shows what activism can accomplish, even in the Yahoo land of Amerikan publishing.

But I had nowhere to go, no way to continue as a writer. So I went on the road—to women's groups who passed a hat for me at the end of my talk, to schools where feminist students fought to get me a hundred dollars or so, to conferences where women sold T-shirts to pay me. I spent weeks or months writing a talk. I took long, dreary bus rides to do what appeared to be only an evening's work and slept wherever there was room. Being an insomniac, I did not sleep much. Women shared their homes, their food, their hearts with me, and I met women in every circumstance, nice women and mean women, brave women and terrified women. And the women I met had suffered every crime, every indignity: and I listened. "The Rape Atrocity and the Boy Next Door" (in this volume) always elicited the same responses: I heard about rape after rape; women's lives passed before me, rape after rape; women who had been raped in homes, in cars, on beaches, in alleys, in classrooms, by one man, by two men, by five men, by eight men, hit, drugged, knifed, torn, women who had been sleeping, women who had been with their children, women who had been out for a walk or shopping or going to school or going home from school or in their offices working or in factories or in stockrooms, young women, girls, old women, thin women, fat women, housewives, secretaries, hookers, teachers, students. I simply could not bear it. So I stopped giving the speech. I thought I would die from it. I learned what I had to know, and more than I could stand to know.

My life on the road was an exhausting mixture of good and bad, the ridiculous and the sublime. One fairly typical example: I gave the last lecture in *Our Blood* ("The Root Cause," my favorite) on my twenty-ninth birthday. I had written it as a birthday present to myself. The lecture was sponsored by a Boston-based political collective. They were supposed to provide transportation and housing for me and, because it was my birthday and I wanted my family with me, my friend and our dog. I had offered to come another time but they wanted me then—en famille. One collective member drove to New York in the most horrible thunderstorm I have ever seen to pick us up and drive us back to Boston. The other cars on the road were blurs of red light here and there. The driver was exhausted, it was impossible to see; and the driver did not like my political views. He kept asking me about various psychoanalytic theories, none of which I had the good sense to appreciate. I kept trying to change the subject—he kept insisting that I tell him what I thought of so-and-so—every time I got so cornered that I had to answer, he slammed his foot down on the gas pedal. I thought that we would probably die from the driver's fatigue and fury and God's rain. We were an hour late, and the jam-packed audience had waited. The acoustics in the room were superb, which enhanced not only my own voice but the endless howling of my dog, who finally bounded through the audience to sit on stage during the question-and-answer period. The audience was fabulous: involved, serious, challenging. Many of the ideas in the lecture were new and, because they directly confronted the political nature of male sexuality, enraging. The woman with whom we were supposed to stay and who was responsible for our trip home was so enraged that she ran out, never to return. We were stranded, without money, not knowing where to turn. A person can be stranded and get by, even though she will be imperiled; two people with a German shepherd and no money are in a mess. Finally, a woman whom I knew slightly took us all in and loaned us the money to get home. Working (and it is demanding, intense, difficult work) and traveling in such endlessly improvised circumstances require that one develop an affection for low comedy and gross melodrama. I never did. Instead I became tired and demoralized. And I got even poorer, because no one could ever afford to pay me for the time it took to do the writing.

I did not begin demanding realistic fees, secure accommodations, and safe travel in exchange for my work until after the publication of *Our Blood*. I had tried intermittently and mostly failed. But now I had to be paid and safe. I felt I had really entered middle age. This presented new problems for feminist organizers who had little access to the material resources in their communities. It also presented me with new problems. For a long time I got no work at all, so I just got poorer and poorer. It made no sense to anyone but me: if you have nothing, and someone offers you something, how can you turn it down? But I did, because I knew that I would never make a living unless I took a stand. I had a fine and growing reputation as a speaker and writer; but still, there was no money for me. When I first began to ask for fees, I got angry responses from women: how could the author of *Woman Hating* be such a scummy capitalist pig, one woman asked in a nearly obscene letter. The letter writer was going to live on a farm and have nothing to do with rat-shit capitalists and bourgeois feminist creeps. Well, I wrote back, I didn't live on a farm and didn't want to. I bought food in a supermarket and paid rent to a landlord and I wanted to write books. I answered all the angry letters. I tried to explain the politics of getting the money, especially from colleges and universities: the money was there; it was hard to get; why should it go to Phyllis Schlafly or William F. Buckley, Jr.? I had to live and I had to write. Surely my writing mattered, it mattered to them or why did they want me: and did they want me to stop writing? I needed money to write. I had done the rotten jobs and I was living in real, not romantic, poverty. I found that the effort to explain really helped—not always, and resentments still surfaced, but enough to make me see that explaining even without finally convincing was worthwhile. Even if I didn't get paid, somebody else might. After a long fallow period I began to lecture again. I lectured erratically and never made enough to live on, even in what I think of as stable poverty, even when my fees were high. Many feminist activists did fight for the money and sometimes got it. So I managed—friends loaned me money, sometimes anonymous donations came in the mail, women handed me checks at lectures and refused to let me refuse them, feminist writers gave me gifts of money and loaned me money, and women fought incredible and bitter battles with college administrators and committees and faculties to get me hired and paid. The women's movement kept me alive. I did not live well or safely or easily, but I did not stop writing either. I remain extremely grateful to those who went the distance for me.

I decided to publish the talks in *Our Blood* because I was desperate for money, the magazines were still closed to me, and I was living hand-to-mouth on the road. A book was my only chance.

The editor who decided to publish *Our Blood* did not particularly like my politics, but she did like my prose. I was happy to be appreciated as a writer. The company was the only unionized publishing house in New York and it also had an active women's group. The women employees were universally wonderful to me—vitally interested in feminism, moved by my work, conscious and kind. They invited me to address the employees of the company on their biennial women's day, shortly before the publication of *Our Blood*. I discussed the systematic presumption of male ownership of women's bodies and labor, the material reality of that ownership, the economic degrading of women's work. (The talk was subsequently published in abridged form under the title "Phallic Imperialism" in *Ms.*, December 1976.) Some men in suits sat dourly through it, taking notes. That, needless to say, was the end of *Our Blood*. There was one other telling event: a highly placed department head threw the manuscript of *Our Blood* at my editor across a room. I did not recognize male tenderness, he said. I don't know whether he made the observation before or after he threw the manuscript.

Our Blood was published in cloth in 1976. The only review of it in a major periodical was in *Ms.* many months after the book was out of bookstores. It was a rave. Otherwise, the book was ignored: but purposefully, maliciously. Gloria Steinem, Robin Morgan, and Karen DeCrow tried to review the book to no avail. I contacted nearly a hundred feminist writers, activists, editors. A large majority made countless efforts to have the book reviewed. Some managed to publish reviews in feminist publications, but even those who frequently published elsewhere were unable to place reviews. No one was able to break the larger silence.

Our Blood was sent to virtually every paperback publisher in the United States, sometimes more than once, over a period of years. None would publish it. Therefore, it is with great joy, and a shaky sense of victory, that I welcome its publication in this edition. I have a special love for this book. Most feminists I know who have read *Our Blood* have taken me aside at one time or another to tell me that they have a special affection and respect for it. There is, I believe, something quite beautiful and unique about it. Perhaps that is because it was written for a human voice. Perhaps it is because I had to fight so hard to say what is in it. Perhaps it is because *Our Blood* has touched so many women's lives directly: it has been said over and over again to real women and the experience of saying the words has informed the writing of them. *Woman Hating* was written by a younger writer, one more reckless and more hopeful both. This book is more disciplined, more somber, more rigorous, and in some ways more impassioned. I am happy that it will now reach a larger audience, and sorry that it took so long.

Andrea Dworkin
New York City
March 1981

Nervous Interview

1978

In 1978 I wrote a whole bunch of short articles. I desperately needed money and wanted to be able to publish them for money. Of these articles, Nervous Interview is probably the most obscure in its concerns and certainly in its form and yet it was the only one that was published at all, not for money. Norman Mailer managed to publish lots of interviews with himself, none of which made much sense, all of which were taken seriously by literati of various stripes. So this is half parody of him and his chosen form and half parody of myself and my chosen movement.

S HE WAS EDGY. Ambivalent would be too polite a word. She came at one, then withdrew. It wasn't a tease, it wasn't coy. Her enemies said Paranoid. She said, Commonsense. In the age of the Glass House, everyone a stone thrower, Commonsense. But the pressure had been mounting. Account for yourself, explain. Ever since that fateful day when she had juxtaposed the two words, "Limp Penis," she had been forced to hide or explain. She didn't count those who wanted apologies. Being a prudent person, she had hidden. An ex-friend had just written her, in accusation, saying that she did not understand "the chemistry of love." Nor, she was willing to admit, the physics or mathematics (or even simple arithmetic) of love. She only understood its laws, the stuff of literature and sexual politics, not science. Now, after nearly two years of absence/exile she was returning to New York. Feeling like a sacrifice. Wondering when the priests would come at her. Determined to defy the gods.

Q: It seems strange that anyone so aggressive in her writing should

56

be so reclusive, so hostile to a public life.
A: I'm shy, that's all. And cold and aloof.

Q: A lot of men in this town think you're a killer.
A: I'm too shy to kill. I think they should be more afraid of each other, less afraid of me.

Q: Why don't you give interviews?
A: Because they're so false. Someone asks a question—very posed and formal, or very fumbling and sincere. Then someone tries to respond in kind. Cult of fame and personality and all that. It's all wrong.

Q: So why this? Why now?
A: I couldn't sleep. Very edgy. Nervous nightmares about New York. Going home. Cesspool and paradise. You see, I've lived many places. I keep leaving them. I keep returning to New York but I can't stay put. But that's what I want most. To stay still. So I'm restless and irritated.

Q: People are surprised when they meet you. That you're nice.
A: I think that's strange. Why shouldn't I be nice?

Q: It's not a quality that one associates with radical feminists.
A: Well, see, right there, that's distortion. Radical feminists are always nice. Provoked to the point of madness, but remaining, at heart, nice.

Q: I could name you a lot of feminists who aren't nice. You yourself have probably had fights with just about everyone I could name. Isn't this a terrible hypocrisy on your part—and silly too—to say that radical feminists are nice?
A: At a distance or very close, nice is true. At any midpoint, it seems false. Also, you see, we love each other. It's a very impersonal love in many cases. But it is a fierce love. You have to love women who are brave enough to do things so big in a world where women are supposed to be so small.

Q: Isn't this just another kind of myth building?
A: No, I think it's a very neutral description. Women who fight fierce battles, as all radical feminists do, encounter so much hostility and

57

conflict in the regular transactions of work and daily life that they become very complex, even if they started out simple. One must learn to protect oneself. This means, inevitably, that one exaggerates some parts of one's personality, some qualities. Or they become exaggerated in the process of trying to survive and to continue to work. So when one sees that in another woman, one loves her for it—even if one does not like the particular defenses she has worked out for herself. That doesn't mean that one wants to be intimate with her. Just that one loves her for daring to be so ambitious. For daring to continue to associate herself with women as a feminist, no matter what the cost, no matter what walls she has to build to keep on doing what's important to her.

Q: What alienates you most from other women?
A: Failures of courage or integrity. Those ever-present human failures. I'm in the midst of the mess, just like everyone else. I expect too much from women. I get bitterly disappointed when women are flawed in stupid ways. As I myself am. And then I resent women who are bitterly disappointed in me because I'm flawed. It's the old double standard, newly cast. I expect nothing from men—or, more accurately, I rarely expect much—but I expect everything from women I admire. Women expect everything from me. Then when we find that we are just ourselves, no matter what our aspirations or accomplishments, we grieve, we cry, we mourn, we fight, and especially, we blame, we resent. Our wrong expectations lead to these difficulties. For me, wrong expectations make me sometimes alienated, sometimes isolated.

Q: People think you are very hostile to men.
A: I am.

Q: Doesn't that worry you?
A: From what you said, it worries them.

Q: I mean, any Freudian would have a field day with your work. Penis envy, penis hatred, penis obsession, some might say.
A: Men are the source of that, in their literature, culture, behavior. I could never have invented it. Who was more penis obsessed than

Freud? Except maybe Reich. But then, what a competition that would be. Choose the most penis obsessed man in history. What is so remarkable is that men in general, really with so few exceptions, are so penis obsessed. I mean, if anyone should be sure of self-worth in a penis-oriented society, it should be the one who has the penis. But one per individual doesn't seem to be enough. I wonder how many penises per man would calm them down. Listen, we could start a whole new surgical field here.

Q: The Women's Movement seems to be more conciliatory towards men than you are, especially these days. There is a definite note of reconciliation, or at least not hurling accusations. What do you think of that?
A: I think that women have to pretend to like men to survive. Feminists rebelled, and stopped pretending. Now I worry that feminists are capitulating.

Q: Isn't there something quite pathological in always looking at sex in male terms? Say you describe male attitudes towards sex accurately. Don't you accept their terms when you analyze everything using their terms?
A: Their terms are reality because they control reality. So what terms should we use to understand reality? All we can do is face it or try to hide from it.

Q: Are there men you admire?
A: Yes.

Q: Who?
A: I'd rather not say.

Q: There are a lot of rumors about your lesbianism. No one quite seems to know what you do with whom.
A: Good.

Q: Can you explain why you are so opposed to pornography?
A: I find it strange that it requires an explanation. The men have made quite an industry of pictures, moving and still, that depict the

torture of women. I am a woman. I don't like to see the virtual worship of sadism against women because I am a woman, and it's me. It has happened to me. It's going to happen to me. I have to fight an industry that encourages men to act out their aggression on women—their "fantasies," as those aspirations are so euphemistically named. And I hate it that everywhere I turn, people seem to accept without question this false notion of freedom. Freedom to do what to whom? Freedom to torture me? That's not freedom for me. I hate the romanticization of brutality towards women wherever I find it, not just in pornography, but in artsy fartsy movies, in artsy fartsy books, by sexologists and philosophes. It doesn't matter where it is. I simply refuse to pretend that it doesn't have anything to do with me. And that leads to a terrible recognition: if pornography is part of male freedom, then that freedom is not reconcilable with my freedom. If his freedom is to torture, then in those terms my freedom must be to be tortured. That's insane.

Q: A lot of women say they like it.
A: Women have two choices: lie or die. Feminists are trying to open the options up a bit.

Q: Can I ask you about your personal life?
A: No.

Q: If the personal is political, as feminists say, why aren't you more willing to talk about your personal life?
A: Because a personal life can only be had in privacy. Once strangers intrude into it, it isn't personal anymore. It takes on the quality of a public drama. People follow it as if they were watching a play. You are the product, they are the consumers. Every single friendship and event takes on a quality of display. You have to think about the consequences not just of your acts vis-à-vis other individuals but in terms of media, millions of strange observers. I find it very ugly. I think that the press far exceeds its authentic right to know in pursuing the private lives of individuals, especially people like myself, who are neither public employees nor performers. And if one has to be always aware of public consequences of private acts, it's very hard to be either spontaneous or honest with other people.

Q: If you could sleep with anyone in history, who would it be?
A: That's easy. George Sand.

Q: She was pretty involved with men.
A: I would have saved her from all that.

Q: Is there any man, I mean, there must be at least one.
A: Well, ok, yes. Ugh. Rimbaud. Disaster. In the old tradition, Glorious Disaster.

Q: That seems to give some credence to the rumor that you are particularly involved with gay men.
A: It should give credence to the rumor that I am particularly involved with dead artists.

Q: Returning to New York, do you have any special hopes or dreams?
A: Yeah. I wish that Bella were King.

Loving Books:
Male/Female/Feminist

1985

After many years of barely being able to publish in magazines at all, the women at Hot Wire, *a magazine about music, asked me to write something about my identity as a writer. Thematically, this follows up on some of what I wrote in* Nervous Interview. *With male writers, people want to know who they are. With women, stereotypes are simply applied. The invitation from* Hot Wire *gave me an exceptionally short chance to say something myself about my own identity and development.*

I LIVE A strange life, but often the strangest thing about it is that I still love books and have faith in them and get courage from them as I did when I was young, hopeful, and innocent. The innocence was particularly about what it takes to endure as a writer—simply to survive, if one is rigorous, unsentimental, radical, extreme, and tells the truth. The books I loved when I was younger were by wild men: Dostoevsky, Rimbaud, Allen Ginsberg among the living, Baudelaire, Whitman, the undecorous. I read Freud and Darwin as great visionaries, their work culled from the fantastic, complex imagination. My own values as a writer were set back then; and work by women (except for *Gone with the Wind* and the Nancy Drew books*) intruded much later. In eighth grade science class, my best girlfriend and I (lovers too) were both writing novels as an

---

* Imagine my surprise when, accidentally and very recently, I discovered that the Nancy Drew books were written by a man under a female pseudonym.

antidote to the boredom of learning by rote—and these novels had women as heroes who had great ambitions. They were named after Belle Starr and Amelia Earhart: strange names, women who were not usual, not grounded, not boring.

I have never wanted to be less than a great writer; and I have never been afraid of failing, the reason being that I would rather fail at that than succeed at anything else. This ambition is deeply rooted in male identification: and many of the characteristics that I value most in myself as a person and as a writer are. When young, I never thought about being homosexual or bisexual or heterosexual: only about being like Rimbaud. *Artiste* in the soon-to-be-dead mode was my sexual orientation, my gender identity, the most intense way of living: dying early the inevitable end of doing everything with absolute passion. I was devoted to Sappho, her existence obscuring the gender specificity of my true devotion. When I read books, I was the writer, not the Lady. I was incorrigible: no matter what happened to me, no matter what price I paid for being in this woman's body, for being used like a woman, treated like a woman, I was the writer, not the Lady. Sexual annihilation, not esthetic burn-out with a magnificent literature left behind, was the real dead-end for women too dense to comprehend.

Feminism provided a way for me to understand my own life: why being free was not just a matter of living without self-imposed or social or sexual limits. My so-called freedom on many occasions nearly cost me my life, but there was neither tragedy nor romance in this: neither Dostoevsky nor Rimbaud had ever ended up being sexually used *and* cleaning toilets.

Sexual Politics was about the writing and sex I had adored; with big doses of lesbianism too. I learned from this book what they were doing to me: see, said Millett, here he does this and this and this to her. I wasn't the writer, after all. I was the *her*. I had plenty of open wounds on my body, and I began to feel them hurt. Had I been the user, not the used, my sensitivity probably would have approximated Henry Miller's. This is not pleasant to face; so I don't. Someday I must.

I have learned tremendously from women writers as an adult; I have learned that great writing from women is genuinely—not romantically—despised, and that the books are written out of an open vein; I have learned about women's lives. My ambitions as a writer still go back, too far, into my obsessions with the men; but what I learned from them, I need every day of my writing life—I am not afraid of confrontation or risk, also not of arrogance or error—I am happy not to even be able to follow the rules of polite discourse, because I learned to hate them so early—I love what is raw and eloquent in writing but not feminine. I have learned to appreciate the great subtlety and strength of women who write within the boundaries of a feminine writing ethic: but I do not accept it for myself.

What I affirm here is that while I did not learn writing from women, I have learned virtually everything important about what it means to be a woman from women writers: and I have also learned much about male power from them, once I cared enough about women as such to realize that male power was the theme my own life had led me to. I know male power inside out, with knowledge of it gained by this female body. I dare to confront it in my writing because of the audacity I learned from male writers. I learned to confront it in life from living feminists, writers and activists both, who lived political lives not bounded by either female frailty or male ruthlessness; instead animated by the luminous self-respect and militant compassion I still hope to achieve.

Mourning Tennessee Williams (1911–1983)

1983

Amerika is hard on writers. The camera is always there to capture failure, decadence, decay. One must be famous or one is worthless. One must be public even though writers need privacy and considerable sheltering. Amerikan writers don't do too well or last too long. They live abroad or fall apart. Some male writers use gender as an aggressive weapon—Mailer, Updike, Bellow. Other male writers, rarer, use gender to explode conceits about identity or power or society or the status quo—Tennessee Williams or Gore Vidal or, in a younger generation, Tim O'Brien in Going After Cacciato. *The male writers who do use gender in a subversive way endanger themselves. The macho boys want them dead. The literary establishment is on the side of the macho boys. Tennessee Williams wrote some true and subversive plays. Amerika didn't treat him very well and isn't sorry.*

WHEN I HEARD that Tennessee Williams was dead, I found myself crying. The tears came almost before I could take my next breath. I was very sad, and in the ensuing days I could not shake my sense of loss and grief. I tried to think about why he meant so much to me.

"His women," as those giants of restlessness and turmoil are called in the popular press, show almost too much of our hidden lives. It is painful even to remember them because their insides were so exposed. He always showed that the circumstances of women's lives were unbearable, which I take to be true. It is almost as if he created women out of the very air that smothers us, showed us breathing in

65

LETTERS FROM A WAR ZONE

that stifling heat, then trying to get rid of it—pushing it out or choking it up. "His women" smother the way I remember smothering under the iron hand of more liberal but still womanly convention. "His women" roam and wander and rebel against the bars the way I did, or they want to, and so they are alone no matter who or what they love, in exile from most of what passes as a woman's proper life. They hide better than I ever did, I suppose, perhaps because they are from an earlier time and had to. They fit in on the surface until the world falls apart for them and they always pay for what they have dared to want. They are great extremists—in suffering, in passion, in desire, in ambition. They know no middle ground. They are greedy and each in her own way is ruthless. Inevitably they fail, they are destroyed, they lose—because life inevitably ends in death and for women especially not much is possible.

For Williams, women were the human protagonists. We embody the human condition in his plays. His men—the sons, brothers, lovers, husbands—are not so different from us, even though they are more brutal. The father, the elder, the patriarch, wounds them and to the degree they want love, they have no chance. Williams, I think, never imagined that men and women had different natures: only different lives. In his static world, our common ground was restlessness, desire, pain, the movement toward love, never coming near enough.

Writing, he said, "became my place of retreat, my cave, my refuge. From what? From being called a sissy by the neighborhood kids, and Miss Nancy by my father, because I would rather read books in my grandfather's large and classical library than play marbles and baseball ... a result of a severe childhood illness and of excessive attachment to the female members of my family, who had coaxed me back into life." It is too cheap to say that Williams' female characters had entirely to do with himself: his own displacement and sense of female stigma. No great artist, which he was, writes without an almost merciless objectivity. Williams' own romanticism and others' trivializing perceptions of his homosexuality obscure the tremendous objectivity of his work: his insides are there (not in any simple way) and so are our own. He was destroyed mostly by his own lucidity, not the drugs or drink that made that lucidity endurable. He thought of writing as an escape from reality, but in an artist of his magnitude it never is. Writing distils reality, so the burden of it is heavier and on the artist alone. "Sometimes," he wrote, still about writing, "the heart dies deliberately, to avoid further pain."

In an introduction to *The Rose Tattoo*, along with *Summer and Smoke* my favorite of his plays, Williams said that we pity and love each other more than we permit ourselves to know. I loved and pitied him much more than I knew, and somewhere, in the generosity of his art, he loved and pitied me back: through Alma and Blanche and Serafina Delle Rose; and through Chance and those other desperate and lonely boys too. I know them all: I know their fear, their heat, their evasion, their failure, inside where no one sees.

I think his work will be reassessed outside the imperatives of commercial theater and that the brilliance of his formal invention—its increasingly surreal complexity and daring long past what is now considered his prime—will be as important as his bold romanticism. But what will always be most important—if a world that does not have much regard for women (or for fragile men excessively attached to women) can only see it—is the remarkable, unique way he used gender—mythically, hauntingly—to get to the root of what is simply and absolutely human: fear of love that takes up time while death comes closer.

"I don't ask for your pity," says Chance at the end of *Sweet Bird of Youth*, "but just for your understanding—not even that—no. Just for your recognition of me in you, and the enemy, time, in us all." Many pitied Williams the man because he suffered many defeats. Few understood him. But as an artist Williams created the "recognition of me in you, and the enemy, time, in us all" with enduring beauty and urgent power. I think he defeated "the enemy, time."

Wuthering Heights

1987

In 1983, I taught a class in literature in the Women's Studies Department at the University of Minnesota. I simply made a list of my favorite books and taught them. I hadn't read Wuthering Heights *since high school. I was astonished by it. The reasons are in this essay.*

"STRONGER THAN A man, simpler than a child, her nature stood alone,"[1] wrote Charlotte Brontë of her deceased sister, Emily. *Wuthering Heights,* her one novel, published under a male pseudonym before her death at thirty, also stands alone. There is nothing like it—no novel of such astonishing originality and power and passion written by anyone, let alone by a nineteenth-century woman who was essentially a recluse. Nothing can explain it: a worldly, obsessed novel of cruelty and love that surpasses, for instance, the best of D. H. Lawrence in both sensuality and range; an act of passion as well as a work of intellectually rigorous art; a romantic, emotionally haunting, physically graphic rendering of sadism as well as an analytical dissection of it; a lyric and at the same time tragic celebration of both love and violence. "It is moorish, and wild, and knotty as a root of heath," wrote Charlotte, who admitted to being somewhat repelled by the book. "Nor was it natural that it should be otherwise; the author being herself a native and nursling of the moors."[2] So was Charlotte, but she wrote *Jane Eyre,* a novel of civilized pain and outspoken dignity. Both women had a deep understanding of male dominance, which does suggest that, for women, the family is Blake's famous grain of sand. Emily did take the family as a paradigm for society, especially for the creation of sadism in men.

She showed how sadism is created in men through physical and psychological abuse and humiliation by other men; and she wrote about femininity as a betrayal of honor and human wholeness. She was indifferent to sex-roles per se, the surface behaviors of men and women. Instead, she exposed the underbelly of dominance: where power and powerlessness intersect; how social hierarchies emphasize difference, fetishizing it, and repudiate sameness; how men learn hate as an ethic; how women learn to vanquish personal integrity. She anticipated contemporary sexual politics by more than a century; and, frankly, I don't think there is a contemporary novelist, man or woman, who has dared to know and say so much. There is nothing to explain her prescience or her prophecy or, for that matter, her radical political acumen; except to say that Emily Brontë seemed to share with her monster creation, Heathcliff, a will that would neither bend nor break. He used his will to create pain for those he hated. She used hers, no less ruthlessly one suspects, to live in a self-determined solitude, to write, and, finally, to die. Shortly after her brother, Branwell, dissolute and self-obsessed, suddenly died, Emily got consumption, and wasted away with what seemed a premeditated fierceness and determination. On the day of her death, she got up and dressed and groomed herself and sat on a sofa and sewed. She said a doctor could be called and soon she died. Branwell had died in September 1848; Emily died in December. "She sank rapidly," wrote Charlotte. "She made haste to leave us. Yet, while physically she perished, mentally she grew stronger than we had yet known her. . . . I have seen nothing like it; but, indeed, I have never seen her parallel in anything."[3]

The love story between Catherine Earnshaw and the outcast child, Heathcliff, has one point: they are the same, they have one soul, one nature. Each knows the other because each is the other. "'Whatever our souls are made of, his and mine are the same; . . .'"[4] says Catherine. Each knows the other because each is the other. This is not altruistic, self-sacrificing love, Christian self-effacement and self-denial; instead, it is greedy and hard and proud, the self not abnegated but doubled, made stronger, wilder, more intemperate. Together, they are human, a human whole, the self twice over; apart, each is insanely, horribly alone, a self disfigured from separation, mutilated. They are wild together, roaming the moors as children outside the bounds of polite society, vagabonds, lawless. They sleep as children in the same cradled bed. The social distinctions between them mean nothing to them, because to each other they are the world: the whole world, mental, emotional, material. This is a love based on sameness, not difference. It is a love outside the conventions or convictions of gender altogether. One might argue that the love between Catherine and Heathcliff is a metaphor for homosexual love; one or the other would be fake-male or fake-female. Or one might argue that they embody an androgynous ideal, a conflation of male and female. These arguments would be wrong because gender means nothing in this love. Gender comes into play once they are separated. But before they are separated, they are companions in a perfect and wild harmony, a sameness of physical and spiritual identity. As adults, separated, in Heathcliff love turned to sadism, each still recognizes the fundamental truth of their unitary being. Catherine, before she dies, says: "'My love for Heathcliff resembles the eternal rocks beneath: a source of little visible delight, but necessary. ... I *am* Heathcliff! He's always, always in my mind: not as a pleasure, any more than I am always a pleasure to myself, but as my own being.'"[5] And after she is dead, Heathcliff, inconsolable, says: "'Be with me always—take any form—drive me mad! only *do* not leave me in this abyss, where I cannot find you! Oh, God! it is unutterable! I *cannot* live without my life! I *cannot* live without my soul!'"[6]

They do not find themselves in each other; they are themselves, which means they are each other. This, says Brontë, is passionate love, real love, unalterable love—not the socialized conflicts and antagonisms of opposites but the deep sameness of two roaming, wild, restless souls; society conspires to destroy the sameness. In destroying the sameness, society destroys the two people. Heathcliff becomes sadistic; Catherine becomes a wife, a shadow of herself. Boy and girl, "the little souls were comforting each other with better thoughts than I could have hit on: no person in the world ever pictured heaven so beautifully as they did, in their innocent talk: ..."[7]; adolescents, "they both promised fair to grow up rude as savages ... it was one of their chief amusements to run away to the moors in the morning and remain there all day, and the after punishment grew a mere thing to laugh at. ... they forgot everything the minute they were together again ..."[8]; adults, Heathcliff wants Catherine to haunt him and she has already promised to—"'I'll not lie there by myself: they may bury me twelve feet deep and throw the church down over me, but I won't rest till you are with me. I never will!'"[9]

Heathcliff is the quintessential outsider, a foundling, dark, "a dirty, ragged, black-haired child," a "gypsy brat,"[10] referred to as *it*: "I was frightened, and Mrs Earnshaw was ready to fling it out of doors . . . all that I could make out . . . was a tale of [Mr Earnshaw's] seeing it starving, and houseless, and as good as dumb, in the streets of Liverpool, where he picked it up and enquired for its owner. . . . and Mr Earnshaw told me to wash it, and give it clean things, and let it sleep with the children."[11]

Being dirty, dark, a gypsy, black-haired, having a black humor, all are synonyms for a virtually racial exclusion, a lower status based on skin and color: this racism is the reason for Heathcliff's exile from the civilized family. The dirt and darkness become his pride and his rebellion, also the hidden source of his pain, the hidden trigger of hate. Still vulnerable and exposed as an adolescent, Heathcliff sees Cathy, as he calls her, being romanced by the gentlemanly Edgar Linton and says: "'. . . if I knocked him down twenty times, that wouldn't make him less handsome or me more so. I wish I had light hair and a fair skin, and was dressed and behaved as well, and had a chance of being as rich as he will be!'"[12] Persecuted by Cathy's older brother, Hindley, because he is dark and dirty and gypsy-like and a foundling, regarded as a savage and treated savagely, Heathcliff's exile is a forced march from money and manners and education and refined language and civilized mating. Cathy, seduced into femininity, finds Heathcliff's attitude and expression "'black and cross'"[13]; she laughs at him because he is dirty, and for herself she takes on the manners of a lady—"pulling off her gloves, and displaying fingers wonderfully whitened with doing nothing and staying indoors."[14] Heathcliff tries to maintain an intellectual equality with Cathy, but hard labor and domestic eviction make that equality impossible: "He struggled long to keep up an equality with Catherine in her studies, and yielded with poignant though silent regret . . ."[15] Social conditions create in him what appears to be a primitive ignorance. He is forced out of the house into hard labor, treated like an animal because he is presumed to have an animal nature, savage and dark. The social conditions create the nature. Education and language become useless to him. He sinks into a rough, hostile silence, animal-like; and Cathy betrays him:

> "It would degrade me to marry Heathcliff now; so he shall never know how I love him; and that, not because he's handsome . . . but because he's more myself than I am. Whatever our souls are made of, his and mine are the same; and Linton's is as different as a moonbeam from lightning, or frost from fire."[16]

Heathcliff overhears her say that to marry him would degrade her, and he runs away, to return later, an adult, educated, rich, still dark, filled with hate and wanting revenge. She chooses white: fair, rich Edgar Linton. The great love is in sameness, not difference. This true love is destroyed by the divisive imperatives of a racist hierarchy that values white, fair, rich, and despises dark, poor. Heathcliff recognizes the brutal and irrevocable meaning of this choice, but Cathy never does. She hides from its meaning in the artifices and moral bankruptcy of femininity. She says she will marry Edgar so that she can use his money to help Heathcliff achieve equality through education and clothes and the other refinements money can buy. "'If I make any sense of your nonsense, miss,'" says Nelly, her servant and the main narrator of the story, "'it goes to convince me that you are ignorant of the duties you undertake in marrying; or else that you are a wicked, unprincipled girl.'"[17] Nelly means that intercourse is a duty of marriage; and it is immoral to have sexual relations with one man while loving another. Cathy, probably ignorant of intercourse per se, is ready to sacrifice herself, her person, for Heathcliff. Because she is self-sacrificing, she never understands why Heathcliff considers himself abandoned and betrayed by her choice of the fair, the rich, over the dark, the poor. He understands the contempt; and he also understands that in abandoning him, she is destroying herself, because they are one. "'*Why* did you despise me?'" Heathcliff asks her when she is dying. "'*Why* did you betray your own heart, Cathy? I have not one word of comfort. You deserve this. You have killed yourself. . . . You loved me—then what *right* had you to leave me?'"[18]

Even before marrying, Cathy had the passionate conviction, based on nothing she could understand, that she was doing the wrong thing; an irrational anguish—"'*Here!* and *here!*' replied Catherine, striking one hand on her forehead, and the other on her breast: 'in which place the soul lives. In my soul and in my heart, I'm convinced that I'm wrong!'"[19]

In betraying Heathcliff, she betrays herself, her own nature, her integrity; this betrayal is precisely congruent with becoming feminine, each tiny step toward white, fair, rich, a step away from self and honor. She slowly becomes a creature of social beauty and grace. She repudiates the ruffian renegade, physically strong and fearless, who roamed the moors: not Heathcliff; herself. She does kill herself: she destroys her own integrity and authenticity. The gowns, the gloves, the whitened, useless, unused skin, are emblems of her contempt for honor, self-esteem. She becomes a social cipher; she is no longer a wild will in a strong body, whole in her own nature and whole in love.

Heathcliff's sadism is not equal and opposite to Cathy's femininity. This is not a "Me Tarzan You Jane" story. There is no male-female symmetry in affliction, no simple exposition of dominance and submission modeled on sex-role stereotypes. Cathy's femininity is a slow, lazy, spoiled abandonment of self, a failure of honor and faith. Heathcliff's sadism has a different genesis: he is patriarchy's scapegoat until he becomes its male prototype. *Wuthering Heights*, perhaps uniquely, shows an interlocking chain of men socialized to hate and to cause pain through abusing power. Heathcliff is but one of many male tyrants in *Wuthering Heights*; but he alone has the self-conscious perspective of one who has been powerless and humiliated because he is dark, dirty. Because his humiliation is based on race, he cannot escape the powerlessness of childhood by growing into dominance: white, fair, rich. The pain he inflicts when he has power is never the accidental, careless dominance of the privileged. His self-consciousness, rooted in race, is necessarily political, foreshadowing *The Wretched of the Earth, The Pedagogy of the Oppressed*: "'The tyrant,'" he says, "'grinds down his slaves and they don't turn against him; they crush those beneath them.'"[20] He is the revolutionary exception, consecrated to revenge; he crushes up, not down. He will destroy those who hurt him, or those who are the descendents of those who hurt him: the family, the class, the kind, the type, anyone whose status is white, fair, rich. "'I have no pity!'" he says. "'I have no pity! The more the worms writhe, the more I yearn to crush out their entrails! It is a moral teething; and I grind with greater energy, in proportion to the increase of pain.'"[21] His sadism is proud and explicit, conjuring up no less a philosopher of cruelty than Sade: "'Had I been born where laws were less strict and tastes less dainty, I should treat myself to a slow vivisection of those two, as an evening's amusement.'"[22] The two he refers to are Cathy's daughter and his own son.

Heathcliff's persecution in childhood is distinct, a racist oppression. But the locus of male dominance, of power abused, is, according to Brontë, in the commonplace experience of being a male child, powerless as all children are, hurt and humiliated by older boys or adult men. Using narrative, Emily Brontë wrote a psychological and physical profile of the power dynamics of the English ruling class, gender male: how boys, treated sadistically, learn to take refuge in a numb, orthodox dominance, insular, hermetically sealed against vulnerability and invasion. A more familiar example might be the socializing rituals in élite English public schools: how ruling class boys are put through sadistic humiliation and physical abuse. A boy escapes this or other choreographed powerlessness into socially secure and physically safe dominance, and he never risks the possibility of being vulnerable to such injury again. This training, occurring in whatever circumstances, destroys any possibility of empathy with the powerless or the socially weak or women or the exiled or the colonialized or the ostracized because one's own body, having experienced the pain and humiliation of being powerless, is safe only in a complete disavowal of social vulnerability, of identification with the injured. Dominance means safety. One is taught, through emotional and physical torture, to snuff out empathy.

The training to sadism begins in childhood. We call it child abuse.

Heathcliff is hit, flogged, beaten, assaulted, insulted, shamed, humiliated, called a vagabond, made homeless, despised as a social inferior, ridiculed. His protector, the elder Mr Earnshaw, is benign, a gentleman of effortless dominance, power in the form of unchallenged patriarchal authority and manners. But he does not give Heathcliff a patriarchal cover, the necessary protection, the name of a father. The outcast is Heathcliff Heathcliff, a patriarchal no one with no rights because he has no last name, no father's lineage or passed-on authority. Having no name means having no earnest protection;

and so even while Mr Earnshaw is still alive, Heathcliff is physically abused by Hindley, the legitimate son, and by the servants, as the wife of the patriarch and mother of his real children says nothing, silently sanctioning the physical abuse. When Mr Earnshaw dies, Heathcliff Heathcliff is not only a nonentity in patriarchy, a nameless boy; he is a dark, dirty pariah, hated with racist malice by Hindley, whose patriarchal legitimacy gives him real power as the head-of-the-family. With Hindley the boss, Heathcliff's bad treatment becomes systematic, no longer random or covert. This physical and psychological abuse is not only his individual affliction or curse; it defines his social and civil status. Heathcliff's adult sadism begins in the mechanisms he develops to survive this cruel childhood: the very capacity to endure mistreatment, to wait, to watch, to hate; the resolve to be avenged, an essential defense against pain. "'I'm trying to settle how I shall pay Hindley back,'" says the young Heathcliff. "'I don't care how long I wait, if I can only do it at last. I hope he will not die before I do!'"[23] Heathcliff learns to take positive delight, to experience real pleasure, in watching "Hindley degrading himself past redemption; ..."[24] This watching and waiting reinforces a strong stoicism:

> He seemed a sullen, patient child; hardened, perhaps, to ill-treatment: he would stand Hindley's blows without a wink or shedding a tear, and my pinches moved him only to draw in a breath and open his eyes, as if he had hurt himself by accident and nobody was to blame.[25]

The vengeful sadism of the adult had in it the more horrible patience of the abused child. Brontë shows the ineluctable logic of what has become a contemporary sociological cliché: child abusers have often been abused as children. She shows how the tree grows from the acorn. We might have short-circuited a century of pain had we bothered to learn from her. (The Brontës are iconized but what they know about life is ignored; why? The question is one of sexual politics; the answer is nasty but inescapable.) Heathcliff survives because he learns the will to revenge and because he turns his desperation for both love and respect into an affirmative pleasure in causing pain. He causes pain to those who stand in for the adults who hurt him when he was a child. To endure as a child, he waits out cruelty, inevitably learning that same cruelty as an ethic and as a substitute for love. As an adult, he acquires the social right—the power—to be cruel: money, property, manners, dress, the language and education to pass as one who has some right to dominance, though he is still perceived as dark, now called morose, not dirty. His distinctive rebellion was to become an oppressor of purposeful, canny, and merciless cruelty: not a slovenly perpetrator of random violence who hurts those in his immediate reach; not a down-and-out drunk whose circle of violence is limited to his own outcast status. Heathcliff's sadism is an energetic upward mobility, but to a political purpose: the radical repudiation of, the violent subversion of, the class system that hurt him. He makes no common bond with others hurt in their powerlessness as children; he has no empathy. Instead, the pariah status of race is the ground he stands on. He could never have the grace of effortless dominance, inherited grace, white grace, patri-archal élan; nor did he want it. He wanted nouveau power, the vulgar display of sadistic revenge. Having been an outcast, he knew how to manipulate the rich, the fair, the white; he knew more about them than they would ever know about themselves (learned through the waiting, the watching, the enduring). He understood power from the outside, as the powerful never can, never have. He knew the vulnerability of those who had hurt him; he knew where they were weak or stupid or ignorant or degenerate or greedy or arrogant. He used their flaws of character against them, a kind of insurgent ju-jitsu, in the hands of a master-survivor of despair and powerlessness a dangerous weapon, one always underestimated by the ruling class. He knows the points of pain and never misses. He causes pain in such a way that those he hurts become cruel against others according to his purposes and plan; he makes them his accomplices in inflicting pain on others and in degrading themselves. He appreciates both emotional and physical suffering, and causes both kinds. In this parable of race oppression, Heathcliff turns on and crushes the class that oppressed him: destroying in himself finally and forever anything fragile or sensitive that might have survived his own training in pain. The sadist as revolutionary can accomplish only revenge, turning-the-tables, a new social order of terror and pain that mimics the old social order of terror and pain. The sadist cannot accomplish transformation or change toward justice or equality. He and the ruling class have too much in common: each is remorseless;

each is incapable of empathy. Heathcliff has learned power's main lesson to its own: feel no empathy. This is a parable of the revolution failed, another coup d'etat just like the last one; the Terror rampant in one oppressed-turned-oppressor's heart.

Hindley marries when Heathcliff is a child; the wife dies in childbirth. Hindley becomes degenerate. He "neither wept nor prayed; he cursed and defied; execrated God and man, and gave himself up to reckless dissipation. The servants could not bear his tyrannical and evil conduct long: ..."26 This was the degradation Heathcliff took pleasure in watching. Hindley's son, Hareton, was another neglected and eventually abused son in this saga of male socialization to brutality. Hindley was a violent drunk. Nelly, the servant, tries to hide the child from Hindley, always in danger from his father's emotional and physical excesses. The child "was impressed with a wholesome terror of encountering either his [Hindley's] wild beast's fondness or his madman's rage; for in one he ran a chance of being squeezed and kissed to death, and in the other of being flung into the fire, or dashed against the wall; and the poor thing remained perfectly quiet wherever I chose to put him."27 He would be secreted away in a cupboard or cabinet or closet to protect him from his father. On one occasion, Hindley takes the child up to the top of a staircase and holds him upside down; distracted by noise, he drops him on his head. Hindley is violent and dissolute; Hareton is a neglected and abused child; Heathcliff as an adult moves back in, managing slowly to buy up Hindley's property by encouraging his dissipation. Heathcliff befriends the abused child, but does nothing to help him, only encourages the self-destruction, with its attendant violence, of the father. Asked why he likes Heathcliff, Hareton says: "'... he pays dad back what he gies to me—he curses daddy for cursing me. He says I mun do as I will.'"28 Heathcliff cultivates the affection of the abused child, meanwhile keeping him uneducated and neglected. Heathcliff encourages the child's hatred for his own father. Hareton's loyalty to Heathcliff is the desperate loyalty an abused animal gives anyone who is kind to it. When Hindley dies, Heathcliff manages to take over Wuthering Heights and the orphan, Hareton. Vengeance on Hareton is part of Heathcliff's plan, a purposeful violation of the innocent, in the commonplace tradition of cruelty from older man to younger boy and also as a conscious act of class retaliation. Hareton, by birth superior, rich, fair, white, will be raised by Heathcliff as a savage, raised like an animal, raised as Heathcliff was raised. "'Now, my bonny lad,'" says Heathcliff when Hindley has died, "'you are *mine!* And we'll see if one tree won't grow as crooked as another, with the same wind to twist it!'"[29] Hareton is already marked by the physical child abuse; Heathcliff need not physically torture him. What terror and pain can do has been done to the child. But he will hurt the child as he was hurt, treat him with the same neglect and contempt, keep him primitive, outcast, a rude, rough animal. Hareton becomes what he is taught to be. He has no means of expressing himself, no language, no gestures, adequate to his genuinely kinder sensibility. The happy ending of *Wuthering Heights*, such as it is, when Hareton begins to learn to read and write from Cathy's daughter, Catherine, and they find in each other an equality of intellectual curiosity and emotional gentleness, provides in affirmative form the great moral the book has been teaching all along: we become what we are taught to be; education is the one civilizing principle, leveling all distinctions of class and status. The narrator of *Wuthering Heights*, Nelly, a servant, is also an equal in learning and discourse; and *Wuthering Heights* is an anguished indictment of bad education—education, like love, based on difference, not sameness, education that creates distinctions instead of creating a community of shared values and pleasures. The physical abuse is recognized as a form of bad education; the neglect also educates. These create the sadist and the savage. Language, books, communication, affection, inclusion on a basis of equality of all persons, is the education that is life-affirming, transforming, humane. The love based on sameness reaches fulfilment in a community that practices education based on sameness: a sameness of rights and dignity and access to intellectual achievement and simple self-respect. Class differences are created through how children are educated; so are sadism, tyranny, and, potentially, equality.

The neglect of children in infancy was particularly commonplace. Childbirth often caused the death of the mother. Cathy dies in childbirth and so does Hareton's mother. The infant no doubt bore some stigma as the instrument of the wife's death, especially if she were cherished. Catherine, the daughter of Heathcliff's love, Cathy, and the gentleman, fair, rich, white Edgar Linton, was born "a puny seven months' child"; her mother died two hours later, and the infant "might have wailed out of life, and nobody cared a morsel, during those first hours of its existence"; the infant was "friendless."[30] She too becomes part of Heathcliff's revenge. He determines that she will marry his son, named Linton by his runaway wife, Isabella, Edgar Linton's sister, because Isabella knew how much Heathcliff hated the Linton name and the Linton heritage. The son was conceived in the carnal brutality of a sadistic marital relation that included physical abuse and emotional torture. Heathcliff's plan was to own Hindley's property, Wuthering Heights, and Edgar Linton's property, and to destroy the heirs of both. To accomplish this, he forced a marriage between his son, Linton, who was close to death, and Catherine, whose father was close to death.

Catherine was a child of her time—she had her own burden of neglect and loneliness to bear. Motherless, raised mostly alone, but treated after neglect as an infant with love and respect, she grows up provincial and protected, isolated, not worldly, somewhat spoiled but decent and essentially kind. She is not brutalized as a child. Mostly, she is lonely. This loneliness and an ignorance of malice prepare her to love her cousin, Linton, first as a child, then as a young adult.

When Heathcliff's runaway wife dies, he takes back their son. Isabella has tried to keep Linton away from Heathcliff. She sends him to his uncle, Edgar Linton. Catherine is enchanted to have a cousin. She thinks of him with childish innocence as a friend, playmate, companion, brother, twin. When Heathcliff manages to get physical custody of the child, Catherine has taken from her this longed for friend. Meeting Linton as an adult, by accident, on the moors, she already has a great tenderness in her heart for him. Her father forbids her to see Linton. This she cannot understand. He is trying to keep her from the harm Heathcliff can do her. She is moved by Linton's apparent suffering and his apparent sensitivity. He is ill and weak. She is stirred to empathy in her first admiration, then to pity as she sees his weaknesses of character. She takes these feelings for love.

Linton is physically weak, chronically ill, probably consumptive, slowly dying. Because Linton is dying and Heathcliff wants Catherine to marry him before he dies, Heathcliff kidnaps Catherine and forces the marriage.

Linton is a tyrant of self-indulgence and passivity. His sadism is no

---

more palatable than his father's, though his character is effete. This is no small part of the brilliance of *Wuthering Heights*. The men are different personalities, and the tyranny of each expands beyond the individual personality to fill the provocative imperatives of male dominance. The sadism or brutality of each is exercised by each according to his need and according to his means. The need is created by the cruelty of man-to-boy. Heathcliff, with the outcast's lucidity, describes his son's character to Catherine:

> "... Linton requires his whole stock of care and kindness for himself. Linton can play the little tyrant well. He'll undertake to torture any number of cats, if their teeth be drawn and their claws pared. You'll be able to tell his uncle fine tales of his *kindness*, when you get home again, I assure you."[31]

(Heathcliff's sadism includes keeping Catherine in captivity to force this marriage while her father is dying.)

Linton's sadism comes out of his weakness. It is terror of his father that motivates him: "Linton had sunk prostrate again in another paroxysm of helpless fear, caused by his father's glance towards him, I suppose: there was nothing else to produce such humiliation."[32] This sadism from fear, the sadism of the weak, is the cowardly relief that comes when his father's cruelty is turned on someone else, not him, a classic defensive posture of the weak. Heathcliff himself physically abuses Catherine, and Linton's vicarious pleasure in the abuse is ambivalent but real:

> "And were you pleased to have her struck?" ...
> "I winked," he answered: "I wink to see my father strike a dog or a horse, he does it so hard. Yet I was glad at first—she deserved punishing for pushing me: but when papa was gone, she made me come to the window and showed me her cheek cut on the inside, against her teeth, and her mouth filling with blood ... and she has never spoken to me since: and I sometimes think she can't speak for the pain. I don't like to think so; but she's a naughty thing for crying continually; and she looks so pale and wild, I'm afraid of her."[33]

Heathcliff has pushed the dying Linton to romance Catherine, to engage her, entice her, enlist her sympathy; in doing this, he pushes Linton to his death: "I could not picture a father treating a dying child as tyrannically and wickedly as I afterwards learned Heathcliff had treated him," says Nelly, "... [Heathcliff's] efforts redoubling the more imminently his avaricious and unfeeling plans were threatened with defeat by death."[34] Afraid that Linton will die before Catherine can be seduced to marry him, Heathcliff uses physical force against her to compel the marriage. But he has destroyed his son. In destroying his son, he brings out Linton's every despicable quality. This is the full depth of Heathcliff's cruelty: the actual destruction of his son but also his moral deconstruction, the unravelling of anything kind or decent in him so that he will be morally degraded and cruel to the fullness of his capacity. He enjoys not only Linton's suffering but the suffering that Linton will cause Catherine: "'It is not I who will make him hateful to you,'" Heathcliff tells her, "'—it is his own sweet spirit. He's as bitter as gall ... I heard him draw a pleasant picture ... of what he would do [to you] if he were as strong as I: the inclination is there, and his very weakness will sharpen his wits to find a substitute for strength.'"[35] The graphic picture of a man driving his son to death, knowing the son will endure his own pain by causing pain to someone else—planning the pain and the pain that the pain will cause—makes one ask as Isabella, Heathcliff's wife, did: "Is Mr Heathcliff a man? If so, is he mad? And if not, is he a devil? ... I beseech you to explain, if you can, what I have married..."[36]

Heathcliff is the worst man, different in degree, not in kind, from the other men who abuse women and children; Brontë emphasizes the abuse of boy children because she is writing about the construction of male dominance. Heathcliff is writ bigger: cruelty is his genius, his ethic; hatred, the radical emotion that fuels his one-man revolution against the rich, the fair, the white, even when they are his own progeny. He destroys everyone precisely because his dominance cannot be passed on; that is the meaning of being an outcast, dark, gypsy-like; he cannot pass on what he is without passing on his degraded status. His radical cruelty, based on class hate, reminds one, however unwillingly, of the more attractive virtues of those born to dominance: an indifferent or even gracious or affable condescension; a security in power and identity that can moderate or sublimate exercises in social sadism. Heathcliff's is a radical, violent revolution incarnated in a socially constructed sadism that appears to have the force of nature: it levels everything before it. Brontë's feminist genius was to show how this sadism was made; how and why. Her political wisdom, a grounding in a profound though not effortless humanism, led her ultimately to disavow radical violence, though her creature, Heathcliff, was so mesmerizing, so grossly misread as a romantic figure, that the author's repudiation of Heathcliff's cruelty and violence has been overlooked or taken as insincere. After all, don't women write romances and fantasize physically brutal heroes? How could she have created him without loving him?—a question asked only of a woman author, who is presumed to be motivated by infatuation, not knowledge; ersatz romanticism, not analytical insight scalpel-like in exposing the viscera of social oppression.

In the narrative itself, Brontë warned against misreading Heathcliff. Isabella, his wife, stands in for the bad reader—a brilliant, ironic political point in itself. The bad reader is the sentimental reader of romance novels when life, love, and art demand a confrontation with the politics of power. The bad reader romanticizes the sadist and reads the rapist, the abuser, the violent man, as a romantic hero: tortured himself, despite proof that he is the torturer. Heathcliff describes this bad reader when he describes Isabella:

> "She abandoned [her family and friends] under a delusion ... picturing in me a hero of romance, and expecting unlimited indulgences from my chivalrous devotion. I can hardly regard her in the light of a rational creature, so obstinately has she persisted in forming a fabulous notion of my character and acting on the false impression she cherished."[37]

She is in the most ordinary relationship with this man: an ingenue in love with an outsider, a mysterious man who is dark and brooding, hurt, sensual; she marries him and it is banal to say that men brutalize their wives. Isabella is ordinary, the way most of us are: taught to be bad readers of men, kept ignorant of the meaning of dominance and sex, in rebellion against the conventional wisdom—the conventions—of the family; the dangerous man is the route for those who must mix ignorance with rebellion.

Heathcliff's contempt for Isabella has in it, again, a stunning lucidity, this time a moral lucidity. She has seen his sadism—she has seen him torture her dog, she has let him do it; "'... no brutality disgusted her,'" says Heathcliff, "'... if only her precious person were secure from injury!'"[38] It is this basic immorality of feminine love—being the exception to the violence—no conscience to stop the brutality against others just so one is exempt from it—that underlines the meaning of femininity: there is no integrity, no wholeness, no honor. The torture of the dog is described twice, once by Nelly who sees it hanging, almost dead, and releases it just in time to save its life; and once by Heathcliff, who describes the little dog's vulnerability, Isabella's pleading for it and then doing nothing to save it, because she inferred that Heathcliff wanted to hang "'every being belonging to her, except one: possibly she took that exception for herself.'"[39] The exception, of course, was Cathy, Edgar's wife. But for this emotional nothing, this inferred regard for her as an exception to his general hatred of her family and friends, she could watch her dog tortured, slowly killed for all she knew, since she did not rescue it. This is a moral bankruptcy familiar to women in love, who will give up everything to be the exception. The real point is that having no honor is an integral part of the female condition, especially the femininity of the woman in love.

Cathy has warned Isabella of her "'deplorable ignorance of his character ... He's not a rough diamond—a pearl-containing oyster of a rustic: he's a fierce, pitiless, wolfish man.'"[40] Her love does not depend on bad reading; she knows Heathcliff.

Heathcliff elopes with Isabella to cut her off from her family, to hurt Edgar and Cathy, to compromise her. In marriage, he brutalizes her. "'She degenerates into a mere slut!'" he tells Nelly. "'She is tired of trying to please me uncommonly early. You'd hardly credit it, but the very morrow of our wedding, she was weeping to go home.'"[41] Isabella confides that she wanted to go home "in twenty-four hours after I left it ..."[42] These are references to the wedding night: for the nineteenth century, they are overt references to a brutal marital rape, particularly underscored when Heathcliff calls his wife a slut to a servant. The carnal abuse of Isabella is unrelenting: "... I'll not repeat his language, nor describe his habitual conduct: he is ingenious and unresting in seeking to gain my abhorrence! I sometimes wonder at him with an intensity that deadens my fear: yet, I assure you, a tiger or a venomous serpent could not rouse terror in me equal to that which he wakens."[43] She runs away. He had the legal authority to find her and bring her back. It is clear that he traces her and knows where she is. But the sexual sadism, the sadism of the marriage relation, has bored him. He leaves her be. Emotionally, she wants revenge; he has managed to turn her into someone who wants to inflict pain because it was inflicted on her: "'. . . but what misery laid on Heathcliff could content me, unless I have a hand in it? I'd rather he suffered *less*, if I might cause his sufferings and he might *know* that I was the cause. Oh, I owe him so much.'"[44] But before she runs away, there is a moment of another kind of violence, a violence rooted more in justice than revenge:

> "I surveyed the weapon inquisitively. A hideous notion struck me: how powerful I should be possessing such an instrument! I took it from his hand, and touched the blade. He looked astonished at the expression on my face assumed during a brief second: it was not horror, it was covetousness."[45]

The weapon is Hindley's; Isabella is supposed to lock Heathcliff's door, because Hindley thinks otherwise he, Hindley, will kill Heathcliff. The moment of recognition that she could kill Heathcliff—the power a weapon would give her—is a moment of dignity. It is a single, lucid perception of a right to self-defense. It is a single, lucid perception of a right to execution: a right morally undeniable to battered wives; a right renounced sometimes for escape, sometimes because women will not kill. This morally relentless book, this radical dissection of violence, gives quiet, quick consideration to what we will not yet discuss: the right of a battered wife to execute the man who tortures her. The point is not an equality of violence, nor is it in an equality of sadism—the point is not that he should suffer. The point is that he must be dead for her to be free. The point is that there is dignity and freedom in executing him. Sadism is in the long, drawn-out vengeance; justice is in stopping the torture.

Charlotte Brontë, trying to defend her sister because Emily had written a rude, untamed book, wrote: "Having formed these beings she did not know what she had done."[46] I think she did; and that we have not yet faced what Emily Brontë knew and said and showed. I want us to read her when we read Fanon and Millett; when we think about race and gender and revolution; when we discuss questions of violence and sadism. "'I've dreamt in my life dreams that have stayed with me ever after,'" says Cathy, "'and changed my ideas: they've gone through and through me, like wine through water, and altered the colour of my mind.'"⁴⁷ To some who have read it, *Wuthering Heights* is such a dream. Now it is time to read it fully awake.

Notes

1. Currer Bell [Charlotte Brontë], "Biographical Notice of Ellis and Acton Bell [Emily and Anne Brontë]," September 19, 1850, xix–xxvi, in Emily Brontë, *Wuthering Heights* (New York: Random House/The Modern Library, 1978), pp. xxiv–xxv.

2. Currer Bell, "Editor's Preface to the New Edition of *Wuthering Heights*," undated, xxvii–xxxii, in Brontë, *Wuthering Heights*, xxviii.

3. Bell, "Editor's Preface," xxiv.

4. Emily Brontë, *Wuthering Heights*, p. 95.

5. Brontë, *Wuthering Heights*, p. 97.

6. Brontë, *Wuthering Heights*, p. 197.

7. Brontë, *Wuthering Heights*, p. 51.

8. Brontë, *Wuthering Heights*, p. 54.

9. Brontë, *Wuthering Heights*, p. 149.

10. Brontë, *Wuthering Heights*, pp. 42–43.

11. Brontë, *Wuthering Heights*, p. 43.

12. Brontë, *Wuthering Heights*, p. 66.

13. Brontë, *Wuthering Heights*, p. 63.

14. Brontë, *Wuthering Heights*, p. 62.

15. Brontë, *Wuthering Heights*, p. 79.

16. Brontë, *Wuthering Heights*, p. 95.

17. Brontë, *Wuthering Heights*, p. 97.

18. Brontë, *Wuthering Heights*, p. 189.

19. Brontë, *Wuthering Heights*, p. 93.

20. Brontë, *Wuthering Heights*, p. 132.

21. Brontë, *Wuthering Heights*, p. 179.

22. Brontë, *Wuthering Heights*, p. 318.

23. Brontë, *Wuthering Heights*, p. 71.

24. Brontë, *Wuthering Heights*, p. 77.

25. Brontë, *Wuthering Heights*, p. 44.

26. Brontë, *Wuthering Heights*, p. 76.

27. Brontë, *Wuthering Heights*, p. 86.

28. Brontë, *Wuthering Heights*, p. 129.

29. Brontë, *Wuthering Heights*, p. 219.

30. Brontë, *Wuthering Heights*, p. 193.

31. Brontë, *Wuthering Heights*, p. 324.

32. Brontë, *Wuthering Heights*, p. 316.
33. Brontë, *Wuthering Heights*, p. 331.
34. Brontë, *Wuthering Heights*, p. 305.
35. Brontë, *Wuthering Heights*, p. 338.
36. Brontë, *Wuthering Heights*, p. 160.
37. Brontë, *Wuthering Heights*, p. 176.
38. Brontë, *Wuthering Heights*, p. 177.
39. Brontë, *Wuthering Heights*, p. 177.
40. Brontë, *Wuthering Heights*, p. 120.
41. Brontë, *Wuthering Heights*, p. 176.
42. Brontë, *Wuthering Heights*, p. 160.
43. Brontë, *Wuthering Heights*, p. 170.
44. Brontë, *Wuthering Heights*, p. 211.
45. Brontë, *Wuthering Heights*, p. 165.
46. Bell, "Editor's Preface," xxix.
47. Brontë, *Wuthering Heights*, p. 93.

Voyage in the Dark:
Hers and Ours

1987

In my class at the University of Minnesota I also taught this book by Jean Rhys. I like her toughness. I like her lack of sentimentality. I hate her twenty-seven-year silence, and it hurts me that she published so little. Her work was lost once, and I see it fading now. To last, work must not only be in print, stay in print, but other writers must use it, be influenced by it, value it. If those other writers are women, their work will disappear too, you see.

VOYAGE IN THE DARK by Jean Rhys, first published in 1934, is a small, terrifying masterpiece. The same could be said of *Quartet* (1928), *Leaving Mr Mackenzie* (1931), *Good Morning, Midnight* (1939), and *Wide Sargasso Sea* (1966). I have not been able to find *The Left Bank*, first published in 1927. The twenty-seven-year silence between *Good Morning, Midnight* and *Wide Sargasso Sea* suggests that writing small, terrifying masterpieces is not a rewarding activity for a woman.

Elegant, hard as nails, without a shred of sentimentality, Rhys writes, usually in the first person, of women as lost ingenues, lonely commodities floating from man to man; the man uses the woman and pays her off when he is tired of her; with each man, the woman's value lessens, she becomes more used, more tattered, more shopworn. These books are about how men use women: not how society punishes women for having sex but how men punish women with whom they want to have sex, with whom they have had sex. The feminist maxim, *Every woman is one man away from welfare*, is true but banal up against Rhys's portrait of the woman alone; there is no welfare; only poverty, homelessness, desperation, and the eventual and inevitable need to find another man.

In *Voyage in the Dark*, Victor is paying off Anna, the narrator, for his friend, Walter. He looks at a photograph of an actress, Anna's friend, Laurie. "'She really is pretty. But hard—a bit hard,' as if he were talking to himself. 'They get like that. It's a pity.'"[1] His stone-cold arrogance is conveyed and so is the narrator's own lonely nonexistence: *as if he were talking to himself.* Her consciousness takes him in—his style, his meaning—and also makes real for the reader the fact that she does not exist for him. Rhys creates women who are perceived by men as pieces, bought on the market, but the woman herself says what life is like: describes the man and the transaction and her feelings before and during and after, her existence within the framework of his existence and simultaneously her existence outside the sphere of his imagination altogether: the woman who is the piece, yes, and who at the same time sees, feels, knows, who has bitter wit and sharp irony, who is caustic, who lives in what men dignify for themselves as an existential despair, who must survive in a world men make smaller than her intelligence. "I was thinking, 'I'm nineteen and I've got to go on living and living and living.'"[2] On the surface the woman is the pretty thing, the ingenue alone and on her way down, and under the surface she has the narrator's consciousness, an objective intelligence that notes every detail of meaning. It is a cold, hard intelligence. Women are judged in a man's world by the surface. Rhys plays the narrator's surface, what it means to men, against the narrator's consciousness. The men meet her body. They never meet her intelligence. They could not hypothesize it or imagine it or withstand it. They never know that she is seeing them; only that they are seeing her.

The arrogance of the men is level, civil, polite, mannered, disdainful but without physical aggression; these are rich johns, not violent rapists. They buy, they don't steal. They buy goods, not people, certainly not people like themselves. The disdain is what they feel for this lower life-form that exists for their pleasure:

> Mr Jones said, "He knew you'd be either eighteen or twenty-two. You girls only have two ages. You're eighteen and so of course your friend's twenty-two. Of course."[3]

The contempt is like some impermeable finish, glossy, polyurethane, a hard, glossy shell; no pores; nothing gets in or out. The narrator captures every nuance of this contempt. "'Poor little Anna,' making his voice very kind. 'I'm so damned sorry you've been having a bad time.' Making his voice very kind, but the look in his eyes was like a high, smooth, unclimbable wall. No communication possible. You have to be three-quarters mad even to attempt it."[4]

Anna is eighteen when the story opens. She is on the road in a vaudeville show. She is used to men picking her up. She has not had sex. Walter takes her to dinner. She discovers it is dinner in a suite of rooms with a bedroom. "He kissed me again, and his mouth was hard, and I remembered him smelling the glass of wine and I couldn't think of anything but that, and I hated him. 'Look here, let me go,' I said."[5] *I remembered him smelling the glass of wine and I couldn't think of anything but that*: in this one detail, the narrator is forcing us to remember that the man is a consumer, not a lover. Refusing him, she goes into the bedroom. She wants love, romance: "Soon he'll come in again and kiss me, but differently. He'll be different and so I'll be different. It'll be different. I thought, 'It'll be different, different. It must be different.'"[6] He doesn't come in; she lies on the bed, cold: "The fire was like a painted fire; no warmth came from it."[7] He waits for her to come out, takes her home, back to an empty, cold, rented room. She becomes ill, and writes him a note asking for help. He visits her, helps her, gives her money, pays the landlady to take care of her, finds other rooms for her for when she is well, and the romance begins. She is not bought for a night; instead, she has the long-term emotional and material security of an affair, being his until he is tired of her. She tells him she is not a virgin, but she is. After making love the first time, she thinks: "'When I shut my eyes I'll be able to see this room all my life.'"[8] She doesn't look in the mirror to see if she has changed. "I thought that it had been just like the girls said, except that I hadn't known it would hurt so much."[9] She was infatuated. She wanted to be valued, loved. Instead, she had to get up in the middle of the night to sneak out of his bedroom and out of his house, a woman alone in the big night. "Of course, you get used to things, you get used to anything."[10] She is happy and she is afraid; she knows her happiness will end. Warned by her friend, Maudie, older and also in vaudeville, she makes the tragic mistake. "'Only, don't get soppy about him' [Maudie] said.

'That's fatal. The thing with men is to get everything you can out of them and not care a damn. You ask any girl in London—or any girl in the whole world if it comes to that [...]'"[11] When Walter is finished with her, she knows it: "I wanted to pretend it was like the night before, but it wasn't any use. Being afraid is cold like ice, and it's like when you can't breathe. 'Afraid of what?' I thought."[12] She sees Walter put money in her purse. She begins the inevitable descent; the first man over and done with; the others waiting; no money of her own; no home. She wanders through a world of men and rented rooms. Nothing assuages her grief: "Really all you want is night, and to lie in the dark and pull the sheet over your head and sleep, and before you know where you are it is night—that's one good thing. You pull the sheet over your head and think, 'He got sick of me,' and 'Never, not ever, never.' And then you go to sleep. You sleep very quickly when you are like that and you don't dream either. It's as if you were dead."[13] (Today we call this grief "depression." Women have it.)

But this is no story of a woman's broken heart. This is the story of a woman who is, in the eyes of the men who behold her, a tart, whether her heart is broken or not. "'I picked up a girl in London and she.... Last night I slept with a girl who....' That was me. Not 'girl' perhaps. Some other word, perhaps. Never mind."[14]

No one has written about a woman's desperation quite like this—the great loneliness, the great coldness, the great fear, in living in a world where, as one man observes, "'a girl's clothes cost more than the girl inside them.'"[15] Eliot and Hardy have written vividly, unforgettably, about women in desperate downfalls, ostracized and punished by and because of a sexual double standard—I think of Hetty in *Adam Bede* and Tess in *Tess of the D'Urbervilles*; Hawthorne also did this in *The Scarlet Letter*. But Rhys simply gives us the woman as woman, the woman alone, her undiluted essence as a woman, how men see her and what she is for. There is a contemporary sense of alienation—distance and detachment from any social mosaic, except that the men and the money are the social mosaic. Society is simpler; exploitation is simpler; survival depends on being the thing men want to use, even as there is no hope at all for survival on those terms, just going on and on, the same but poorer and older. Anna observes the desperate masquerade of women to get from day to day:

The clothes of most of the women who passed were like caricatures of the clothes in the shop-windows, but when they stopped to look you saw that their eyes were fixed on the future. "If I could buy this, then of course I'd be quite different." Keep hope alive and you can do anything [...] But what happens if you don't hope any more, if your back's broken? What happens then?[16]

She paints a deep despair in women, each, for the sake of tomorrow, continually aware of her own worth on the market, thinking always of the dressed surface that does cost more than she costs.

Anna becomes pregnant from one of her casual encounters and *Voyage in the Dark* ends with a graphic, virtually unbearable description of an illegal abortion and Anna's subsequent near death from bleeding. The doctor can be called once there are complications, told she fell down the steps. "'Oh, so you had a fall, did you?[...] You girls are too naive to live, aren't you?[...] She'll be all right [...] Ready to start all over again in no time, I've no doubt.'"[17]

Anna is eighteen when the book begins, nineteen when it ends.

In *Voyage in the Dark*, Rhys uses race to underline Anna's total estrangement from what is taken to be middle-class reality. Anna has been raised in the West Indies, fifth-generation West Indian on her mother's side, as she brags to Walter. This boast and an accusation from her stepmother suggest that Anna's mother was black. But her status is white, the legitimate daughter of a white father who has many illegitimate black children. Being white estranges her from these undeniable relatives and from the black society in which she lives. She is alien. Her stepmother blames Anna's inability to marry up in England on her closeness with blacks in her childhood: "I tried to teach you to talk like a lady and behave like a lady and not like a nigger and of course I couldn't do it. Impossible to get you away from the servants.... Exactly like a nigger you talked—and still do."[18] Having sex with Walter, all she can think about is something she saw when she was a child, an old slave list, the mulatto slaves: "Maillotte Boyd, aged 18, mulatto, house servant."[19] She is eighteen, possibly mulatto; in the sex act, this other woman, like her, haunts her. But Anna knows she is an outsider to blacks, not accepted by the servants: "But I knew that of course she disliked me too because I was white; and that I would never be able to explain to her that I hated being white. Being white and getting like Hester [the stepmother] and all the things you get—old and sad and everything. I kept thinking, 'No. . . . No. . . .' And I knew that day that I'd started to grow old and nothing could stop it."[20] She hates London: "This is London—hundreds of thousands of white people white people [. . .]"[21] She contrasts the white people with the dark houses, the dark streets; in literary terms, she makes the white skin stand out against the dark backdrop of the city. Anna is a total outsider, belonging nowhere. *Voyage in the Dark* exposes and condemns the colonial racism of the English; and it also uses Anna's outsider state-of-being to underscore the metaphysical exile of any woman alone, any woman as a woman per se, an exile from the world of men and the human worth they have, the money and power they have; an exile especially from the legitimacy that inheres simply in being male.

Now: in 1934 Jean Rhys published a book about women as sexual commodities; sophisticated and brilliant, it showed the loneliness, the despair, the fear, and by showing how men look at and value and use women, it showed how all women live their lives in relation to this particular bottom line, this fate, this being bought-and-sold. And in 1934, Jean Rhys published a book that described an illegal abortion, showed its often terminal horror, and also showed how it was simply part of what a woman was supposed to undergo, the same way she was supposed to be used and then abandoned, or poor, or homeless, or at the mercy of a male buyer. Jean Rhys is one of many "lost women" writers rediscovered and widely read in the 1970s because of the interest in women's writing generated by the current wave of feminism. People are happy to say she was a great writer without much meaning it and certainly without paying any serious attention to the substance of her work: to what she said. She wrote about the loneliness of being a woman, poor and homeless, better than anyone I know of. She wrote about what being used takes from you and how you never get it back. Women who should have been reading her read *The Catcher in the Rye* or Jean Genet instead because her books were gone. We had books by men on prostitution and street life: Genet's broke some new ground, but there is a long history of men writing on prostitution. In fact, at the beginning of *Voyage in the Dark*, Rhys makes a writerly joke about those books. Anna is reading Zola's *Nana*: "Maudie said, 'I know; it's about a tart. I think it's disgusting. I bet you a man writing a book about a tart tells a lot of lies one way and another. Besides, all books are like that—just somebody stuffing you up.'"22 Well, *Voyage in the Dark*, a book by a woman, doesn't just "stuff you up." It is, finally, a truthful book. It is, at the very least, a big part of the truth; and, I think, a lot closer to the whole truth than the women's movement that resurrected her work would like to think.

Sometimes I look around at my generation of women writers, the ones a little older and a little younger too, and I know we will be gone: disappeared the way Jean Rhys was disappeared. She was better than most of us are. She said more in the little she wrote—with her twenty-seven-year silence. Her narrative genius was just that: genius. We expect our mediocre little books to last forever, and don't even think they have to risk anything to do so. Yet, the fine books of our time by women go out of print continually; some are brought back, most are not. I wish I had grown up reading Jean Rhys. I did grow up reading D. H. Lawrence and Jean Genet and Henry Miller. But her truth wasn't allowed to live. To hell with their fights against censorship; she was obliterated. I couldn't learn from her work because it wasn't there. And I needed Jean Rhys a hell of a lot more than I needed the above-named bad boys: as a woman and as a writer. I don't know why we now, we women writers, think that our books are going to live. There is nothing to indicate that things in general have changed for women writers. I know the children of the future will have a lot of sexy literary trash from men; but I don't think they will have much by women that shows even as much as Jean Rhys showed in 1934. This disappearance of women writers costs us; this is a lot worse than having to reinvent the wheel. When a woman writer is "lost," the possibilities of the women after her are lost too; her true perceptions are driven out of existence and we are left with books by men that tell "a lot of lies one way and another." These are lies that keep women lost in all senses: the writers, the Annas. We have not done much to stop ourselves from being wiped out because we think that we are the exceptional generation, different from all the ones that came before: the lone generation to endure male dominance (we say we are fighting it) by writing about it. Our dead sisters, their books buried with them, try not to laugh.

Notes

1. Jean Rhys, *Voyage in the Dark* (New York: Popular Library, n.d.), p. 149.
2. Jean Rhys, *Voyage in the Dark*, p. 93.
3. Jean Rhys, *Voyage in the Dark*, p. 11.
4. Jean Rhys, *Voyage in the Dark*, p. 148.
5. Jean Rhys, *Voyage in the Dark*, p. 19.
6. Jean Rhys, *Voyage in the Dark*, p. 20.
7. Jean Rhys, *Voyage in the Dark*, p. 20.
8. Jean Rhys, *Voyage in the Dark*, p. 31.
9. Jean Rhys, *Voyage in the Dark*, p. 32.
10. Jean Rhys, *Voyage in the Dark*, pp. 34–35.
11. Jean Rhys, *Voyage in the Dark*, p. 38.
12. Jean Rhys, *Voyage in the Dark*, p. 74.
13. Jean Rhys, *Voyage in the Dark*, p. 120.
14. Jean Rhys, *Voyage in the Dark*, pp. 134–35.
15. Jean Rhys, *Voyage in the Dark*, p. 39.
16. Jean Rhys, *Voyage in the Dark*, p. 112.
17. Jean Rhys, *Voyage in the Dark*, p. 160.
18. Jean Rhys, *Voyage in the Dark*, p. 55.
19. Jean Rhys, *Voyage in the Dark*, p. 44.
20. Jean Rhys, *Voyage in the Dark*, p. 60.
21. Jean Rhys, *Voyage in the Dark*, p. 15.
22. Jean Rhys, *Voyage in the Dark*, p. 9.

III

TAKE BACK
THE DAY

One must talk, after all; share interests
with the people one's surrounded by. What
kind of humbug, in a city of rapists, holds out
for the dignity of womanhood?
                              John Gardner, *Shadows*

A Feminist Looks at Saudi Arabia

1978

It's hard to fight liberals. They slip and slide. Jimmy Carter had a human rights dimension to his foreign policy so that South Africa was held accountable for its racism. Countries that systematically segregate women, like Saudi Arabia, had nothing to fear from this human rights president. Now that Reagan's support of apartheid is Amerikan foreign policy, people may think the points made in this essay are glib or cheap. I hate apartheid, in South Africa and in Saudi Arabia, on the basis of race or on the basis of sex. Do women matter or not? Is there a single standard of human rights that includes women or not?

S OMETIMES I CANNOT believe the world I live in. Usually I go along, believing. As a feminist and a writer, I study rape, pornography, wife-beating. I see the abused bodies of women, in life and in newspapers. I meet, in life and in books, the torn minds, the locked-in victims. I grieve, I rage, but through it all, I believe. This ability to believe comes, no doubt, from hearing as a child the desperate memories of those, some in my own family, who survived Nazi concentration camps and Russian pogroms. Being a Jew, one learns to believe in the reality of cruelty and one learns to recognize indifference to human suffering as a fact.

Sometimes though, my credulity is strained. The fact that women, after over half a century of struggle, apparently will not have equal rights under the law in this country is difficult to believe, especially on those grotesque days when Mr Carter makes impassioned statements on the importance of human rights elsewhere. Disbelief leads me to wonder why the plight of male dissidents in Russia overtakes Mr Carter's not very empathetic imagination when women in this

97

country are in mental institutions or lobotomized or simply beaten to death or nearly to death by men who do not like the way they have done the laundry or prepared dinner. And on days when this sanctimonious president makes certain that poor women will not have access to life-saving abortion, and tells us without embarrassment that "life is unfair," my disbelief verges on raw anguish. I ask myself why the pervasive sexual tyranny in this country—the tyranny of men over women, with its symptomatic expression in economic deprivation and legal discrimination—is not, at least, on the list of human rights violations that Mr Carter keeps on the tip of his forked tongue.

But mostly, inability to believe surfaces on days when Mr Carter and his cronies—and yes, I must admit, especially Andrew Young—discuss our good friend, Saudi Arabia. That is, *their* good friend, Saudi Arabia. I hear on newscasts that Mr Carter was enchanted by Saudi Arabia, that he had a wonderful time. I remember that Mrs Carter used the back door. I remember that the use of contraceptives in Saudi Arabia is a capital crime. I remember that in Saudi Arabia, women are a despised and imprisoned caste, denied all civil rights, sold into marriage, imprisoned as sexual and domestic servants in harems. I remember that in Saudi Arabia women are forced to breed babies, who had better be boys, until they die.

Disbelief increases in intensity as I think about South Africa, where suddenly the United States is on the side of the angels. Like most of my generation of the proud and notorious sixties, a considerable part of my life has been spent organizing against apartheid, there and here. The connections have always been palpable. The ruthless economic and sexual interests of the exploiters have always been clear. The contemptuous racism of the two vile systems has hurt my heart and given me good reason to think "democracy" a psychotic lie. Slowly activists have forced our government, stubborn in its support of pure evil, to acknowledge in its foreign policy that racist systems of social organization are abhorrent and intolerable. The shallowness of this new commitment is evident in the almost comical slogan that supposedly articulates the aspirations of the despised: One *Man*, One Vote. Amerikan foreign policy has finally caught up, just barely, with the human rights imperatives of the early nineteenth century, rendered reactionary if not obsolete by the Seneca Falls Convention in 1848.

Seductive mirages of progress notwithstanding, nowhere in the world is apartheid practiced with more cruelty and finality than in Saudi Arabia. Of course, it is women who are locked in and kept out, exiled to invisibility and abject powerlessness within their own country. It is women who are degraded systematically from birth to early death, utterly and totally and without exception deprived of freedom. It is women who are sold into marriage or concubinage, often before puberty; killed if their hymens are not intact on the wedding night; kept confined, ignorant, pregnant, poor, without choice or recourse. It is women who are raped and beaten with full sanction of the law. It is women who cannot own property or work for a living or determine in any way the circumstances of their own lives. It is women who are subject to a despotism that knows no restraint. Women, locked out and locked in. Mr Carter, enchanted with his good friends, the Saudis. Mr Carter, a sincere advocate of human rights. Sometimes even a feminist with a realistic knowledge of male hypocrisy and a strong stomach cannot believe the world she lives in.

A Battered Wife Survives
1978

This essay is now ten years old. Wife-beating is the most commonly committed violent crime in the United States, according to the FBI. In New Hampshire, I meet eighteen-year-old women who work in a battered women's shelter. One talks about how she feels when women decide to go home and she has to drive them. In Toronto, I meet two women who travel through rural Canada in the dead of winter to find and help battered women. In a project called "Off the Beaten Path," Susan Faupel is walking 600 miles—from Chicago, Illinois, to Little Rock, Arkansas—for battered women. In a southern state, I am driven to the airport by an organizer of the rally I have just spoken at; the car keeps veering off the road as she says she is being battered now; when? I keep asking; now, now, she says; she has gone to the organizing meetings for the antipornography demonstrations with make-up covering the bruises on her face. In the South especially I meet lesbians, married with children, who are being beaten by their husbands—afraid to leave because they would lose their children, battered because they are lesbian. In Seattle, I find safe houses, secret from most feminists, for women being beaten by their women lovers. In small towns where there are no shelters, especially in the North and Midwest, I find safe houses organized like an underground railroad for women escaping battery.

I knew not but the next
Would be my final inch—
Emily Dickinson

IN A FEW days, I will turn thirty-one. I am filled with both pride and dread.

The pride comes from accomplishment. I have done what I wanted to do more than any other thing in life. I have become a writer, published two books of integrity and worth. I did not know what those two books would cost me, how very difficult it would be to write them, to survive the opposition to them. I did not imagine that they would demand of me ruthless devotion, spartan discipline, continuing material deprivation, visceral anxiety about the rudiments of survival, and a faith in myself made more of iron than innocence. I have also learned to live alone, developed a rigorous emotional independence, a self-directed creative will, and a passionate commitment to my own sense of right and wrong. This I had to learn not only to do, but to want to do. I have learned not to lie to myself about what I value—in art, in love, in friendship. I have learned to take responsibility for my own intense convictions and my own real limitations. I have learned to resist most of the forms of coercion and flattery that would rob me of access to my own conscience. I believe that, for a woman, I have accomplished a great deal.

The dread comes from memory. Memory of terror and insupportable pain can overpower the present, any present, cast shadows so dark that the mind falters, unable to find light, and the body trembles, unable to find any solid ground. The past literally overtakes one, seizes one, holds one immobile in dread. Each year, near my birthday, I remember, involuntarily, that when I was twenty-five I was still a battered wife, a woman whose whole life was speechless desperation. By the time I was twenty-six I was still a terrorized woman. The husband I had left would come out of nowhere, beat or hit or kick me, disappear. A ghost with a fist, a lightning flash followed by riveting pain. There was no protection or safety. I was ripped up inside. My mind was still on the edge of its own destruction. Smothering anxiety, waking nightmares, cold sweats, sobs that I choked on were the constants of my daily life. I did not breathe; I gulped in air to try to get enough of it each minute to survive a blow that might come a second, any second, later. But I had taken the first step: he had to find me; I was no longer at home waiting for him. On my twenty-fifth birthday, when I had lived one quarter of a century, I was nearly dead, almost catatonic, without the will to live. By my twenty-sixth birthday, I wanted more than anything to live. I was one year old, an infant born out of a corpse, still with the smell of death on her, but hating death. This year I am six years old, and the anguish of my own long and dreadful dying comes back to haunt me. But this year, for the first time, I do more than tremble from the fear that even memory brings, I do more than grieve. This year, I sit at my desk and write.

Rape is very terrible. I have been raped and I have talked with hundreds of women who have been raped. Rape is an experience that pollutes one's life. But it is an experience that is contained within the boundaries of one's own life. In the end, one's life is larger.

Assault by a stranger or within a relationship is very terrible. One is hurt, undermined, degraded, afraid. But one's life is larger.

A battered wife has a life smaller than the terror that destroys her over time.

Marriage circumscribes her life. Law, social convention, and economic necessity encircle her. She is roped in. Her pride depends on projecting her own satisfaction with her lot to family and friends. Her pride depends on believing that her husband is devoted to her and, when that is no longer possible, convincing others anyway.

The husband's violence against her contradicts everything she has been taught about life, marriage, love, and the sanctity of the family. Regardless of the circumstances in which she grew up, she has been taught to believe in romantic love and the essential perfection of married life. Failure is personal. Individuals fail because of what is wrong with them. The troubles of individuals, pervasive as they are, do not reflect on the institution of marriage, nor do they negate her belief in the happy ending, promised everywhere as the final result of male-female conflict. Marriage is intrinsically good. Marriage is a woman's proper goal. Wife-beating is not on a woman's map of the world when she marries. It is, quite literally, beyond her imagination. Because she does not believe that it could have happened, that *he* could have done that to *her*, she cannot believe that it will happen again. He is her *husband*. No, it did not happen. And when it happens again, she still denies it. It was an accident, a mistake. And when it happens again, she blames the hardships of his life outside the home. There he experiences terrible hurts and frustrations. These account for his mistreatment of her. She will find a way to comfort him, to make it up to him. And when it happens again, she blames herself. She will be better, kinder, quieter, more of whatever he likes, less of whatever he dislikes. And when it happens again, and when it happens again, and when it happens again, she learns that she has nowhere to go, no one to turn to, no one who will believe her, no one who will help her, no one who will protect her. If she leaves, she will return. She will leave and return and leave and return. She will find that her parents, doctor, the police, her best friend, the neighbors upstairs and across the hall and next door, all despise the woman who cannot keep her own house in order, her injuries hidden, her despair to herself, her smile amiable and convincing. She will find that society loves its central lie—that marriage means happiness—and hates the woman who stops telling it even to save her own life.

The memory of the physical pain is vague. I remember, of course, that I was hit, that I was kicked. I do not remember when or how often. It blurs. I remember him banging my head against the floor until I passed out. I remember being kicked in the stomach. I remember being hit over and over, the blows hitting different parts of my body as I tried to get away from him. I remember a terrible leg injury from a series of kicks. I remember crying and I remember screaming and I remember begging. I remember him punching me in the breasts. One can remember that one had horrible physical pain, but that memory does not bring the pain back to the body. Blessedly, the mind can remember these events without the body reliving them. If one survives without permanent injury, the physical pain dims, recedes, ends. It lets go.

The fear does not let go. The fear is the eternal legacy. At first, the fear infuses every minute of every day. One does not sleep. One cannot bear to be alone. The fear is in the cavity of one's chest. It crawls like lice on one's skin. It makes the legs buckle, the heart race. It locks one's jaw. One's hands tremble. One's throat closes up. The fear makes one entirely desperate. Inside, one is always in upheaval, clinging to anyone who shows any kindness, cowering in the presence of any threat. As years pass, the fear recedes, but it does not let go. It never lets go. And when the mind remembers fear, it also relives it. The victim of encapsulating violence carries both the real fear and the memory of fear with her always. Together, they wash over her like an ocean, and if she does not learn to swim in that terrible sea, she goes under.

And then, there is the fact that, during those weeks that stretch into years when one is a battered wife, one's mind is shattered slowly over time, splintered into a thousand pieces. The mind is slowly submerged in chaos and despair, buried broken and barely alive in an impenetrable tomb of isolation. This isolation is so absolute, so killing, so morbid, so malignant and devouring that there is nothing in one's life but it, it. One is entirely shrouded in a loneliness that no earthquake could move. Men have asked over the centuries a question that, in their hands, ironically becomes abstract: "What is reality?" They have written complicated volumes on this question. The woman who was a battered wife and has escaped knows the answer: reality is when something is happening to you and you know it and can say it and when you say it other people understand what you mean and believe you. That is reality, and the battered wife, imprisoned alone in a nightmare that *is* happening to her, has lost it and cannot find it anywhere.

I remember the isolation as the worst anguish I have ever known. I remember the pure and consuming madness of being invisible and unreal, and every blow making me more invisible and more unreal, as the worst desperation I have ever known. I remember those who turned away, pretending not to see the injuries—my parents, dear god, especially my parents; my closest female friend, next door, herself suffocating in a marriage poisoned by psychic, not physical, violence; the doctor so officious and aloof; the women in the neighborhood who heard every scream; the men in the neighborhood who smiled, yes, lewdly, as they half looked away, half stared, whenever they saw me; my husband's family, especially my mother-in-law, whom I loved, my sisters-in-law, whom I loved. I remember the frozen muscles of my smile as I gave false explanations of injuries that no one wanted to hear anyway. I remember slavishly conforming to every external convention that would demonstrate that I was a "good wife," that would convince other people that I was happily married. And as the weight of social convention became insupportable, I remember withdrawing further and further into that open grave where so many women hide waiting to die—the house. I went out to shop only when I had to, I walked my dogs, I ran out screaming, looking for help and shelter when I had the strength to escape, with no money, often no coat, nothing but terror and tears. I met only averted eyes, cold stares, and the vulgar sexual aggression of lone, laughing men that sent me running home to a danger that was at least familiar and familial. Home, mine as well as his. Home, the only place I had. Finally, everything inside crumbled. I gave up. I sat, I stared, I waited, passive and paralyzed, speaking to no one, minimally maintaining myself and my animals, as my husband stayed away for longer and longer periods of time, slamming in only to thrash and leave. No one misses the wife who disappears. No one investigates her disappearance. After awhile, people stop asking where she is, especially if they have already refused to face what has been happening to her. Wives, after all, belong in the home. Nothing outside it depends on them. This is a bitter lesson, and the battered wife learns it in the bitterest way.

The anger of the survivor is murderous. It is more dangerous to her than to the one who hurt her. She does not believe in murder, even to save herself. She does not believe in murder, even though it would be more merciful punishment than he deserves. She wants him dead but will not kill him. She never gives up wanting him dead.

The clarity of the survivor is chilling. Once she breaks out of the prison of terror and violence in which she has been nearly destroyed, a process that takes years, it is very difficult to lie to her or to manipulate her. She sees through the social strategies that have controlled her as a woman, the sexual strategies that have reduced her to a shadow of her own native possibilities. She knows that her life depends on never being taken in by romantic illusion or sexual hallucination.

The emotional severity of the survivor appears to others, even those closest to her, to be cold and unyielding, ruthless in its intensity. She knows too much about suffering to try to measure it when it is real, but she despises self-pity. She is self-protective, not out of arrogance, but because she has been ruined by her own fragility. Like Anya, the survivor of the Nazi concentration camps in Susan Fromberg Schaeffer's beautiful novel of the same name, she might say: "So what have I learned? I have learned not to believe in suffering. It is a form of death. If it is severe enough it is a poison; it

kills the emotions." She knows that some of her own emotions have
been killed and she distrusts those who are infatuated with suffering,
as if it were a source of life, not death.

In her heart she is a mourner for those who have not survived.

In her soul she is a warrior for those who are now as she was then.

In her life she is both celebrant and proof of women's capacity and
will to survive, to become, to act, to change self and society. And each
year she is stronger and there are more of her.

A True and Commonplace Story
1978

This has never been published before.

L AST DECEMBER, IN the midst of a blizzard, I had to fly from a small airport in New England to Rochester, New York, to do a benefit for four women charged with committing a felony: breaking a window to tear down a poster advertising the sadistic, pornographic film, *Snuff*, which had been playing in a cinema adjacent to and owned by a local Holiday Inn. The women neither admitted nor denied committing the dastardly act, though the evidence against them is ephemeral, because they were convinced, as was the whole Rochester feminist community, that the act needed doing. And a felony charge, with a maximum sentence of four years, was transparently more vendetta than justice. Being intelligent and sensitive women given to fighting for the rights of women, they had noticed that the law enforcement officials in Rochester were singularly indifferent to the presence of a film that celebrates the dismemberment of a woman as an orgasmic act; and that these same officials were highly disturbed, to the point of vengeance, by the uppity women who made a stink about the casual exhibition of this vicious film.

Airports are not congenial places for women traveling alone, especially on snowy days when planes are delayed interminably. Most of the bored passengers-to-be are men. As men wait, they drink. The longer they wait, the more they drink. After a few hours, an airport on a stormy day is filled with drunken, cruising men who fix their sloppy attention on the few lone women. Such a situation may or may not be dangerous, but it is certainly unpleasant. Having been followed, harassed, and "seductively" called dirty names, I was pleased to notice another lone female traveler. We looked at each other, then around at the ready-to-pounce men, and became immediate and fast friends. My new traveling companion was a student, perhaps twenty, who was studying theater at a small liberal arts college. She was on her way to Rochester to visit friends. We discussed books, plays, work, our aspirations, and the future of feminism. In this warm and interesting way, time passed, and eventually we arrived in Rochester. Exiting from the plane, I was, in the crush, felt up quickly but definitively by one of the men who had been trailing me. My friend and I anguished over "the little rapes" as we parted.

In subsequent months, back in New England, I sometimes ran into my friend in the small town where I live. We had coffee, conversation.

The season changed. Spring blossomed. In Rochester, feminists had spent these months preparing for the trial. Because of their effective grassroots organizing and a firm refusal by the defendants to plea-bargain, the district attorney had been forced to reduce the charge to a misdemeanor, which carries a maximum sentence of one year.

Then, one day, I received a letter from a Rochester feminist. The trial date was set. Expert witnesses were lined up to testify to the fact that violent pornography does verifiable harm to women. Money had been raised. Everyone, while proud of what had been accomplished, was exhausted and depleted. They wanted me to come up and stay for the duration of the trial to give counsel, comfort, and encouragement. On this same day, I took a walk and saw my friend, but she had changed. She was somehow frail, very old even in her obvious youth, nearly shaking. She was sitting alone, preoccupied, but, even observed from a distance, clearly drained and upset.

How are things, I asked. Well, she had left school for a month, had just returned. Silence. No intimacy or eager confidence. I asked over and over: why? what had happened? Slowly, terribly, the story came out. A man had attempted to rape her on the college campus where she lived. She knew the man, had gone to the police, to the president of the college. She had moved off campus, in fear. Had the police found the man? No, they had made no attempt to. They had treated her with utter contempt. And what had the president of the college, a woman, done? Well, she had said that publicity would not be "good for the college." Entirely undermined by the callous indifference of those who were supposed to help and protect her, she had left school, to recover as best she could. And the worst of it, she said, was that people would just look right through her. Well, at least he didn't rape you, they said, as if, then, nothing had really happened. She did not know where the man was. She was hoping desperately that he had left the area. In her mind, she took a gun and went to find him and shot him. Over and over. She could not quiet herself, or study, or concentrate, or recover. She knew she was not safe anywhere. She thought she might leave school, but where would she go and what would she do? And how would she ever regain her self-confidence or sense of well-being? And how would she ever contain or discipline her anger at the assault and then the betrayal by nearly everyone?

In Rochester, the trial of four feminists for allegedly breaking a window was postponed, dragging out the ordeal more months. In a small New England town, one young woman quaked and raged and tried to do simple things: drink coffee, study, forget. And somewhere, one aspiring rapist with nothing to fear from the law or anyone is doing who knows what.

Biological Superiority:
The World's Most Dangerous and Deadly Idea

1977

---

*One of the slurs constantly used against me by women writing in behalf of
pornography under the flag of feminism in misogynist media is that I endorse a
primitive biological determinism.* Woman Hating *(1974) clearly repudiates
any biological determinism; so does* Our Blood *(1976), especially "The Root
Cause." So does this piece, published twice, in 1978 in* Heresies *and in 1979
in* Broadsheet. Heresies *was widely read in the Women's Movement in
1978. The event described in this piece, which occurred in 1977, was fairly
notorious, and so my position on biological determinism—I am against it—is
generally known in the Women's Movement. One problem is that this essay, like
others in this book, has no cultural presence: no one has to know about it or take it
into account to appear less than ignorant; no one will be held accountable for
ignoring it. Usually critics and political adversaries have to reckon with the
published work of male writers whom they wish to malign. No such rules protect
girls. One pro-pornography "feminist" published an article in which she said I
was anti-abortion, this in the face of decades of work for abortion rights and
membership in many pro-choice groups. No one even checked her allegation; the
periodical would not publish a retraction. One's published work counts as
nothing, and so do years of one's political life.*

1

All who are not of good race in this world are chaff.

Hitler, *Mein Kampf*[1]

It would be lunacy to try to estimate the value of man according to his race,
thus declaring war on the Marxist idea that men are equal, unless we are

110

determined to draw the ultimate consequences. And the ultimate consequence of recognizing the importance of blood—that is, of the racial foundation in general—is the transference of this estimation to the individual person.

Hitler, *Mein Kampf* [2]

H ISSES. WOMEN SHOUTING at me: slut, bisexual, she fucks men. And before I had spoken, I had been trembling, more afraid to speak than I had ever been. And, in a room of 200 sister lesbians, as angry as I have ever been. "Are you a bisexual?" some woman screamed over the pandemonium, the hisses and shouts merging into a raging noise. "I'm a Jew," I answered; then, a pause, "and a lesbian, and a woman." And a coward. Jew was enough. In that room, Jew was what mattered. In that room, to answer the question "Do you still fuck men?" with a No, as I did, was to betray my deepest convictions. All of my life, I have hated the proscribers, those who enforce sexual conformity. In answering, I had given in to the inquisitors, and I felt ashamed. It humiliated me to see myself then: one who resists the enforcers out there with militancy, but gives in without resistance to the enforcers among us.

The event was a panel on "Lesbianism as a Personal Politic" that took place in New York City, Lesbian Pride Week 1977. A self-proclaimed lesbian separatist had spoken. Amidst the generally accurate description of male crimes against women came this ideological rot, articulated of late with increasing frequency in feminist circles: women and men are distinct species or races (the words are used interchangeably); men are biologically inferior to women; male violence is a biological inevitability; to eliminate it, one must eliminate the species/race itself (means stated on this particular evening: developing parthenogenesis as a viable reproductive reality); in eliminating the biologically inferior species/race Man, the new *Übermensch* Womon (prophetically foreshadowed by the lesbian separatist* herself) will have the earthly dominion that is her true

* SuperWomon's ideology is distinguished from lesbian separatism in general (that is, lesbians organizing politically and/or culturally in exclusively female groups) by two articles of dogma: (1) a refusal to have anything to do with women who have anything to do with males, often including women with male children and (2) the absolute belief in the biological superiority of women.

biological destiny. We are left to infer that the society of her creation will be good because she is good, biologically good. In the interim, incipient SuperWoman will not do anything to "encourage" women to "collaborate" with men—no abortion clinics or battered woman sanctuaries will come from her. After all, she has to conserve her "energy" which must not be dissipated keeping "weaker" women alive through reform measures.

The audience applauded the passages on female superiority/ male inferiority enthusiastically. This doctrine seemed to be music to their ears. Was there dissent, silent, buried in the applause? Was some of the response the spontaneous pleasure that we all know when, at last, the tables are turned, even for a minute, even in imagination? Or has powerlessness driven us mad, so that we dream secret dreams of a final solution perfect in its simplicity, absolute in its efficacy? And will a leader someday strike that secret chord, harness those dreams, our own nightmare turned upside down? Is there no haunting, restraining memory of the blood spilled, the bodies burned, the ovens filled, the peoples enslaved, by those who have assented throughout history to the very same demagogic logic?

In the audience, I saw women I like or love, women not strangers to me, women who are good not because of biology but because they care about being good, swept along in a sea of affirmation. I spoke out because those women had applauded. I spoke out too because I am a Jew who has studied Nazi Germany, and I know that many Germans who followed Hitler also cared about being good, but found it easier to be good by biological definition than by act. Those people, wretched in what they experienced as their own unbearable powerlessness, became convinced that they were so good biologically that nothing they did could be bad. As Himmler said in 1943:

We have exterminated a bacterium [Jews] because we did not want in the end to be infected by the bacterium and die of it. I will not see so much as a small area of sepsis appear here or gain a hold. Wherever it may form, we will cauterize it. All in all, we can say that we have fulfilled this most difficult duty for the love of our people. And our spirit, our soul, our character has not suffered injury from it.[3]

So I spoke, afraid. I said that I would not be associated with a movement that advocated the most pernicious ideology on the face of the earth. It was this very ideology of biological determinism that had licensed the slaughter and/or enslavement of virtually any group one could name, including women by men. ("Use their own poison against them," one woman screamed.) Anywhere one looked, it was this philosophy that justified atrocity. This was one faith that destroyed life with a momentum of its own.

Insults continued with unabated intensity as I spoke, but gradually those women I liked or loved, and others I did not know, began to question openly the philosophy they had been applauding and also their own acquiescence. Embraced by many women on my way out, I left still sickened, humiliated by the insults, emotionally devastated by the abuse. Time passes, but the violence done is not undone. It never is.

<h1 style="text-align:center">2</h1>

I am told that I am a sexist. I *do* believe that the differences between the sexes are our most precious heritage, even though they make women superior in the ways that matter most.

George Gilder, Sexual Suicide [4]

Perhaps this female wisdom comes from resignation to the reality of male aggression; more likely it is a harmonic of the woman's knowledge that ultimately she is the one who matters. As a result, while there are more brilliant men than brilliant women, there are more good women than good men.

Steven Goldberg, The Inevitability of Patriarchy [5]

As a class (not necessarily as individuals), we can bear children. From this, according to male-supremacist ideology, all our other attributes and potentialities are derived. On the pedestal, immobile like waxen statues, or in the gutter, failed icons mired in shit, we are exalted or degraded because our biological traits are what they are. Citing genes, genitals, DNA, pattern-releasing smells, biograms, hormones, or whatever is in vogue, male supremacists make their case which is, in essence, that we are biologically too good, too bad, or too different to do anything other than reproduce and serve men sexually and domestically.

The newest variations on this distressingly ancient theme center on hormones and DNA: men are biologically aggressive; their fetal

113

brains were awash in androgen; their DNA, in order to perpetuate itself, hurls them into murder and rape; in women, pacifism is hormonal and addiction to birth is molecular. Since in Darwinian terms (interpreted to conform to the narrow social self-interest of men), survival of the fittest means the triumph of the most aggressive human beings, men are and always will be superior to women in terms of their ability to protect and extend their own authority. Therefore women, being "weaker" (less aggressive), will always be at the mercy of men. That this theory of the social ascendancy of the fittest consigns us to eternal indignity and, applied to race, conjures up Hitler's identical view of evolutionary struggle must not unduly trouble us. "By current theory," writes Edward O. Wilson reassuringly in *Sociobiology: The New Synthesis*, a bible of genetic justification for slaughter, "genocide or genosorption strongly favoring the aggressor need take place only once every few generations to direct evolution."[6]

3

> I have told you the very low opinion in which you [women] were held by Mr Oscar Browning. I have indicated what Napoleon once thought of you and what Mussolini thinks now. Then, in case any of you aspire to fiction, I have copied out for your benefit the advice of the critic about courageously acknowledging the limitations of your sex. I have referred to Professor X and given prominence to his statement that women are intellectually, morally and physically inferior to men ... and here is a final warning ... Mr John Langdon Davies warns women "that when children cease to be altogether desirable, women cease to be altogether necessary." I hope you will make note of it.
>
> Virginia Woolf, *A Room of One's Own*[7]

In considering male intellectual and scientific argumentation in conjunction with male history, one is forced to conclude that men as a class are moral cretins. The vital question is: are we to accept *their* world view of a moral polarity that is biologically fixed, genetically or hormonally or genitally (or whatever organ or secretion or molecular particle they scapegoat next) absolute; or does our own historical experience of social deprivation and injustice teach us that to be free in a just world we will have to destroy the power, the dignity, the efficacy of this one idea above all others?

Recently, more and more feminists have been advocating social, spiritual, and mythological models that are female-supremacist and/or matriarchal. To me, this advocacy signifies a basic conformity to the tenets of biological determinism that underpin the male social system. Pulled toward an ideology based on the moral and social significance of a distinct female biology because of its emotional and philosophical familiarity, drawn to the spiritual dignity inherent in a "female principle" (essentially as defined by men), of course unable to abandon by will or impulse a lifelong and centuries-old commitment to childbearing as *the* female creative act, women have increasingly tried to transform the very ideology that has enslaved us into a dynamic, religious, psychologically compelling celebration of female biological potential. This attempted transformation may have survival value—that is, the worship of our procreative capacity as *power* may temporarily stay the male-supremacist hand that cradles the test tube. But the price we pay is that we become carriers of the disease we must cure. It is no accident that in the ancient matriarchies men were castrated, sacrificially slaughtered, and excluded from public forms of power; nor is it an accident that some female supremacists now believe men to be a distinct and inferior species or race. Wherever power is accessible or bodily integrity honored on the basis of biological attribute, systematized cruelty permeates the society and murder and mutilation contaminate it. We will not be different.

It is shamefully easy for us to enjoy our own fantasies of biological omnipotence while despising men for enjoying the reality of theirs. And it is dangerous—because genocide begins, however improbably, in the conviction that classes of biological distinction indisputably sanction social and political discrimination. We, who have been devastated by the concrete consequences of this idea, still want to put our faith in it. Nothing offers more proof—sad, irrefutable proof—that we are more like men than either they or we care to believe.

Notes

1. Adolf Hitler, *Mein Kampf*, trans. Ralph Manheim (Boston: Houghton Mifflin Company, 1962), p. 296.

2. Hitler, *Mein Kampf*, p. 442.

3. Jeremy Noakes and Geoffrey Pridham, ed., *Documents on Nazism 1919-1945* (New York: The Viking Press, 1975), p. 493.

4. George Gilder, *Sexual Suicide* (New York: Quadrangle, 1973), v.

5. Steven Goldberg, *The Inevitability of Patriarchy* (New York: William Morrow and Company, Inc., 1973), p. 228.

6. Edward O. Wilson, *Sociobiology: The New Synthesis* (Cambridge, Mass.: The Belknap Press of Harvard University Press, 1975), p. 573.

7. Virginia Woolf, *A Room of One's Own* (New York: Harcourt, Brace and World, Inc., 1957), pp. 115-16.

Sexual Economics:
The Terrible Truth

1976

This was given as a speech to women at Harper & Row, the original publishers of
Our Blood. *I refer to it in the preface to* Our Blood *in this volume: men in
suits took notes and my goose was cooked. Later,* Ms. *published an "edited"
version. This is the original text. I was very pleased to be asked by the women
employees at Harper & Row to speak on a day they had organized in behalf of
women workers. Harper & Row was, at the time, the only unionized publisher in
New York, and in addition there was a women's group. Most workers in
publishing are women, low paid with no power. Organized with lawyers and
money to defend the speech rights of pornographers, publishers do not allow those
who work for them to organize as workers or as women; nor do they pay any
attention to the rights of writers to economic dignity or creative integrity.
Publishing is a stinking, sick industry in the United States. The low-paid editors
and clerical workers who listened to this speech had a lot in common with the
woman who wrote it: that is what the essay is about. I thank the women of
Harper & Row for inviting me in.*

IN WOMEN AND ECONOMICS (first published in 1898), Charlotte
Perkins Gilman wrote, "The female of genus homo is economically
dependent on the male. He is her food supply."[1] Men are our food
supply, whether we are mothers, housewives, prostitutes, workers in
industry, clerical workers, or in the professions. Men are our food
supply whether we are heterosexual or lesbian, promiscuous or
celibate, whatever our racial, ethnic, or male-defined class identities.
Men are our food supply whether we work for love or for money.

Men are our food supply whether we live in capitalist countries where men control industry, agriculture, and the state, or in socialist countries where men control industry, agriculture, and the state. Women know that material survival and well-being derive from men, whether those men are fathers, husbands, tricks, foremen, employers, or government officials. People say that the way to a man's heart is through his stomach, but it is women who give their hearts to ward off hunger.

Under the male-supremacist system that now blights our planet, women are defined first by our reproductive capacities. We produce babies. We are the first producers of the first product. A product is that which is made by human labor. Our labor is the first labor, and we are the first laborers. Even though in actuality not all women can produce babies, all women are defined as the producers of babies. That is why radical feminists regard women as a class of persons who have in common the same relationship to production (reproduction).

We labor and produce babies. The raw materials out of which babies are formed are the mother's flesh and blood, the nutrients which nourish her, the very stuff of her own physical existence. An embryo literally feeds from and is formed out of the mother's body. It is as if the embryo were knit, stitch by stitch, from her flesh and blood.

Once the baby is born, this product of the mother's labor, made from the raw materials of her body, does not belong to her. It belongs to a man. It belongs to one who did not and cannot produce it. This ownership is systematized in law, theology, and national mores; it is sanctioned by the state, sanctified in art and philosophy, and endorsed by men of all political persuasions. A baby who is not owned by a man does not have a legitimate civil existence.

The relationship between the woman who labors and produces and the man who owns the product is at once sexual and economic. In reproduction, sex and economics cannot be separated nor can they be distinguished from each other. The woman's material reality is determined by a sexual characteristic, a capacity for reproduction. The man takes a body that is not his, claims it, sows his so-called seed, reaps a harvest—he colonizes a female body, robs it of its natural resources, controls it, uses it, depletes it as he wishes, denies it freedom and self-determination so that he can continue to plunder it, moves on at will to conquer other land which appears more verdant and alluring. Radical feminists call this exclusively male behavior "phallic imperialism" and see in it the origins of all other forms of imperialism.

Fucking is the means by which the male colonizes the female, whether or not the intended goal is impregnation (reproduction). Fucking authenticates marriage and, in or out of marriage, it is regarded as an act of possession. The possessor is the one with a phallus; the possessed is the one without a phallus. Society in both capitalist and socialist countries (including China) is organized so as to guarantee the imperial right of each man to possess, to fuck, at least one woman.

In fucking, as in reproduction, sex and economics are inextricably joined. In male-supremacist cultures, women are believed to embody carnality; women *are* sex. A man wants what a woman has—sex. He can steal it (rape), persuade her to give it away (seduction), rent it (prostitution), lease it over the long term (marriage in the United States), or own it outright (marriage in most societies). A man can do some or all of the above, over and over again.

As Phyllis Chesler and Emily Jane Goodman wrote in *Women, Money, and Power*: "It is an ancient drama, a miracle of currency—this buying of women. . . . Being bought, especially for a high price, or for a lifetime, is exactly how most women learn what they are worth. In a money culture, their self-knowledge can be very exact."[2]

The act of rape establishes the nadir in female worthlessness. Rape signifies that the individual victim and all women have no dignity, no power, no individuality, no real safety. Rape signifies that the individual victim and all women are interchangeable, "all the same in the dark." Rape signifies that any woman, no matter how uppity she has become, can be reduced by force or intimidation to the lowest common denominator—a free piece of ass, there for the taking.

Seduction is often difficult to distinguish from rape. In seduction, the rapist bothers to buy a bottle of wine. Some expenditure of money is made to encourage the woman into sexual surrender, though many forms of coercion are typically used in seductions to make certain that the seducer's outlay of time and money will not be in vain. Seduction often means to a woman that she has worth because her value to a man (the only real criterion of female worth in a male-supremacist culture) can be measured in wine, food, and other material attentions.

In prostitution, a woman is paid outright for her sexual services. In male-supremacist cultures (except for a few socialist countries where serious efforts have been made to end the exploited sexual labor of women as prostitutes), prostitution is the one profession genuinely and whole-heartedly open to women. Hard-working prostitutes earn enormous gross sums of money (compared to gross sums typically earned by other women), but they do not go on to become financiers or founders of universities. Instead, their money goes to men, because men control, profit from, and perpetuate female prostitution. The men their money goes to are pimps, racketeers, lawyers, police, and the like, all of whom, because they are men and not women, can turn that money into more money, social status, and influence. The prostitute herself is marked with a scarlet "W"—stigmatized as whore, ostracized as whore, exiled as whore into a world circumscribed by organized crime, narcotics, and the notorious brutality of pimps. The prostitute's utterly degraded social status functions to punish her for daring to make money at all. The abuse that accrues to her prevents her from translating money into dignity or self-determination; it serves to keep her in her place, female, cunt, at the mercy of the men who profit from her flesh. Also, as Kate Millett wrote in *The Prostitution Papers*, "the whore is there to show the rest of us how lucky we are, how favored of our lords, how much worse it could go for us."[3] For that lesson to be vivid, the prostitute's money cannot be allowed to bring with it self-esteem, honor, or power.

In marriage, male ownership of a woman's body and labor (reproductive, carnal, and domestic) is sanctified by god and/or state. In marriage, a man acquires legal, exclusive right of carnal access to a woman, who is ever after known as "his wife." "His wife" is the highest embodiment of female worth in a male-supremacist society. "His wife" is the exemplary female, and for a very good reason: in a world with no viable sexual-economic options for the female, "his wife" has struck the best possible bargain. She has sold herself (or, still in many places, has been sold) not only for economic support from one man, which may or may not be forthcoming, but also for protection—protection from being raped, seduced, or forced to prostitution by other men, protection from the dangers of being female prey in a world of male predators. This protection often is not worth very much, since wife-beating and sexual assault are commonplace in marriage.

In marriage, a woman not only provides sex for the male; she also cleans his house. She does housework whether or not she also works for a wage outside the house. She does housework whether she lives in a capitalist or a socialist country. She does housework because she is a woman, and housework is stigmatized as women's work. Not coincidentally, it is also the most menial, isolating, repetitious, and invisible work there is. (When the man is rich his wife does not clean the house. Instead, she is turned into an ornament and used as a symbol of his wealth. The situation of the lady is a bizarre variation on a consistently cruel theme.)

According to contemporary socialist theory, the incarceration of women in the home as unpaid domestics is the distinctive feature of women's oppressed condition under capitalism. When women do productive labor for a wage outside the home under capitalism, they are viewed by socialists as doubly exploited—exploited first as workers by capitalist profiteers and exploited second as unpaid domestics inside the home. In the socialist analysis, women in the home are exploited by the "capitalist system," not by the men who profit from women's domestic labor.

Marx himself recognized that under capitalism women were viciously exploited, as men were not, as domestic servants. He therefore favored protective labor legislation to shield women from the worst ravages of industrial exploitation so that they would be better able to perform their domestic labors. Socialists since Marx have supported protective labor legislation for women. The effect of this socialist chivalry is to keep women from being able to compete for jobs on the same terms as men or to match male earning power. Consequently, the role of the woman as unpaid domestic is reinforced and men are also assured an adequate supply of reproductive and carnal servants.

This "solution" to "the woman question," which entirely serves to uphold the dominance of men over women, typifies socialist theory and practice. In Russia, in Czechoslovakia, in China, housework is women's work, and the women remain exploited as domestics. The ideology that justifies this entrenched abuse is accepted as self-evident truth in socialist and capitalist countries alike: women are defined first as the class of persons who reproduce and so, it is postulated, there is a "natural division of labor in the family" which is why "the man devotes himself more intensively to his work, and perhaps to public activity or self-improvement connected with his job or his function, while the woman concentrates on the children and the household."[4] The notion that capitalism, instead of systematized male supremacy from which all men profit, is the source of women's misery—even when that misery is narrowly defined as exploited domestic labor with no reference to the brutal sexual abuses which characterize women's oppressed condition—is not borne out by that final authenticator, history.

Everywhere, then, the female is kept in captivity by the male, denied self-determination so that he can control her reproductive functions, fuck her at will, and have his house cleaned (or ornamented). And everywhere, when the female leaves the house to work for wages, she finds that she carries her inferior and servile status with her.

The inferior status of women is maintained in the labor market in both capitalist and socialist countries in four mutually reinforcing ways:

(1) *Women are paid lower wages than men for doing the same work.* In the United States, the male-female wage differential has actually increased in the last ten years, despite the fact that equal pay for equal work has been required by law. In industrialized communist countries, inequities in male and female wages were huge as late as 1970—a staggering fact since the law has required equal pay for equal work in the Soviet Union since 1936 and in the Eastern-bloc countries since the late 1940s.

(2) *Women are systematically excluded from work of high status, concrete power, and high financial reward.* Strangely, in China, where women allegedly hold up half the sky, the government is overwhelmingly male; so too in the Soviet Union, Hungary, Algeria. In all socialist countries, women do most of the low-skilled, poorly paid work; women are not to be found in significant numbers in the upper echelons (and there are upper echelons) of industry, agriculture, education, or culture. The typical situation of women in socialist

countries was described by Magdalena Sokolowska, a Polish expert on women's employment in that country: "As long as women worked in factories and in the fields it didn't bother anyone very much. As soon as they started to learn skills and to ask for the same money for the same work, men began to worry about [women's] health, their nerves, to claim that employment doesn't agree with them, and that they are neglecting the family."[5] Of course, capitalist males have identical worries and so, in capitalist countries, women are also denied access to high rank, authority, and power.

(3) *Women are consigned to the lowest ranks within a field, no matter what the field.* In the United States, for instance, doctors, lawyers, and full professors are male while nurses, legal secretaries, and research assistants are female. Even when a profession is composed almost entirely of women, as are library science (librarians) in the United States and medicine (doctors) in the Soviet Union, the top positions in those professions are held by men.

(4) *When women enter any industry, job, or profession in great numbers, the field itself becomes feminized, that is, it acquires the low status of the female.* Women are able to enter a field in large numbers because it is low paid relative to other areas where men can find employment. In the United States, for instance, clerical work is a recently feminized field. Male clerical workers, who in 1949 earned an average of $3213 a year compared to $2255 for women, moved out of the field as women moved in—to the lower female salaries, which were seventy percent of the male wage. With the influx of women doing menial work for menial wages, clerical work became women's work—low paid and dead-ended. In 1962, female clerical workers earned sixty-nine percent of the male wage; in 1970, they earned sixty-four percent of the male wage; and in 1973, they earned only sixty-one percent of the male wage.

In the Soviet Union and Czechoslovakia, doctoring, that exalted profession in the West, has become feminized. Women became doctors in these countries because the work was low paid compared to manual labor available to men. Today in those countries female physicians are mundane service workers whose low pay is appropriate because women need not be well paid. Male medical professionals are high-status, highly paid research scientists and surgeons.

In general, then, women do the lowest work of the society whatever that lowest work is perceived to be; and when women are the primary workers in a field, the field itself takes on the females' low status. Therefore, it is false to think that the inferior status of women will dissolve when women do productive labor or enter freely into high status professions. When women enter any field in great numbers, the status of the field itself is lowered. The men who are in it leave it; the men looking for work will not enter it. When men leave a field, they take its prestige with them; when men enter a field, they bring prestige to it. In this way, the subordination of women to men is perpetuated even when women work for a wage and no matter what work women do.[6]

When we dare to look at these embittering sexual-economic realities, it is as if we look into Medusa's eyes. We look at her and see ourselves; we see our condition and it is monstrous; we see our rage and anguish in her hideous face and, terrified to become her, we turn instead to stone. Then, for solace and out of fear, we turn to look elsewhere—anywhere—to Democrats, to socialists, to union leaders, to working men, to gay men, or to a host of authoritarian father figures who promise freedom in conformity and peace in self-delusion.

But there will be no freedom or peace until we, women, are free to determine for ourselves the integrity and boundaries of our own bodies, the uses to which we will put our own bodies—that is, until we have absolute reproductive freedom and until the crimes of sexual violence committed against us by men are ended.

If these revolutionary necessities are not our first priority, we will be led down the garden path and into the sunset by seducers and pimps of all persuasions who will do what they have always done—pillage our bodies, steal our labor, and bury us in unmarked graves under the weeds of centuries of contempt.

Notes

1. Charlotte Perkins Gilman, *Women and Economics*, ed. Carl Degler (New York: Harper Torchbooks, 1966), p. 22.

2. Phyllis Chesler and Emily Jane Goodman, *Women, Money, and Power* (New York: William Morrow and Company, Inc., 1976), p. 19.

3. Kate Millett, *The Prostitution Papers: A Candid Dialogue* (New York: Avon Books, 1973), p. 87.

4. Radoslav Selucký, "Emancipation or Equality?" *Literarni noviny*, March 6, 1965, cited by Hilda Scott in *Does Socialism Liberate Women? Experiences from Eastern Europe* (Boston: Beacon Press, 1974), p. 123.

5. Scott, *Does Socialism Liberate Women?*, p. 5.

6. For data on these same processes in underdeveloped and developing countries, see Ester Boserup, *Women's Role in Economic Development* (New York: St. Martin's Press, 1970).

Look, Dick, Look. See Jane Blow It.

1979

This was originally given as a speech at a Women's Week Conference at Smith College in Northampton, Massachusetts. There had been open warfare between those on the nominal Left, the only Left in Amerika, and feminists. Male leftists had made a strong effort to close down the annual Women's Week Conference held for students from the five colleges and universities in the area. Of course, some women were on their side. One consequence of the fight was conflict among women, a devaluing of feminism following the priorities of the men. It was a volatile audience. I tried to set an ethical and honest course. Every warning about what would happen to the Women's Movement if we caved into male pressure from the Left has come true, has happened, in my view. Local women published this speech in their own newspaper, Valley Women's News, *and a Rochester, New York, newspaper,* New Women's Times, *with a more national audience (and now defunct) also published it.*

O NE OF THE hazards of trying to discuss strategies for social change is that abstractions have a nasty way of taking over. One wants to clarify the elements necessary to sustain effective radical action—or effective reformist or remedial action. One ends up with a list of "isms" that become more and more unreal each time one refers to them. This happens, for instance, when one must use a word like "lesbianism." The erotic reality, without which, after all, the lesbian would not exist, is "ismed" out of the word; an intimidating collective dimension is added to it; the experiences of lesbians and the political realities associated with lesbian acts and commitments are increasingly obscured. We lose our rootedness to the necessities that compelled us to "ism" the word to begin with. The word becomes a

126

code word, both shorthand and symbol. We begin to measure ourselves against it instead of measuring it against ourselves. Then, we begin to use the word as a weapon against others, to factor out their experiences which somehow do not quite warrant the "ism" part of the word: not being weighty enough, being personal-not-political-enough, being too slight to deserve the grandeur of a whole "ism." At this point, we have lost the word, we have lost ourselves, we have lost our connectedness to our own original impulses, meanings, and necessities. Inevitably, then, another "ism" comes along to knock our "ism" out of the sphere of legitimate concern altogether, and political discourse is reduced to a war of the "isms," to which "ism" indicates the greater atrocity, the greater pain. "Ism-ism"—if you will please pardon the coining of yet another "ism"—is perhaps the most destructive, and reactionary, disease of political movements. Tyranny comes from it, and so does defeat. But by the time a movement can be reduced to its "isms," it deserves defeat because it has been taken over by an acquiescence to authority that intrinsically negates any possibility of real rebellion, real creation, an infusion of new values based on what we can learn from reality when we face it unarmed by ideological orthodoxies.

The purpose of theory is to clarify the world in which we live, how it works, why things happen as they do. The purpose of theory is understanding. Understanding is energizing. It energizes to action. When theory becomes an impediment to action, it is time to discard the theory and return naked, that is, without theory, to the world of reality. People become slaves to theory because people are used to meeting expectations they have not originated—to doing what they are told, to having everything mapped out, to having reality prepackaged. People can have an antiauthoritarian intention and yet function in a way totally consonant with the demands of authority. The deepest struggle is to root out of us and the institutions in which we participate the requirement that we slavishly conform. But an adherence to ideology, to any ideology, can give us the grand illusion of freedom when in fact we are being manipulated and used by those whom the theory serves. The struggle for freedom has to be a struggle toward integrity defined in every possible sphere of reality—sexual integrity, economic integrity, psychological integrity, integrity of expression, integrity of faith and loyalty and heart.

Anything that shortcuts us away from viewing integrity as an essential goal or anything that diverts our attention from integrity as a revolutionary value serves only to reinforce the authoritarian values of the world in which we live.

One may discover integrity in the companionship of others, but one does not ever discover integrity by bowing to the demands of peer pressure. The heavier the pressure is toward conformity—no matter how lofty the proposed final goal—the more one must be suspicious of it and antagonistic to it. History has one consistent lesson in it: one by one, people give up what they know to be right and true for the sake of something loftier that they do not quite understand but *should* want in order to be good; soon, people are the tools of despots and atrocities are committed on a grand scale. And then, it is too late. There is no going back.

Women are especially given to giving up what we know and feel to be right and true for the sake of others or for the sake of something more important than ourselves. This is because the condition in which women live is a colonized condition. Women are colonized by men, in body, in mind. Defined everywhere as evil when we act in our own self-interest, we strive to be good by renouncing self-interest altogether.

Feminists are now threatened in every area of activity because men are trying to recolonize our minds—minds that have been trying to be free of male control. Everywhere, women are confronted by the urgency of male demands, all of which are supposed to supersede in importance the demands which women must make toward our own integrity. This story is so old that it should be tired and dead, but it is not. Feminists tell the tales over and over: how women contributed to this and that revolution and were sold out in the end, sent packing back to the house to clean it up after the revolutionary dust had settled, pregnant and poor; how women contributed to this and that movement for social change and were raped and exploited and abused, and then sent back to clean the house, pregnant and poor. But the colonized mind cannot remember. The colonized mind does not have the pride or militancy of memory. The colonized mind refuses to politicize anger or bitterness. The colonized mind must meet the demands of the colonizer: devotion and good behavior, clean thoughts and no ugly wrath.

Look, Dick, Look. See Jane Blow It.

The mind struggling toward integrity does not accept someone else's version of the story of life: this mind demands that life itself must be confronted, over and over, by all who live it. The mind struggling toward integrity confronts the evidence and respects experience.

One characteristic especially defines the colonized mind of a woman: she will put the experience of men before her own; she will grant a male life greater importance than her own. The mind struggling toward integrity will fight for the significance of her own life and will not give up that significance for any reason. Rooted in the reality of her own experience—which includes all that has happened to her faced squarely and all that she has seen, heard, learned, and done—a woman who understands that integrity is the first necessity will find the courage not to defend herself from pain. The colonized mind will use ideology to defend itself from both pain and knowledge.

Right now, the Left is making every effort to recolonize the minds of women. This is partly because women's fight for freedom demanded a renunciation of leftist alliances. Women who were on the Left were there because they cared passionately for freedom. They were abused by men who said that they too cared for freedom, but not for the freedom of women. Women found the courage to include women in every demand for freedom, to make women primary, to make women essential. This angered the men, but more importantly, it left them without an abundance of sexual partners, envelope fillers, organizers, and dishwashers. It also left them without women to bear their (sic) children, a loss insufferable to all men.

For nearly a decade, women who rightly called themselves feminists delved into what is rightly characterized as sexual politics: sex as power, the power relationships and values inherent in sex and sexuality as cultural and social institutions. The men fretted, moaned, had encounter groups, did primal therapy and rebirth therapy and water therapy, ate brown rice, and continued to seek out acquiescent women, colonized women, who would continue to inflate masculine esteem by subservient behavior. The men also withdrew their money, labor, energy, and moral support from the causes defined by women as primary. For instance, during the 1960s, access by women to safe abortion was important to leftist men. Access to safe abortion made more women more willing to be fucked more often by more

129

men. With a feminist redefinition of the importance of abortion—that is, with abortion defined as an essential component of a woman's right to control her own body, that control also including and often necessitating the use of the dreaded word, No—men became apathetic or simply changed sides. They created a vacuum, which the organized Right lost no time in filling. We won the right to legal abortion on our own, but the Right is now piece by piece taking it away from us: enter the conquering heroes, those who abdicated all responsibility when it mattered so much, who will help us now at a price. The price is reinvolvement with politics as they define it, an acceptance of their political priorities. For the last decade, the male Left has been the frontline of the male Right, buttressing it by strategies geared toward destroying feminists. As our right-wing enemies have gained in strength and arrogance, women have become more and more afraid—more and more afraid of crossing leftist men, more and more afraid of defining our priorities in our own terms. Women running scared are more subject to the pressure of men on us to conform, to reenter the world of the colonized women. And women have been capitulating at an alarming rate. Rather than participating in the world from a woman-defined sense of urgency, women have been retreating into the world of male political discourse and priorities. Suddenly, once again, everything is more important than the crimes committed against women by men. Suddenly, once again, men are golden (not tin) allies and male supremacy, though ever so distasteful, must not distract us from The Real Issues. There are women calling themselves feminists though they have no particular commitment to women as a group and no credible interest in sexual politics as such. They are in the service of male "isms," and both they and the "isms" are being manipulated to dissuade women from political, sexual, and social confrontation with men. So, we have women insisting that capitalism is the source of male supremacy, even though all history and contemporary reality demonstrate clearly that the hatred of women permeates all societies regardless of their economic organization. We have women defending the pornography pimps on the basis of the First Amendment—civil libertarianism—even though women have no viable protection derived from the First Amendment because women have no meaningful access to media; and even with access would not have the economic means to defend any claim we might make since lawyers who specialize in the field of First Amendment litigation cost $150 an hour and their fees are only a small part of the expense involved. We have women charmed once again by the pacifist Left. In all these cases and more, we have women who manage to defend the political priorities of men who continue to manipulate and exploit them, to deny their most basic claims to human dignity and autonomy; we have women who want to be good in male terms at any cost to themselves and to other women; we have women willing to forget everything substantive we have learned over the past decade so that they can begin again, arm in arm, with men who have slightly improved their manners and not much more. More and more, those who found the strength to struggle toward integrity are reentering the shadowy world of purposeful male confusion: they are giving up their own lives, and they will take the lives of the rest of us with them if we do not stand up to them. With increasing frequency, these women are used by the male Left to impugn our basic decency, condemn our loyalty to women, to shout us down, to slander and slur us; and because we too are women, we are expected to give in, our minds are expected to collapse under the impact of their antagonism. I have seen too much of female self-delusion not to fear it more than anything. I have been under its sway too often not to fear it more than anything. Those who take the priorities of men as their own priorities are colonized: we must name it to stay free of it.

I came here to say one simple thing: our honor and our hope is in our ability to name integrity the essential reality of revolution; our future will bring that integrity to realization only if we put it first; we put it first by keeping our relationship to real life immediate and by respecting our capacity to understand experience ourselves, not through the medium of male ideology, male interpretation, or male intellection. Male values have devalued us: we cannot expect to be valued by honoring male values. This is a contradiction without resolution except in our obliteration.

In these next few years, we are going to see attempts on every front to recolonize us, to bring us back to the fold as women who do the dirty work and spread our legs when the men will it. We have to know and to acknowledge that our buttons can be pushed, that we are prone to guilt—which is political in and of itself—and to fear, which is entirely realistic. We have to be brave enough to confront in ourselves the desire to be reassimilated back into the male world, to know that we might lie to ourselves—especially about the righteousness of male political imperatives—to get back in. We always think it is safer there. But, if we dare to keep facing it, we know that there lies madness, there lies rape, there lies battery, there lies forced pregnancy and forced prostitution and forced mutilation, there lies murder. If we go back, we cannot go forward. If we do not go forward, we will disappear.

Feminism:
An Agenda

1983

This too was a speech, given April 8, 1983, at Hamilton College in upstate New York. It was published at the invitation and by the initiative of a male student in the college literary magazine, The ABC's of Reading, *in 1984. I remember flying up in a plane that was more like a tin can, just me and the pilot. I remember the semicircle of hundreds of young faces. That night, fraternity boys tried to break into the rooms I was staying in on campus in a generally deserted building. There were two immovable, institutional doors between me and them. I couldn't get an outside line and the switchboard didn't answer to get security. I waited. They went away.*

I still think that prostitution must be decriminalized, as I say in this speech; but, increasingly, I think there must be simple, straightforward, enforced criminal laws against exploiting women in commercial sexual transactions. The exploiter—pimp or john—needs to be recognized and treated as a real criminal, much as the batterer now is.

I REPRESENT THE morbid side of the women's movement. I deal with the shit, the real shit. Robin Morgan calls it "atrocity work." And that's pretty much what it is.

I deal with what happens to women in the normal course of women's lives all over this planet: the normal stuff that is abusive, criminal, violating—the point being that it is considered *normal* by the society at large. It is so systematic that it appears that women are not being abused when these commonplace things happen to women because these abuses are so commonplace.

Because women are everywhere, and because, as Shulamith Firestone said, a sex class is invisible because everyone takes it to be nature, and because many of the abuses that women systematically suffer are called sex, and because women are socialized in a way to make us indifferent to the plight of other women, and because there are no institutional means of redress for the crimes committed against us, feminism sometimes seems as if a group of women are standing in front of a tidal wave with one hand up saying: "Stop." That is why people say, "Well, it's hopeless." And from "it's hopeless," people say: "Well, it's life."

The stance of the women's movement is that it is not "just life." It is politics; it is history; it is power; it is economics; it is institutional modes of social organization: it is not "just life." *And that applies to all of it*: the sexual abuse, the economic degradation, the "natural" relationship between women and children (to paraphrase Firestone again: women and children are not united by biology, we are united by politics, a shared powerlessness; I think this is true).

The women's movement is like other political movements in one important way. Every political movement is committed to the belief that there are certain kinds of pain that people should not have to endure. They are unnecessary. They are gratuitous. They are not part of the God-given order. They are not biologically inevitable. They are acts of human will. They are acts done by some human beings to other human beings.

If you believe that God made women to be submissive and inferior, then there is almost nothing that feminism can say to you about your place in society. A political movement against the will of God does not sound like a very reasonable form of organizing. And in fact frequently a misogynist will say: "Your argument isn't with me. It's with God." And we say: "Well, since you're created in His image, you're the best we can do. So stand there and let's discuss this. You represent Him, you do that all the time anyway."

Another mode of argument about women's inferiority—a pervasive mode—has to do with biology. There are a lot of ways to address this issue. It is, in a certain sense, the basic issue of women's rights, of what women's rights should be: because there is a question as to what rights we women should have. If it were a common supposition that we should enjoy the same rights as men and that our lives had the same worth, we would be living in a very different world. There is not that supposition. There is not that premise. So in trying to discuss what rights women should have, many people refer to biology, and they do so in a myriad of ways. For instance, they may find—they go to great great lengths to find—various crawling things that behave in certain specified ways and they say: "Look at that! Seven million years ago you were related to that." This is an abuse of Charles Darwin to which any literate person should object; one should cringe to see such formidable theoretical work used in such a vile way. But these same people point to primates, fish, they point to anything that moves, anything that is actually alive, anything that they can find. And they tell us that we should infer our rights from the behaviors of whatever they are pointing to. Frequently they point to things that *aren't* alive, that are only postulated to have been alive at some previous moment in prehistory. One outstanding example is the cichlid, which is my personal favorite. It is a prehistoric fish—or, to be more precise, some men think it *was* a prehistoric fish. The followers of Konrad Lorenz—and these are scientists, okay?—say that the male cichlid could not mate unless his partner demonstrated *awe*. Now is this a projection or is this... a fish? Kate Millett wondered in *Sexual Politics* how a fish demonstrates awe. People who look to other animals (I will concede that we are also animals) to find reasons why women, human women, should be subordinate jump from species to species with alarming dexterity and ignore all information that contradicts their ideological point of view. Now, this is a quite human failing, and *that* is the point: it is a human failing. One need not postulate that a chimpanzee or an insect has the same failing to locate something human.

The women's movement is concerned first of all with this virtually metaphysical premise that women are biologically inferior. I don't know how many times in your own lives you have experienced the sense that you were being treated in a certain way because those around you considered you to be biologically inferior to them. I suspect that if you trace backwards, many of the humiliating events of your lives—and I am talking to the women in this room—would have at their base a commitment on the part of the person who created the humiliation that you deserved to be treated in the way in which you were treated because you were a woman. This means that there is some sense in which you are biologically not entitled to the same dignity and the same human respect to which men are entitled. This belief in the biological inferiority of women is, of course, not limited to men. Not only men have this belief. Women are raised to believe this same thing about ourselves, and many of us do. This belief is really the underpinning of the sexual system in which we live, whether you as an individual encounter it directly or indirectly. It is also the justification for most of the systematic sexual assault that women experience.

I am going to talk a lot today about sexual assault, but first I want to make a generalization about the women's movement and its relationship to knowledge—its purpose, in fact. The women's movement is not a narrowly political movement. It is not only an electoral movement. It is not only a reform movement, however you understand the word reform, because when you are dealing with a presumption of biological inferiority or God-given inferiority, there is no reform that addresses that question. There is no way to change the status of women in any society without dealing with basic metaphysical assumptions about the nature of women: what we are, what we want, what we have a right to, what our bodies are for, and especially to whom our bodies belong. The women's movement is a movement *for* knowledge, toward knowledge. I come here to a college to speak to you, and many of you are students here, and you are here for a lot of different reasons, personal reasons; but you are also here for social reasons. You are sent to college to learn how to become adults in this society, adults of a certain class, adults of a certain type, adults who will fit into a certain place. And the women here are here in part to be taught how to be women. As far back as you can go, when you were first taken to kindergarten, that is why you were taken there. And the same thing is true for the men. If what they wanted to teach you is not sealed, if it isn't fixed, if anything is loose and rattling around, *this* is their last chance to fix it. Most of the time they succeed. You get fixed. And yet these institutions are supposed to exist so that you can acquire knowledge. The women's movement, like other political movements before it, has unearthed a tremendous body of knowledge that has not been let into colleges and universities, into high schools, into grade schools, for political reasons. And for that reason, your relationship to knowledge has to be a questing one:

136

not learning what you are given, but finding what questions you must ask. The women's movement in general, with many exceptions, with many failures, with many imperfections, has been dedicated to that process of *finding out* which questions to ask and asking those questions.

A lot of the questions are considered unspeakable. They are unspeakable questions. And when they are asked, those who ask them are greeted with extraordinary hostility. I am sure you have experienced something similar whenever you have asked a question that somebody didn't want asked. Everything that you have been taught about the liberal tradition of education, about the value of books, the beauty of art, the meaning of creativity, is *lost*, means nothing, unless you retain the independence to ask your own questions, always, throughout your lives. And it is easier now than it will be in ten years, and it is easier now than it will be when you are fifty or sixty or seventy. It is one of the most extraordinary things about getting older: everything that people say about becoming more conservative is *true*. Everything that people say about selling out is *true*. If you are not brave enough now to ask the questions that you think need to be asked, you will never be brave enough. So don't ever put it off. The women's movement cannot survive unless you make that commitment. The women's movement is not a movement that just passes down an ideology: it's a movement that creates ideology, and that is very different. It creates ways of understanding the world in which women live, ways of understanding the social construction of masculinity and femininity, ways of understanding what prejudice is as a social construction, how it works, how it is transmitted. It creates ways of understanding what the hatred of women is, why it exists, how it is transmitted, what function it serves in this society or in any other society, regardless of how that society is organized economically, regardless of which side of the Iron Curtain it is on, whether or not it is a nuclear society. So we are dedicated to questions and we try to find answers.

We are also a movement against human suffering. There is no way to be a feminist and to forget that. If you are a feminist, and if you have forgotten that our purpose is to *end* the suffering of countless unnamed and invisible women from the crimes committed against them—and yes, we may also end the suffering of the men who are committing the crimes, yes, we probably think we can—then your feminism is hollow and it doesn't matter, it doesn't count. This is a movement against suffering. So, in between the lines, when you hear people say that this is a movement for freedom, for justice, for equality—and all of that is entirely and deeply true—you must remember that we are trying to eliminate suffering too. Freedom, justice, and equality have become slogan words, Madison Avenue words: so has *revolution*. Nobody tries to sell suffering: in Amerika, suffering is barely acknowledged. Suffering does not fit into the advertising scheme of things as a goal for a happy Amerikan. So it is a good measure of your own commitment to understand that in the end, in the end, the positives that we are searching for have to be measured against the true condition of women that we know and that we understand. The goal of the society we live in is to achieve Happiness, consumer Happiness. You are supposed to get Happiness from lip gloss and twenty-four hours of television every day. That means that you are not supposed to feel pain: you might not know what it is you do feel, but you must not feel pain. One of the things the women's movement does is to make you feel pain. You feel your own pain, the pain of other women, the pain of sisters whose lives you can barely imagine. You have to have a lot of courage to accept that if you commit yourself, over the long term, not just for three months, not for a year, not for two years, but for a lifetime, to feminism, to the women's movement, that you are going to live with a lot of pain. In this country that is not a fashionable thing to do. So be prepared for the therapists. And be prepared for the prescriptions. Be prepared for all the people who tell you that it's your problem, it's not a social problem, and why are you so bitter, and what's wrong with you? And underneath that is always the presumption that the rape was delusional, that the battery did not happen, that the economic hardship is your own unfortunate personal failing. Hold onto the fact that that's not true: it has never been true.

There have been many ways of defining the essential concerns of feminism. There are many differences of opinion. There are many ideological strains in the women's movement. There are many different sets of priorities. I am going to discuss mine as an individual feminist who writes books, who travels around the country a lot, who hears from women all over the world. You decide what that means.

I think that women's fundamental condition is defined literally by the lack of physical integrity of our bodies. I think that our subordinate place in society begins there. I do not think we can talk about women's condition in strictly economic terms, though I do not want to see any exclusion of economics from any discussion of women's condition. But I would say that what is fundamental and what must always be considered is the sexual and reproductive integrity of a woman's body. A woman is an individual and women are a class. The class of women includes women of every race, economic and social condition, in every society on the face of this globe.

It used to be that some feminists would speak at college campuses and would say, "You're too young to know anything, what do you know, what have you ever experienced, wait until you get out there, wait until the bastards start fucking with you, *then* you'll see what feminism is about." The search for knowledge has revealed that by the time women are the age of most of the women in this room, one in four has been sexually assaulted already. In fact since most of you are over eighteen, I suspect that more than a quarter of you have had this experience of sexual assault.

Incest is the first assault. We never had any idea of how common it was. We have always heard of the incest taboo, but, as I am sure you have heard in other contexts, laws are meant to be broken: this one especially. Most incest victims are girls. They are assaulted in a variety of ways, frequently by their fathers, often by step-fathers. We are talking about assault by men who are in intimate situations of power: adults with children, beloved adults. Very little incest is committed by women with children. There is beating of children by women, a lot of it. We must not leave that out. A lot of women are forced to have children they do not want, and there is a lot of battery especially on those children. But there does not seem to be very much sexual abuse.

Incest is terrifically important in understanding the condition of women. It is a crime that is committed against someone, a crime from which many victims never recover. Now, life is hard, or, as Jimmy Carter said, life is unfair. Horrible things happen from which people never recover. That is true. Probably no woman ever recovers from a rape; probably no woman ever recovers from battery. But this is different, because the child does not have a chance in the world. Her whole system of reality, her whole capacity to form attachments, her whole capacity to understand the meaning of self-respect, is destroyed by someone whom she loves. Incest victims are now organizing in this country, and they are organizing politically. One of the reasons that they are organizing politically and not psychiatrically is because they understand that it is the power of the father in the family that creates the environment that licenses the abuse. They understand that probably better than anyone who hasn't had the experience understands it. They have seen the mother's fear of the father; they know their own fear of the father; they have seen the community support for the father; they have seen the psychiatric community's defense of the father; they have seen the legal system's refusal to treat the father like a criminal; they have seen the religious leaders' refusal to take incest as seriously as the grave crime of homosexuality. They understand the world in which women live. Most important, I think, they understand the fear of their mothers, which is not to say that they ever forgive their mothers for what happened to them. This is a society in which it is very hard to forgive your mother, no matter what happens to you. But incest victims are truly at the center of our political situation. They have been, in my opinion, the bravest among us for speaking out about what happened to them when they were children. And they are organizing to get children some protection, some rights: and the women's movement has to be more serious in understanding that the connection between women and children really is political. The power of the father is what makes women and children a political underclass.

Marital rape is also very important in understanding the condition of women. Now I will tell you a story. I have a godson. It is a surprise to me that I have this godson, but I do. My godson's father is a civil liberties lawyer. I do not like civil liberties lawyers because they defend pornographers and racists and rapists and Nazis. In many ways we are ideological and political enemies. My godson's mother, who is my close friend, is an anti-rape feminist. That means that she understands feminism through understanding rape. My godson's father tells me, and he publishes an article in a newspaper that tells a lot of people, that when a woman is raped by someone she knows it is not so bad. He also says, to me and the public, that in marriage rape is impossible, not because the law says so—although the law frequently does say so—but because we can never know what the woman really wanted. My godson's father is a very nice man, a very sensitive man. He defends rapists in court—even though his doing so causes his wife unbearable personal pain—because he believes that women consistently accuse men of rape when they have only had sex and because he believes that penalties for rape are too severe anyway. It is impossible for him to even consider that being raped by someone you know—like a husband—might be *worse* than being raped by a stranger; that it can destroy your ability to go on; that it is the rape of your body and also the total destruction of your integrity and your self-esteem, your trust, your deepest privacy. The physical injuries that women suffer in marital rape are no less grave than the physical injuries that women suffer in any other kind of rape. Nevertheless, in the home the right to privacy has guaranteed the husband total access to his wife's body. Very specific statutes have guaranteed him that access, those rights. At the same time we have in this country a climate in which people are terrified of crime on the streets. Women are scared to death of rape. But the truth is—factually, not just polemically—that every woman is more likely to be raped by someone she knows, especially by a father or a husband; and the home, which is being promoted as a place of peace and harmony and Christian bliss is the most dangerous place in the world for a woman. That is the truth. A woman who is murdered is likely to be murdered in her home by a husband or lover. It is very hard to find out how many women are actually battered: the estimates based on research are now close to fifty percent of married women—fifty percent of married women have perhaps been battered at some point in a marriage. That's war. That's not life, that's war.

Recently there was a gang rape in New Bedford. You had a vigil here. Forty-three percent of all the rapes committed in this country are pair or gang rapes. Forty-three percent. Twenty-seven percent are three or more men; sixteen percent are two men. Gang rape is common, and it is almost never successfully prosecuted because the men are witnesses for each other: they all tell the same story. They all say that the victim came with them willingly or took money. It doesn't matter what happened to the woman. There will not be a prosecution at all for that rape. The implications of this are staggering because it means that any group of men can rape any individual woman, and that is in fact the case.

The Kinsey Institute, which studied such diverse phenomena as sex, sex, and sex, called gang rape "polyandrous attention." A woman, according to Kinsey research, walked down a street. Actually, the Kinsey categories are such that a woman is defined as someone fifteen years old or more. So maybe a teenager is walking down the street. She is gang-raped: male predators follow her, seek her out, force her. It is "polyandrous attention." That is the most recognition that gang rape has had until feminists began to analyze rape.

In talking about rape, we often talk about strangers who rape women, because that is the stereotype of rape, and also because strangers do rape women, though in less than half the rapes committed. Most women will be raped by somebody they know. So why is it that we are brought up to believe that rape is committed by strangers when mostly it isn't? In my view, rape is simply a matter of access. There is no qualitative distinction about men here. The group of men that we know are worse to us than the group of men that we don't know because they have the most access to us. Rape is a question of access. Men will rape women to whom they have access. The stranger in rape is used in a very important political way, especially in organizing women on the right: the stranger is used as a scapegoat. In the United States the stranger is black and he is a rapist. In Nazi Germany the stranger was a Jew and he was a rapist.

This use of rape associated with a stranger is a basic component of racism. Women's fears of rape are legitimate. Those fears are manipulated to serve the ends of racism.

We now see the same scapegoat strategy being used against homosexual men, who are accused of child molestation when most child molestation is of little girls. It is not that homosexual men do not rape. They do. So do black men and Jewish men. Men in all classes and of all races and ethnicities rape, which is not to say that all men rape. It is to say that all men benefit from rape, because all men benefit from the fact that women are not free in this society; that women cower; that women are afraid; that women cannot assert the rights that we have, limited as those rights are, because of the ubiquitous presence of rape.

When feminists began paying attention to rape, our intrusion into this area of male thought and male study and male activity was not much appreciated. We were told that we were making things worse for certain groups of men, especially for black men. Before the feminist movement, rape was treated by politically progressive people as a complete figment of a woman's imagination or as a vengeful, reactionary, racist effort to destroy somebody else or as an act of personal vengeance. The distinction I am making here is very important because rape is real. The selective use of the identity of the rapist has been false. That is a staggeringly dangerous piece of information, because when we look especially at white male anger with feminists for dealing with rape at all, we find that suddenly for the first time in the history of this country white men were included in the category of potential rapists. Somebody was onto their game at last. They did not like it. It is precisely the white liberals who have been saying that they have been fighting universally fraudulent claims against black men all these years who were most stubborn in refusing to understand that rape was real and that rape was committed by all kinds and classes of men, *including them.* They were perpetuating the racist stereotyping by refusing to acknowledge that all kinds of men do rape, thus leaving black men as the rapists in the public mind.

We frequently find ourselves in these dangerous and difficult situations because we are challenging not only power—and power is serious, power is important—but notions of reality with which people have become comfortable even though they protest them. It is not true that because people protest a condition they really want to see it eliminated. It is an ugly but basic fact of life that too frequently protest is a form of attachment to a condition, and when you eliminate the condition, you eliminate the function that the person has created for himself. The ultimate goal of feminism is to make feminism unnecessary. And that makes feminism different from other political movements in this country.

Connected with forced sex is forced pregnancy. As a radical feminist, one is constantly accused of many things: hating men, for instance, but also not knowing anything. People say, well, if you only knew this you wouldn't think that. I think that I must be the only woman alive who at over the age of thirty has been taken aside by people, radical people, kindly people, so that they could explain to me how the sperm unites with the egg so that I could understand the basis of sexuality and reproduction and why this system in which we now live is essential for our continued survival. So what can you do? When people keep telling you that you don't understand something, you have to try to understand it. So I tried to understand it, and it led to an astonishing conclusion: because when the sperm and egg unite there is the possibility of fertilization and a baby can be born, it doesn't matter whether the sex act was voluntary or involuntary. The pregnancy does not depend on the consent of the woman to sex; it only depends on the act taking place, the act of intercourse. Then look at what we know about women and forced sex. We know that possibly fifty percent of married women are or have been battered. We know that rape is endemic, that incest is endemic. We know that women get pregnant a lot, all the time. We know that women are blamed for their pregnancies when they want to terminate them; we know that women are held responsible for sex all the time whether they are responsible or not. We know that all the responsibility for the child will ultimately rest on the woman. She will feed it, she will clothe it, she will decide through her behavior whether the child lives or dies. She is the one who will be responsible for the child's life.

I am not going to talk about reproductive rights now; I want to talk about abortion, only abortion. Killing is central to it: the killing that takes place in forced sex. The killing is in sex that is forced, and every single synonym for sex in this society says so. All the words. Killing me softly; violation: all the words that have to do with sex are hostile words, dangerous words, so-called dirty words. The word *vagina* means sheath. All the pornographic imagery has to do with hostility: and there are weapons, knives, the use of the penis as a weapon. We didn't do this; feminists didn't do this. We are not responsible for creating it, but we are making people face it. So the practical reality is that as long as sex is forced on women, women must have the right to abortion, absolutely, no matter what it means, no matter what you think it means.

Abortion is also ideologically central to understanding women's condition. What abortion means to women is the absolute right to control the reproductive functions of our own bodies. There are other reproductive rights we need: not to be sterilized against our will as is happening systematically in some populations because of race

144

and class (sex being the precondition). But abortion is the symbol of a woman's life: and that is because when abortion was criminal in this country, women died in huge numbers, and women died horrible, horrible deaths. Death by criminal abortion was death by torture. Death by putrefaction. Gangrenous death. Drawn-out bleeding-to-death. That *is* what it was like and that is why the women who lived through it will never give up on the struggle for the total decriminalization of abortion, free funding, the absolute availability of safe abortion for all women. Which brings us to money. Now women with money get abortions when they want them and women without money do not. Women as a class are poor. Women who work earn fifty-six to fifty-nine cents on the dollar to what men get for comparable work. These figures are important. They really matter. Women get 100 percent of the pregnancies, but only half the dollar. One of the reasons that women are kept in a state of economic degradation—because that's what it is for most women—is because that is the best way to keep women sexually available. We can also talk about the way capitalism is organized, the way multinationals work, the way cheap labor is exploited by exploiting all kinds of people on the basis of race and class; but the fact of the matter is that when women are economically dependent, women are sexually available. Women have got to sell sex—at home, at work; and some women only have sex to sell because they are kept illiterate and untrained and because women are paid so little for "honest" work anyway. Systematic economic debasement turns every woman into a woman who can be bought, a woman who will be bought, and it is better to be a woman who has a high market value.

Instead of having a direct relationship to real work, and being able to go out and earn money (and having the same economic and political responsibilities for the economic system and its exploitation of workers in general that men have) women work for pittances and barter sex. Equality across sex means equal blessings and equal responsibilities, including equal economic and political responsibilities for the economic system. Equal pay for equal work would mean, too, that women would begin to break away sexually from men in a whole host of ways. This has nothing to do with being straight or being gay. It has nothing to do with any of the propaganda against the women's movement that says we hate men, want to destroy them, castrate them—I can't even think of all the things we are supposed to want to do to them once we can do whatever we want. Every woman lives with a knife in her kitchen; every woman can do what she wants right now. But the assertion of independence is a lot more complex, isn't it? It really means that you have to take some responsibility for your life, and a lot of women's problems are tied up with the enforced dependence on men that we are forced to develop. Some of that is expressed in sexual neediness; some of it is expressed in self-denigration. And even if none of that applies, the fact of the matter is that if you want to be an economically solvent woman in this society, you had damn well better be attached to a man—if not in your home, then in the workplace. Somewhere. If you don't have that connection somewhere you are in a lot of trouble.

The economic exploitation of women as a class means that we have to sell sex and that makes us, as a class, not irrationally viewed as prostitutes by men whether they call us prostitutes or not. A lot of the laws that we deal with are based on the assumption that a woman will sell herself to anyone for anything. If you have a group of people who are poor enough, the likelihood is that they will, and many women are poor enough. When you have endemic sexual harassment in the workplace, it is based on the presumption that the woman is there as a sexual being and is by her nature some kind of a prostitute—she will give sex for money or she will give sex for employment. That is part of what she is for. That is part of what she *is*.

There are differences between marriage and prostitution. Like prostitution, marriage is an institution that is extremely oppressive and dangerous for women. Women lose civil rights when they get married in most states. There is a whole continuum of rights that you don't have once you become a married woman in most places. They range from the inability to own your own property (in Louisiana, for instance, which is still governed by laws derived from the Napoleonic code, if you can believe it) to the loss of your own rights over your own body. You must have sex with your husband when he wants. That is his legal right and your legal obligation. One of the differences between marriage and prostitution is that in marriage you only have to make a deal with one man. A lot of women prefer marriage to prostitution for that reason. It is safer, a better deal. That is one of the major reasons that right-wing women defend the sanctity and insularity of the home. They don't want to be out on the streets selling their asses. Are you going to say they're stupid or wrong? They're not stupid. They're smart. They understand the system that they live in, and they understand what it is they have to trade for shelter and decent health and a little security. And then, like all good gamblers, they take their chances. Like all *women*, they take their chances.

Briefly, about prostitution: it is very much in our interest as women to see that prostitution is decriminalized. The criminalization of prostitution leaves poor women open to the most extraordinary kind of abuse and exploitation—by pimps, by pornographers, by professional buyers and sellers of women. It is also very important to us as women that prostitution not be legalized. In other words, there should be no laws against prostitution and there should be no laws regulating prostitution. In countries where prostitution is legalized, women are frequently kept prisoners in brothels. I recommend that you read Kathy Barry's *Female Sexual Slavery*, which is about forced prostitution on a global scale. I have lived in Amsterdam, Holland, where prostitution is de facto legalized, that is, regulated by the police rather openly. People there live to be a very old age, except for the prostitutes, who die very young. There is virtually no junkie problem, except among the prostitutes. They use heroin, they use morphine, they smoke opium. Women who are prostitutes in systems where prostitution is legalized never escape prostitution, and one of the reasons that they never escape is that the police don't let them. So it is against the interests of women to do anything that will put other women, some women, any women, in the position where they must be prostitutes for the rest of their lives. Then, there is the question of what prostitution does to the woman herself, the individual person. It is a question, I think, that we all have to ask ourselves, because we all make deals. The woman who is a professional prostitute is in a particularly abject situation. Current studies have shown that in some cities up to seventy percent of the women who are working in prostitution have been incest victims. Women become prostitutes often because they run away from home at a very early age. They run

147

away because they are being abused. They are particularly vulnerable to the pimps because they have not learned any system of self-protection or any form of self-respect; and also because what they are coming from in their minds *has* to be worse than what they are going toward. We have to change their situation.

Pornography is very closely related to prostitution, certainly for the women who are in it. For the women who are in it, very often pornography is a step up. Anything indoors is a step up. It's cold out there.

Pornography is many things. It is an industry. We estimate that it is an $8-billion-a-year industry. It is larger than the conventional film and record industries combined. Think of what that means about the consumption of pornography and how that consumption relates to the men, the vast numbers of men, who are committing the sexual assaults I am talking about. The content of pornography is almost always the same. It has a universal quality. Either the woman wants to be raped and wants to be hurt and really likes it *or* she doesn't, in which case all of these things are still done to her and she discovers, lo and behold, that she loved it all along, and really her life was so empty before all these things happened to her. Pornography is hate propaganda against women. It not only encourages acts of violence against us but it says that we love them. Pornography is an extremely vital and vigorous and effective belief system. It is also behavioral training. People say, "Oh, well, pornography—that's for mastur-bation, nobody can get hurt that way." But orgasm is a very serious reward, isn't it? Think of Pavlov's little dogs, right? They don't just think about salivating; they salivate. They do it because they learned it. Period. Now think about pornography. The dehumanization is a basic part of the content of all pornography without exception. Pornography in this country in the last ten years has become increasingly violent by every measure, including *Playboy*, including all the stuff you take for granted; and every single orgasm is a reward for believing that material, absorbing that material, responding to that value system: having a sexual response to stuff that makes women inferior, subhuman.

Nothing in this system is unrelated to anything else, and there is a relationship between rape and pornography. Pornography celebrates rape. We have a tremendous amount of information on the use of

pornography in rapes that no authority would consider important.*
We have a tremendous amount of information from incest victims
that their fathers used pornography. So let me just talk to you briefly
about how the women's movement gets its information, and why we
are almost always right. In the last ten years there has been a pattern.
Feminists have said that something happens or is true and then ten
thousand authorities have said "that's bullshit." And then somebody
started doing studies, and then three years later they say, "well, well,
rape is endemic." Right? They say to us, well, your figure was too low,
it's ten times that, right? The FBI discovers rape, right?

The same thing happened with battery. Women love to be beaten:
that is what authorities think and say. Battered wives begin speaking.
Women begin to emerge from situations in which they have been
held captive and terrorized for ten years, twelve years, fifteen years.
"Oh, what crap," the authorities say. Five years later we have
sociologists telling us that they did a study in California and found out
that fifty percent of married women had been beaten. It wasn't news
to us. We have a terrific trick. We listen to the women. It is an
unbelievably top secret method that we don't let anybody else know
about. It is how we found out about incest. When women started
talking about having been incestuously abused three or four or five
years ago everyone said it did not happen. Now the authorities use
our figure: one in four. We now think the figure is too low, and we're
right. They'll find out that we're right.

So the relationship between rape and pornography is not really a
matter of speculation. The studies are being done, some have been
done, they will be done, we can discuss them if you want to discuss
them: but I am telling you that we have the stories of women who say
that pornography was centrally involved in the rape. We know that it
is true. Pornography is how-to material. There are rapists who use it
that way. There are batterers who use it that way. There are Daddy-
rapists who use it that way. There are *loving*, battering husbands who
use it that way, and it will be established beyond any doubt that it is
used that way by *masses* of men. Now, where does this leave us?

* In Minneapolis on December 12 and 13, 1983, the Minneapolis City Council held
hearings that established the centrality of pornography in sexual abuse as experienced
by women along the whole continuum of forced and hostile sex acts imposed classically
on females. The proof is now all in one place, and it is irrefutable.

It is a total non sequitur to me, but some people feel that we are left with questions about freedom of speech. Some people think that questions about freedom of speech are a logical political response to what I have just said about harm. They do not mean the freedom of speech of the victims; they mean the freedom of speech of the pornographers. Say something about pornography and somebody says, "what about freedom of speech?" Well, what *about* freedom of speech? Who has it? *Who has it?* Where does it begin? I say it begins with the incest victim; I say that's where it begins. It begins with *that* child who is captive in *that* home who cannot say no. Or freedom of speech might begin on a pool table in New Bedford: freedom of speech might begin with the woman gang-raped on the pool table in public. *Her* freedom of speech: did she have any? About six weeks before that gang rape took place, *Hustler* had precisely, *precisely*, the same gang rape. It was in the January issue: on a pool table, in the same kind of bar, everything in that lay-out is what happened in that bar. Coincidence? A copy-cat rape? We now have as part of our social fabric and virtual public policy the public celebration of rape. People go to films to celebrate rape. People say that the fact that Linda Marchiano, who was known as Linda Lovelace, was beaten and raped and forced to make *Deep Throat* doesn't matter. *Deep Throat* is more important. *Deep Throat* is speech. We need *Deep Throat*, right? The fact that someone was held in captivity and terrorized in order to make the film is not supposed to diminish the importance of the film to our freedom. Maybe free speech begins with Linda Marchiano.

The First Amendment was written by white men who were literate and who owned land. Many of them owned slaves and many of them owned women. It was illegal to teach slaves to read or write, and none of them worried about the First Amendment. The First Amendment was written by those men because literacy and ownership of property were linked. Literacy was a sign of upper-class power. The First Amendment was written to preserve that power. Now it protects a different kind of power, a more vulgar power. It is not an aristocratic power. It is the pure power of money. It is the pimp's power. That is what it does now. It does not empower women. It does nothing for us when we write our books, when we sing our songs. It was never intended to, and if we're concerned about freedom of speech, what we have to do is to find a way to get it.

Feminists have asked—just pro forma—the ACLU (American Civil Liberties Union) to help us. We've said, "look, women are excluded historically and economically from any possible participation in this media world that costs so much money. And so are blacks. And so are Hispanics. And so are other dispossessed people in this country. What about our rights to speech? How do we get them?" The ACLU defends the corporations. They defend NBC; they defend the owners of newspapers to print what they want. They do not defend your right or my right to be heard in those places. They defend the rights of the *owners* to decide what will or will not be said. We need a political approach to civil liberties in this country—not a liberal, sentimental, nonsensical approach. Where is power? Who has it? Who has freedom of expression? What does it mean? What does it amount to? How does it work out in real life? Who does the State come down on and why? And who are the people so dispossessed that the State doesn't even worry about them? The State controls those dispossessed people in other ways. I say to you as a writer and as a woman that literacy, writing a book, speaking here before you, are signs of tremendous privilege. These are not common rights we can all exercise.

We all want to think of ourselves as individuals. We all want to think that our qualities make a difference in the world, and it is a brutal thing to find out that because you're a woman, or because you're black, or because you're Jewish, or because you are anything else, because of your condition of birth, certain expressions of individuality are closed off to you.

Many women rebel against feminism because many women think we are the ones insisting that their full human uniqueness cannot be expressed because they are women. We are the bringers of the terrible message. We found this out by being women in the world. We want to change it. This is not a condition imposed by a political movement. This is a condition imposed by male supremacy. That is what we want to change, so that each individual can be herself, need not conform to a definition of her function and a definition of her body and a definition of her worth that has nothing whatsoever to do with her personally. Sometimes, though, the political movement against male supremacy is confused with male supremacy itself, as if we're the ones who are telling you, "because you are women, you're going to have to do this and this and this." We're reporters. We're telling you that because you're women you live in this world I'm describing, and that the only way to do anything about it is to take some political responsibility for its existence and to work collectively together, which *never* means the abandonment of your integrity as individuals. It also never means the abandonment of common sense or common decency. If it does, there is something wrong with the way you are going about organizing against what it is that's upsetting you and making you angry and exploiting you and hurting you.

There is nothing that feminists want more than to become irrelevant. We want the end of the exploitation of women; but as long as there is rape—as long as there is rape—there is not going to be any peace or justice or equality or freedom. You are not going to become what you want to become or who you want to become. You are not going to live in the world you want to live in. And so you have to organize an agenda. I don't have an agenda. My agenda is everything I can think of, everything I think of doing, all the time: movement, movement, physical and intellectual and political confrontations with power. You have to write the picket signs, march, scream, yell, write the fucking letters. It's your responsibility to yourselves and to other women.

There is one thing that is not practical, and it's the thing I believe in most, and that is the importance of vision in the midst of what has to be done, never forgetting for one minute the world that you really want to live in and how you want to live in it and what it means to you and how much you care about it—what you want for yourselves and what you want for the people that you love. Everywhere in this country now people are told to be complacent because change is impossible. Change is not impossible. It is not impossible. Many things have to be changed in the world. It is now time to change the condition of women, finally and absolutely and for all time. That is my agenda, and I thank you for listening.

Margaret Papandreou:
An American Feminist in Greece

1982

It is important to understand that a published interview is not a transcript of a conversation. This, like virtually all interviews, is cut-and-pasted from a much longer literal text. I am against this process and was aghast at how many changes were made in the interview before publication. I don't think I could ever interview anyone again because the published interview is always artifice. Margaret Papandreou is not misrepresented, nor am I; but this is not what went down. As someone who has been interviewed a lot, I hate the distortions introduced by editorial excision and revision. In this case, even with my care and the care of Robin Morgan, who as an editor at Ms. *was responsible for the piece, I am not at peace with either the process or the result. Things were not said in this way, in this order, and a lot is missing. Think of it as edited tape: the fragments you see on television documentaries culled from long dialogues that you can never either recreate or imagine.*

WHEN THE MILITARY junta took over Greece on April 21, 1967, many of the friends I had on Crete, where I had lived in 1965 and 1966, were arrested. Those friends spanned many generations. Some had been imprisoned under the right-wing Metaxas dictatorship in the 1930s or their parents had been. Some had survived the Nazi occupation of Crete. Some had been jailed—or older friends had been—after the 1946–49 civil war because they were Communists. All remembered, as if it had happened to them, the Turkish occupation (more than 400 years, ending in 1829).

Everyone I met understood political terror and feared the police. All, no matter what their politics, were reticent, discreet, aware that the liberal government of George Papandreou, then Prime Minister, was in trouble and that the Right, with American support, might well impose harsher restraints on civil liberties. The Communist Party was illegal, and those who were or had been members or sympathizers were particularly in jeopardy. Especially irritating to the Right was a leftist economist named Andreas Papandreou, son of George, and a visible, persuasive radical who came to represent the political aspirations many had to hide.

During my first days on Crete, George Papendreou came to speak. Three days before his speech, people began coming into the city from the mountains—in wagons, on mules, on foot, whole families, women carrying infants, thousands of peasants. Two years later, the military junta was in power and George Papandreou and his dissident son were in jail. There were 6000 political prisoners.

George Papandreou died in 1968. Andreas, who in 1939 had been tortured under the Metaxas dictatorship, was kept in solitary confinement for eight months and allowed to exercise in isolation in a specially built cage. Pressure from John Kenneth Galbraith, Gloria Steinem, and others persuaded Lyndon Johnson to persuade the colonels to allow Andreas to go into exile. He returned to Greece when the junta fell in 1974; and in 1981, the founder of a new socialist political party, he became Prime Minister of Greece.

He is married to an American, Margaret Chant from Elmhurst, Illinois, a feminist activist with whom I had the pleasure of speaking when she was in the United States to visit her family. I was particularly excited to have the opportunity to meet with her. To me, the election of her husband was a vindication of the friends I loved who had been jailed (despite the fact that many of them are in leftist parties that oppose Andreas Papandreou). But also, Margaret is a feminist in a country in which only two out of every hundred women have attended college and only nine out of every hundred have completed secondary school; in which women were not given the vote until 1952; in which a woman cannot legally be the guardian of her own children, even when the father dies. It is hard to imagine the wife of a chief executive who is not only the president of the Women's Union of Greece, but also a *real* feminist organizer. Margaret

Papandreou is such a woman. These are excerpts from our conversation.

Andrea Dworkin: In Greece, women are socially segregated, certainly in public. How has this segregation affected you?

Margaret Papandreou: I suppose it's the condition that caused me to make women's rights my major political struggle. When I first went to Greece I saw the second-class, third-class—it's even worse than second-class—status of women in the country. It affected me very much. Many Greek women feel the same way. They have lived with this thing and are dedicated to fighting against it. And that's been extremely positive for me, to find women who desperately want this kind of political activism.

A.D.: In the United States, consciousness-raising was instrumental in the development of a women's movement, because even though we are socially integrated into the world, we found ourselves in total isolation from one another. Greek women live much more together than we do, in extended families, in village structures, and so on. Do they realize what they have in common? Or are they still isolated from what happens to one another?

M.P.: I would say they're still isolated. They still feel it necessary to defend their husbands, to show that each has the best husband in the group. Especially in the village areas, it's very hard for them to open up and say what is in their hearts. Their sole source of prestige and upward mobility is through their husbands.

Only thirty percent of our women work outside the home. So we have two-thirds of women who are solely housewives. (Every woman who works outside the home is also a housewife.) It's very important to them that they give a view to the neighbor or to the village that they have a good marriage.

When we go out and organize women in the villages, we don't ask them directly if they've been beaten by their husbands. We ask if they know of beatings. Most of them will shake their heads "no." Some younger women will say, "What do you mean, what are you saying? We know there are beatings going on in this village." But the majority will not want to say it. When I say "young women," I should correct that: sometimes it is an older woman, a woman of about seventy-five or eighty.

A.D.: Do you have any notion of what the level of violence is that Greek women experience in the home? The intensity? The frequency?

M.P.: We don't have any statistics as far as I know, but I think it's a very great deal. In a male-dominated society, in a patriarchal society with the hierarchy of the family that exists, and in the attitude toward the women, there couldn't be anything but violence in the family. The wife is there as an animal, that is, the person who carries the water, who serves the man, so then she can be kicked, too. It's not so hard, she's not a human being. I'm not talking about the very young generation, but there's not *that* much change from generation to generation.

A.D.: One of my most vivid memories of Crete was the old women, many of them survivors from the Nazi occupation, when whole villages of men were killed. Are they any part of your organizing? They're formidable women.

M.P.: Yes, they are. When they come out and speak, we usually know we've got the makings of a good chapter of our feminist organization. There are some of them yet who feel that they have the ideas but because they are illiterate they don't want to take an active role. They're intimidated. And then we have other women—we've recorded their statements—and they really give it to all the men in the village, to the whole goddamned system. I would say that when you find a strong Greek woman, you find a really strong woman, because she's had to struggle through all kinds of odds. When she comes out of that and decides to play a leadership role, you can count on tremendous strength and she's ready for almost anything.

A.D.: Is there anything in that system of sex segregation that you think is a political plus for Greek women? Is there any particular strength or pride developed that can be built on politically?

M.P.: I can't see where that kind of sex segregation gives any particular strength to women. But what we do in the Women's Union—I think it's very important that we don't have men because we are doing political education—we take women who have never had any organization experience, never any political thinking that they could adopt, and in that environment which is supportive and pushes them to move ahead, they learn things they never would learn if they went into a mixed organization at the very beginning. It's like a school. I have seen some remarkable developing. We've been functioning since 1975, and some of these women who couldn't face a public meeting are deputies in Parliament today. So they have a fantastic pace of development once they get into it, even more than a man has who is in it from the time he's born.

A.D.: Do the male-dominated political parties object to all-women political groups?

M.P.: Yes, they tend to ridicule us, to call us bourgeois, middle-class, educated, elitist, and say that all we do is drink tea. Suffragettes, we're called. And also we are told that it weakens the major struggle, which is the struggle for socialism. If you manage to get socialism, they say, then your worries are over, the woman is suddenly equal and everything's fine. We've had to fight against all those things.

A.D.: I want to ask you something that is very important to me. When I first went to Crete I was aware of what the Nazis had done on the island and what the Turks had done. I know that under Metaxas and again after the civil war a tremendous number of Greeks experienced prison and police brutality at the hands of other Greeks, and certainly with the junta there were seven years of systematic police brutality and torture. When men are tortured, it's always viewed as political. When women are tortured, as in rape, battery, pornography, it's viewed as sexual; women are seen to be natural victims. It seems to me that in Greece there is a unique historical circumstance: there's a political generation that has a basis for really understanding what torture is, the kind of total psychic as well as physical abuse inherent in it. Do you think it's possible for that to provide some kind of basis for really understanding what violence against women is, and for really transforming the sexual oppression of women?

M.P.: That's a good thought—a good possible tactic to use in terms of the education of our men. So far, unfortunately, even those who have gone through this kind of experience make the division between that and sexual abuse and torture. They haven't made the jump, and maybe it's also because women have not yet reached the stage where they can sit down and talk to men and try to discuss these issues. But I have never heard a man in Greece talk that way, certainly not men who have gone through tremendous torture themselves. What success would you say there has been in the United States in making the connection?

A.D.: Very little. We can't even make people understand that when you torture a woman in pornography, when you do to a woman what you wouldn't do to a dog or cat, there might be something wrong with it.

M.P.: But what you're saying is that with the specific experience of Greek men during the period of the dictatorship, there might be a basis for some better understanding?

A.D.: Yes. Also, in my experience on Crete, while I encountered intense male domination—the kind you feel only in a sex-segregated society, especially if you're an outsider and female—there was also the most extraordinary belief in democracy. It wasn't silly or romantic; it seemed to be visceral.

M.P.: But the belief in democracy as a political ideal is still not carried through, for example, to form a democratic family. The woman is in a separate compartment, whether it has to do with democracy, with socialism, with practically any political philosophy you can find. The woman's issue is a separate issue; it is compartmentalized; it is shoved away. Men don't want to think about it. And they don't even find difficulty in reconciling these things. It is not a philosophical issue for them. It's amazing. Sometimes we've had banquets that our women's chapter has given in the villages. Men and women come, and I will talk to some of those who are members of PASOK.* They will sit at my table. And a man will say to me, "I'm a socialist, you know, but when it comes to women—" And he thinks this is all right, that a woman's place is in the home. If you say, "Wouldn't the woman like to go out and also experience some political action, shouldn't she belong to the local organization of PASOK?"—well, then, he'll ask, "But who's going to take care of the children?"

I remember one discussion in which we were talking about the change in the family law. The speaker was saying that there's no reason why a man, if a child gets sick, could not stay home from work himself for some days; they should divide this responsibility. There

---

* An acronym for the Panhellenic Socialist Movement, the party founded by Andreas Papandreou.

was a farmer there. He was obviously trying to understand these things. And he raised his hand afterward and he said, "But you said I should stay home with the baby." He put his hands out, like this, you know: "How could I hold that baby, I mean what could I—?" He was struggling to understand how he could hold a baby. He couldn't fathom it. So there's a wall.

A.D.: What do you hope for, realistically, organizing women in the next decade?

M.P.: First of all, I hope to raise the level of consciousness on this whole issue. And I think this is being done. From then on, I believe as women understand the sources of their oppression, they understand also their need to struggle against it. That means they will unite more and more, join some kind of group—they don't have to join ours. What I'd like to see is that they get active with organizations. That, then, is a movement. I believe that this is happening and I believe that it is growing.... During this visit to the States I am going to the United Nations where our government representative there is going to sign the international resolution for the abolishment of discrimination against women, which the former Greek government refused to ratify and sign.† So we have accepted a kind of international framework for the whole question of discrimination against women.

The changing of attitudes and traditions will be a long, long thing, and to me that's the most difficult of all. I don't expect to see it in my lifetime. But legally we can do some things *now*—and we will do them.

Margaret Papandreou on Women's Organizations in Greece

Seven years of dictatorship kept women away from any kind of political activity. All the women's organizations were abolished and women were actually put in jail for having belonged to women's organizations. Their lists were confiscated. When I came back, the first two years the whole society was functioning under fear but women were especially afraid. There were those courageous women who really started rebuilding women's organizations. In those first

† The United States has not ratified this resolution.

few years, it was very hard. So we've had to go through a different experience than women in the United States.

We have three mass women's organizations. One is the Women's Union, to which I belong. Another is most closely tied to the Communist Party. A third is the Organization of Democratic Women, which belongs to the splinter party of the Communist Party, the Euro-Communists. They are the most feminist in their approach and their positions.

Within our own organization, we have some women who express conservative ideas, some religious people—we have a really wide spectrum. The main thrust is very progressive and socialist. Our doors are open to any women who accept our organization's constitution, but most of the women who come to our organization are either members or friends of PASOK. We are not controlled or given direction by the party. But when you have a number of party members in the organization, they will push the party line in some cases. So we have this socialist-feminist kind of mentality. The word "feminist" in Greece is a much worse word than "socialist." Socialism has become a little bit respectable. Feminism has not.

We have two women deputy ministers in the government and one—Melina Mercouri—as Minister of Culture and Sciences. All three women have what you might call women's posts. Also, in terms of the hierarchy of ministries, they are not at the top. We didn't manage to get women appointed to really nontraditional posts—for instance, Mitterand in France did appoint a woman Minister of Agriculture. We didn't manage to do that.

Margaret Papandreou on:

The Family Law: The Family Code virtually defines the woman as incapable of independent and intelligent judgment. She must always be under the control of a male. The man is the head of the family. He has all of the rights over the children. If there is a divorce and the man is stripped of his parental authority for some reason, the court assigns a guardian or adviser for her—a man.

Dowry: The woman has the right to hold onto the dowry that she brought into marriage, but the man has the right to invest or make decisions about that capital or property, and he takes the income.

Adultery: The decriminalization of adultery is a women's issue. [At the time of our interview, adultery was a crime with jail sentences of up to a year, mostly falling to the women. In July 1982, adultery was decriminalized.]

Battery: I don't believe it is even an issue legally.

Rape: The law defines rape only as entry into the vagina. Oral or anal rape or any other kind of sexual abuse is not considered rape. There is rape presumably only when there is a potential that the woman can get pregnant. The concept of marital rape is not included.

Prostitution: There are legalized houses of prostitution. The women are asked to report for health examinations. The police pretty much control the houses.

Abortion: Abortion is not legal. We have about the highest abortion rate of any European country. Abortion is the means of birth control. There is no sex education in schools or elsewhere and no public information on birth-control techniques. Doctors who perform abortions never give women information on how to avoid pregnancy. It's a very profitable income for the doctors. I've talked to women who have had as many as twenty abortions.

Lesbianism: We're very much behind on some issues. But if you look at the development of the feminist movement in the United States, lesbianism was not one of the first issues. The Women's Movement had to grow and understand what the key issues were, the really feminist issues. We haven't gone through this yet.

I Want A Twenty-Four-Hour Truce During Which There Is No Rape

1983

This was a speech given at the Midwest Regional Conference of the National Organization for Changing Men in the fall of 1983 in St Paul, Minnesota. One of the organizers kindly sent me a tape and a transcript of my speech. The magazine of the men's movement, M., published it. I was teaching in Minneapolis. This was before Catharine MacKinnon and I had proposed or developed the civil rights approach to pornography as a legislative strategy. Lots of people were in the audience who later became key players in the fight for the civil rights bill. I didn't know them then. It was an audience of about 500 men, with scattered women. I spoke from notes and was actually on my way to Idaho—an eight-hour trip each way (because of bad air connections) to give a one-hour speech on Art—fly out Saturday, come back Sunday, can't talk more than one hour or you'll miss the only plane leaving that day, you have to run from the podium to the car for the two-hour drive to the plane. Why would a militant feminist under this kind of pressure stop off on her way to the airport to say hi to 500 men? In a sense, this was a feminist dream-come-true. What would you say to 500 men if you could? This is what I said, how I used my chance. The men reacted with considerable love and support and also with considerable anger. Both. I hurried out to get my plane, the first hurdle for getting to Idaho. Only one man in the 500 threatened me physically. He was stopped by a woman bodyguard (and friend) who had accompanied me.

I HAVE THOUGHT a great deal about how a feminist, like myself, addresses an audience primarily of political men who say that they are antisexist. And I thought a lot about whether there should be a qualitative difference in the kind of speech I address to you. And then I found myself incapable of pretending that I really believe that that qualitative difference exists. I have watched the men's movement for many years. I am close with some of the people who participate in it. I can't come here as a friend even though I might very much want to. What I would like to do is to scream: and in that scream I would have the screams of the raped, and the sobs of the battered; and even worse, in the center of that scream I would have the deafening sound of women's silence, that silence into which we are born because we are women and in which most of us die.

And if there would be a plea or a question or a human address in that scream, it would be this: why are you so slow? Why are you so slow to understand the simplest things; not the complicated ideological things. You understand those. *The simple things.* The clichés. Simply that women are human to precisely the degree and quality that you are.

And also: that we do not have time. We women. We don't have forever. Some of us don't have another week or another day to take time for you to discuss whatever it is that will enable you to go out into those streets and do something. We are very close to death. All women are. And we are very close to rape and we are very close to beating. And we are inside a system of humiliation from which there is no escape for us. We use statistics not to try to quantify the injuries, but to convince the world that those injuries even exist. Those statistics are not abstractions. It is easy to say, "Ah, the statistics, somebody writes them up one way and somebody writes them up another way." That's true. But I hear about the rapes one by one by one by one by one, which is also how they happen. Those statistics are not abstract to me. Every three minutes a woman is being raped. Every eighteen seconds a woman is being beaten. There is nothing abstract about it. It is happening right now as I am speaking.

And it is happening for a simple reason. There is nothing complex and difficult about the reason. Men are doing it, because of the kind of power that men have over women. That power is real, concrete, exercised from one body to another body, exercised by someone who feels he has a right to exercise it, exercised in public and exercised in private. It is the sum and substance of women's oppression.

It is not done 5000 miles away or 3000 miles away. It is done here and it is done now and it is done by the people in this room as well as by other contemporaries: our friends, our neighbors, people that we know. Women don't have to go to school to learn about power. We just have to be women, walking down the street or trying to get the housework done after having given one's body in marriage and then having no rights over it.

The power exercised by men day to day in life is power that is institutionalized. It is protected by law. It is protected by religion and religious practice. It is protected by universities, which are strongholds of male supremacy. It is protected by a police force. It is protected by those whom Shelley called "the unacknowledged legislators of the world": the poets, the artists. Against that power, we have silence.

It is an extraordinary thing to try to understand and confront why it is that men believe—and men do believe—that they have the right to rape. Men may not believe it when asked. Everybody raise your hand who believes you have the right to rape. Not too many hands will go up. It's in life that men believe they have the right to force sex, which they don't call rape. And it is an extraordinary thing to try to understand that men really believe that they have the right to hit and to hurt. And it is an equally extraordinary thing to try to understand that men really believe that they have the right to buy a woman's body for the purpose of having sex: that that is a right. And it is very amazing to try to understand that men believe that the seven-billion-dollar-a-year industry that provides men with cunts is something that men have a right to.

That is the way the power of men is manifest in real life. That is what theory about male supremacy means. It means you can rape. It means you can hit. It means you can hurt. It means you can buy and sell women. It means that there is a class of people there to provide you with what you need. You stay richer than they are, so that they have to sell you sex. Not just on street corners, but in the workplace. That's another right that you can presume to have: sexual access to any woman in your environment, when you want.

Now, the men's movement suggests that men don't want the kind of power I have just described. I've actually heard explicit whole sentences to that effect. And yet, everything is a reason not to do something about changing the fact that you do have that power.

Hiding behind guilt, that's my favorite. I love that one. Oh, it's horrible, yes, and I'm so sorry. You have the time to feel guilty. We don't have the time for you to feel guilty. Your guilt is a form of acquiescence in what continues to occur. Your guilt helps keep things the way they are.

I have heard in the last several years a great deal about the suffering of men over sexism. Of course, I have heard a great deal about the suffering of men all my life. Needless to say, I have read *Hamlet*. I have read *King Lear*. I am an educated woman. I know that men suffer. This is a new wrinkle. Implicit in the idea that this is a different kind of suffering is the claim, I think, that in part you are actually suffering because of something that you know happens to someone else. That would indeed be new.

But mostly your guilt, your suffering, reduces to: gee, we really feel so bad. Everything makes men feel so bad: what you do, what you don't do, what you want to do, what you don't want to want to do but are going to do anyway. I think most of your distress is: gee, we really feel so bad. And I'm sorry that you feel so bad—so uselessly and stupidly bad—because there is a way in which this really is your tragedy. And I don't mean because you can't cry. And I don't mean because there is no real intimacy in your lives. And I don't mean because the armor that you have to live with as men is stultifying: and I don't doubt that it is. But I don't mean any of that.

I mean that there is a relationship between the way that women are raped and your socialization to rape and the war machine that grinds you up and spits you out: the war machine that you go through just like that woman went through Larry Flynt's meat grinder on the cover of *Hustler*. You damn well better believe that you're involved in this tragedy and that it's your tragedy too. Because you're turned into little soldier boys from the day that you are born and everything that you learn about how to avoid the humanity of women becomes part of the militarism of the country in which you live and the world in which you live. It is also part of the economy that you frequently claim to protest.

And the problem is that you think it's out there: and it's not out there. It's in you. The pimps and the warmongers speak for you. Rape and war are not so different. And what the pimps and the warmongers do is that they make you so proud of being men who can

165

get it up and give it hard. And they take that acculturated sexuality and they put you in little uniforms and they send you out to kill and to die. Now, I am not going to suggest to you that I think that's more important than what you do to women, because I don't.

But I think that if you want to look at what this system does to you, then that is where you should start looking: the sexual politics of aggression; the sexual politics of militarism. I think that men are very afraid of other men. That is something that you sometimes try to address in your small groups, as if if you changed your attitudes towards each other, you wouldn't be afraid of each other.

But as long as your sexuality has to do with aggression and your sense of entitlement to humanity has to do with being superior to other people, and there is so much contempt and hostility in your attitudes towards women and children, how could you not be afraid of each other? I think that you rightly perceive—without being willing to face it politically—that men are very dangerous: because you are.

The solution of the men's movement to make men less dangerous to each other by changing the way you touch and feel each other is not a solution. It's a recreational break.

These conferences are also concerned with homophobia. Homophobia is very important: it is very important to the way male supremacy works. In my opinion, the prohibitions against male homosexuality exist in order to protect male power. *Do it to her.* That is to say: as long as men rape, it is very important that men be directed to rape women. As long as sex is full of hostility and expresses both power over and contempt for the other person, it is very important that men not be declassed, stigmatized as female, used similarly. The power of men as a class depends on keeping men sexually inviolate and women sexually used by men. Homophobia helps maintain that class power: it also helps keep you as individuals safe from each other, safe from rape. If you want to do something about homophobia, you are going to have to do something about the fact that men rape, and that forced sex is not incidental to male sexuality but is in practice paradigmatic.

Some of you are very concerned about the rise of the Right in this country, as if that is something separate from the issues of feminism or the men's movement. There is a cartoon I saw that brought it all

166

together nicely. It was a big picture of Ronald Reagan as a cowboy with a big hat and a gun. And it said: "A gun in every holster; a pregnant woman in every home. Make America a man again." Those are the politics of the Right.

If you are afraid of the ascendancy of fascism in this country—and you would be very foolish not to be right now—then you had better understand that the root issue here has to do with male supremacy and the control of women; sexual access to women; women as reproductive slaves; private ownership of women. That is the program of the Right. That is the morality they talk about. That is what they mean. That is what they want. And the only opposition to them that matters is an opposition to men owning women.

What's involved in doing something about all of this? The men's movement seems to stay stuck on two points. The first is that men don't really feel very good about themselves. How could you? The second is that men come to me or to other feminists and say: "What you're saying about men isn't true. It isn't true of me. I don't feel that way. I'm opposed to all of this."

And I say: don't tell me. Tell the pornographers. Tell the pimps. Tell the warmakers. Tell the rape apologists and the rape celebrationists and the pro-rape ideologues. Tell the novelists who think that rape is wonderful. Tell Larry Flynt. Tell Hugh Hefner. There's no point in telling me. I'm only a woman. There's nothing I can do about it. These men presume to speak for you. They are in the public arena saying that they represent you. If they don't, then you had better let them know.

Then there is the private world of misogyny: what you know about each other; what you say in private life; the exploitation that you see in the private sphere; the relationships called love, based on exploitation. It's not enough to find some traveling feminist on the road and go up to her and say: "Gee, I hate it."

Say it to your friends who are doing it. And there are streets out there on which you can say these things loud and clear, so as to affect the actual institutions that maintain these abuses. You don't like pornography? I wish I could believe it's true. I will believe it when I see you on the streets. I will believe it when I see an organized political opposition. I will believe it when pimps go out of business because there are no more male consumers.

You want to organize men. You don't have to search for issues. The issues are part of the fabric of your everyday lives.

I want to talk to you about equality, what equality is and what it means. It isn't just an idea. It's not some insipid word that ends up being bullshit. It doesn't have anything at all to do with all those statements like: "Oh, that happens to men too." I name an abuse and I hear: "Oh, it happens to men too." That is not the equality we are struggling for. We could change our strategy and say: well, okay, we want equality; we'll stick something up the ass of a man every three minutes.

You've never heard that from the feminist movement, because for us equality has real dignity and importance—it's not some dumb word that can be twisted and made to look stupid as if it had no real meaning.

As a way of practicing equality, some vague idea about giving up power is useless. Some men have vague thoughts about a future in which men are going to give up power or an individual man is going to give up some kind of privilege that he has. That is not what equality means either.

Equality is a practice. It is an action. It is a way of life. It is a social practice. It is an economic practice. It is a sexual practice. It can't exist in a vacuum. You can't have it in your home if, when the people leave the home, he is in a world of his supremacy based on the existence of his cock and she is in a world of humiliation and degradation because she is perceived to be inferior and because her sexuality is a curse.

This is not to say that the attempt to practice equality in the home doesn't matter. It matters, but it is not enough. If you love equality, if you believe in it, if it is the way you want to live—not just men and women together in a home, but men and men together in a home and women and women together in a home—if equality is what you want and what you care about, then you have to fight for the institutions that will make it socially real.

It is not just a matter of your attitude. You can't think it and make it exist. You can't try sometimes, when it works to your advantage, and throw it out the rest of the time. Equality is a discipline. It is a way of life. It is a political necessity to create equality in institutions. And another thing about equality is that it cannot coexist with rape. It cannot. And it cannot coexist with pornography or with prostitution or with the economic degradation of women on any level, in any way. It cannot coexist, because implicit in all those things is the inferiority of women.

I want to see this men's movement make a commitment to ending rape because that is the only meaningful commitment to equality. It is astonishing that in all our worlds of feminism and antisexism we never talk seriously about ending rape. Ending it. Stopping it. No more. No more rape. In the back of our minds, are we holding on to its inevitability as the last preserve of the biological? Do we think that it is always going to exist no matter what we do? All of our political actions are lies if we don't make a commitment to ending the practice of rape. This commitment has to be political. It has to be serious. It has to be systematic. It has to be public. It can't be self-indulgent.

The things the men's movement has wanted are things worth having. Intimacy is worth having. Tenderness is worth having. Cooperation is worth having. A real emotional life is worth having. But you can't have them in a world with rape. Ending homophobia is worth doing. But you can't do it in a world with rape. Rape stands in the way of each and every one of those things you say you want. And by rape you know what I mean. A judge does not have to walk into this room and say that according to statute such and such these are the elements of proof. We're talking about any kind of coerced sex, including sex coerced by poverty.

You can't have equality or tenderness or intimacy as long as there is rape, because rape means terror. It means that part of the population lives in a state of terror and pretends—to please and pacify you—that it doesn't. So there is no honesty. How can there be? Can you imagine what it is like to live as a woman day in and day out with the threat of rape? Or what it is like to live with the reality? I want to see you use those legendary bodies and that legendary strength and that legendary courage and the tenderness that you say you have in behalf of women; and that means against the rapists, against the pimps, and against the pornographers. It means something more than a personal renunciation. It means a systematic, political, active, public attack. And there has been very little of that.

I came here today because I don't believe that rape is inevitable or natural. If I did, I would have no reason to be here. If I did, my political practice would be different than it is. Have you ever wondered why we are not just in armed combat against you? It's not because there's a shortage of kitchen knives in this country. It is because we believe in your humanity, against all the evidence.

We do not want to do the work of helping you to believe in your humanity. We cannot do it anymore. We have always tried. We have been repaid with systematic exploitation and systematic abuse. You are going to have to do this yourselves from now on and you know it.

The shame of men in front of women is, I think, an appropriate response both to what men do do and to what men do not do. I think you should be ashamed. But what you do with that shame is to use it as an excuse to keep doing what you want and to keep not doing anything else; and you've got to stop. You've got to stop. Your psychology doesn't matter. How much you hurt doesn't matter in the end any more than how much we hurt matters. If we sat around and only talked about how much rape hurt us, do you think there would have been one of the changes that you have seen in this country in the last fifteen years? There wouldn't have been.

It is true that we had to talk to each other. How else, after all, were we supposed to find out that each of us was not the only woman in the world not asking for it to whom rape or battery had ever happened? We couldn't read it in the newspapers, not then. We couldn't find a book about it. But you do know and now the question is what you are going to do; and so your shame and your guilt are very much beside the point. They don't matter to us at all, in any way. They're not good enough. They don't do anything.

As a feminist, I carry the rape of all the women I've talked to over the past ten years personally with me. As a woman, I carry my own rape with me. Do you remember pictures that you've seen of European cities during the plague, when there were wheelbarrows that would go along and people would just pick up corpses and throw them in? Well, that is what it is like knowing about rape. Piles and piles and piles of bodies that have whole lives and human names and human faces.

I speak for many feminists, not only myself, when I tell you that I am tired of what I know and sad beyond any words I have about what has already been done to women up to this point, now, up to 2:24 p.m. on this day, here in this place.

And I want one day of respite, one day off, one day in which no new bodies are piled up, one day in which no new agony is added to the old, and I am asking you to give it to me. And how could I ask you for less—it is so little. And how could you offer me less: it is so little. Even in wars, there are days of truce. Go and organize a truce. Stop your side for one day. I want a twenty-four-hour truce during which there is no rape.

I dare you to try it. I demand that you try it. I don't mind begging you to try it. What else could you possibly be here to do? What else could this movement possibly mean? What else could matter so much?

And on that day, that day of truce, that day when not one woman is raped, we will begin the real practice of equality, because we can't begin it before that day. Before that day it means nothing because it is nothing: it is not real; it is not true. But on that day it becomes real. And then, instead of rape we will for the first time in our lives—both men and women—begin to experience freedom.

If you have a conception of freedom that includes the existence of rape, you are wrong. You cannot change what you say you want to change. For myself, I want to experience just one day of real freedom before I die. I leave you here to do that for me and for the women whom you say you love.

Violence Against Women:
It Breaks the Heart, Also the Bones

1984

Early in 1983, I went to the Republic of Ireland to speak at a conference on pornography organized by the Committee Against Sexual Exploitation (CASE) in Dublin. I fell in love with Ireland. The women I met were so special. I was stunned by their endurance, their humor, their strength, their kindness, their warmth. Because I was on Irish television, vast numbers of people recognized me and talked with me: old women ran out of houses and down the street to thank me for what I had said about women's rights; joggers stopped to say they agreed about how pornography hurt women (the television interview had been acrimonious, so they were letting me know they appreciated my holding my own); people at concerts and in pubs and everywhere I went wanted to say hello. Some very bitter but nevertheless friendly men wanted to say that I was wrong about everything. I forged close ties with feminists in the Republic and also went up North and met feminists from a more desperate Ireland. I remain devoted to the Irish Women's Movement. I was pleased to be asked to contribute this essay to Personally Speaking, a collection of writings by Irish feminists published by an Irish feminist press. This essay has never been published in the United States.

WHAT BREAKS THE heart about violence against women is that people, including women, do not know it when they see it, when they do it or collaborate in it, when they experience it—even as victims of it. What breaks the spirit of those fighting for women's rights is that one can never take for granted a realization that a woman is an actual human being who, when hurt, is hurt.

The hurting of women is so basic to the sexual pleasure of men, to the social and sexual dominance that men exercise over women, to

172

the economic degradation imposed on women by men, that women are simply considered those creatures made by God or biology for what would be abuse if it were done to men (human beings); but it is being done to women, so it is not abuse; it is instead simply what women are for.

The natural relation of the sexes means that women are made to be used the way men use us now, in a world of civil, social, and economic inequality based on sex; a world in which women have limited rights, no physical integrity, and no real self-determination. This condition of inequity is even good for us, because we are different from men. When men are deprived of social equality, they are hurt in their rights to self-respect and freedom. Inequality actually causes women to thrive, and provides the best environment for sexual pleasure and personal fulfillment.

This nature of ours has entirely to do with sex: sex is our natural function, and our lives are supposed to be predetermined by this natural use to which our bodies are put for reproduction or for pleasure, depending on the ideology of the person making the claim. Our nature is such that we crave the cruelties men so generously provide. We like pain, especially in sex. We make men hurt us. We especially like to be forced to have sex while refusing to have it; our refusal encourages men to use physical force, violence, and humiliation against us, which is why we refuse in the first place. As our hormones secretly surge and our genes smirk in self-satisfied delight, we say no, intending through refusal to provoke an antagonism sufficiently destructive to satisfy us when finally it is vented on us in sex. We are hungry for a certain vulgar brutality, which is lucky for us, since we get so much of it. In marriage, being beaten is proof to us that we are loved. Evidence is cited of obscure villages in remote places where, if a man does not beat his wife, she feels unloved, since no woman at hand seems to find it proof at all. (In those obscure villages, no doubt the women of New York and Dublin are cited to the same end.) We particularly enjoy being sold on street corners (does bad weather increase our fun?). We entice our fathers to rape us, because even little girls are born women. In technologically advanced societies, we eschew becoming brain surgeons for the delight of finding photographers who will shoot our genitals: camera or gun, we don't mind.

One thing should be clear, but apparently it is not: if this were indeed our nature, we would be living in paradise.

If pain, humiliation, and physical injury made us happy, we would be ecstatic.

If being sold on street corners were a good time, women would jam street corners the way men jam football matches.

If forced sex were what we craved, even we would be satisfied already.

If being dominated by men made us happy we would smile all the time.

Women resist male domination because we do not like it.

Political women resist male domination through overt, rude, unmistakable rebellion. They are called unnatural, because they do not have a nature that delights in being debased.

Apolitical women resist male domination through a host of bitter subversions, ranging from the famous headache to the clinical depression epidemic among women to suicide to prescription-drug tranquilization to taking it out on the children; sometimes a battered wife kills her husband. Apolitical women are also called unnatural, the charge hurled at them as nasty or sullen or embittered individuals, since that is how they fight back. They too are not made happy by being hurt or dominated.

In fact, a natural woman is hard to find. We are domesticated, tamed, made compliant on the surface, through male force, not through nature. We sometimes *do* what men say we *are*, either because we believe them or because we hope to placate them. We sometimes try to become what men say we should be, because men have power over our lives.

Male domination is a system of social institutions, sexual practices, economic relations, and emotional devastations. At the same time, it is something men do to women through commonplace behaviors. It is not abstract or magical; and any woman's life illustrates the ways in which male dominance is used on real women by real men. Underlying the big social realities of male dominance are the flesh-and-blood realities of rape, battery, prostitution, and incest, as well as being used in banal, demeaning ways in sex, as domestics, to have children *for* men. We are treated as if we are worthless in how we are talked to, looked at, in common social interchanges. The acts of violence and the acts of insult are justified by the nature we are presumed to have: an inferior nature, specially marked by its compulsive need for force in sex. The inferiority of women is best described as an immovable, barely comprehensible stupidity. Getting hurt is what we want.

Women do not simply endure having this peculiar nature. We celebrate it by actively seeking to be dominated and hurt, that is, fulfilled. Men only respond; we provoke. A man is going about his business, bothering no one, when a woman calls attention to herself—by walking down the street, for instance. The man, intending no harm, tries to please the woman by doing to her whatever her language and behavior suggest she does not want. As he inflicts this kindness on her, strictly through solicitude for her real desire, indicated by her resistance and repugnance, he is only responding to what has been her purpose from the beginning: she has wanted his attention so that he would do whatever she is appearing to resist. He knows what she wants because he knows what she is.

In the world of male domination, there are no individual women who are unique persons. There is only a generic *she*, frequently called *cunt* so that what defines the genus is clear. She is the hole between her legs. Her nature justifies whatever men need to do to make that hole accessible to them on their terms. She is valued insofar as men value entry into her. For the rest, she is decorative or does housework.

Feminists think that many of the so-called normal uses of women under male domination are abuses of women. This is because feminists think that women are human beings. This means that when a woman is hurt, she is hurt, not fulfilled. When she is forced, she is forced, not fulfilled. When she is humiliated, she is humiliated, not fulfilled. Inequality wrongs her. Pain hurts her. Exploitation robs her of her rights over herself. Broken bones and bruises are physical injuries, not grandiose romantic gestures. Feminism is an esoteric and nasty politic, practiced only by unnatural women who do not like being hurt at all.

If women are human beings, as feminists suspect, then crimes of violence against women are human rights violations that occur on a massive, almost unimaginable scale. These crimes are committed most frequently in private, in intimacy; but they are committed all the time, every day and every night, all over the world, by normal men. Unbending, powerful social institutions, including church and state, cloak these crimes in a protective legitimacy, so that, for instance, forced sex in marriage is a legally secured right of marriage for the man, socially acceptable, commonplace, unremarkable. Battery, incest, forced pregnancy, prostitution, and rape originate in this same sanctioned ownership of men over women. That ownership is both collective and class-based (men as a class own women as a class) and it is particular, private, individual, one human being (male) having rights over sexual and reproductive chattel (female).

In practice, a man can rape his wife or daughter, beat his wife or daughter, or prostitute his wife or daughter, with virtually no state interference, except in exceptional circumstances (for instance, if the victim dies). The state in fact actively supports male dominance achieved through or expressed in violence. Marriage, for example, is a legal license to rape: it is a state-backed entitlement to fuck a woman without regard for her will or integrity; and a child finds herself in the same feudal relationship to her father because of his state-backed power as head-of-the-household.

Sometimes, laws prohibit acts of violence against women. Battery is illegal, but no police will interfere; husbands are rarely arrested for beating their wives, even though an experimental program in Minneapolis showed that immediate arrest and real convictions with real jail sentences had a serious impact on stopping battery. It ended the legal impunity of the batterer, and it also introduced, frequently for the first time, the idea that it was not natural or right for husbands to hit their wives—it introduced the idea to the husband.*

Rape is illegal. A man is not supposed to be able to rape anyone but his own wife with impunity. But rape is widespread, rarely even reported to the police (one in ten or eleven rapes are reported in the

---

* In Seattle, a judge ordered the police force to enforce laws against "domestic violence," i.e. wife-battery. As a result, police began arresting any woman who fought back or resisted marital rape. One woman was arrested because she had scratched her husband's face when he tried to force sex on her. The police claim they have no choice: if they must enforce these laws that they do not want to enforce, they must enforce them against any spouse who commits any act of violence. This is one example of how the legal system works to make reforms meaningless and women's rights ludicrous.

United States), more rarely prosecuted, and convictions are unusual and unlikely. This is because juries view the woman as responsible for the sex act, no matter how abusive it is. The woman's sexual history is explored to convict her of being wanton: any sexual experience is used to show that her nature is responsible for what happened to her, not the man who did it.

The right to rape as a male right of dominance is never the issue in rape cases. Historically, rape was considered a crime against the man to whom the woman belonged as chattel: her husband or her father. In her husband's house, she was private property. In her father's house, she was a virgin to be sold as such to a husband. Rape was rather like stealing a car and smashing it into a tree. The value of the property is hurt. If the woman was already damaged goods—not private enough as property before the rapist got hold of her—or if she consented (a corpse could meet the legal standard for consent in a rape case)—then the putative rapist was not responsible for her low value and he would not be convicted of rape. The woman as a separate human being with rights over her own body does not exist under traditional rape laws. That is why feminists want rape laws changed: so that rape is a crime against the woman raped, not her keeper. The difficulty in accomplishing this is unpleasantly simple: the injuries of rape to a human being are self-evident; but the injuries of rape to a woman are not injuries at all—they are sexual events that she probably liked, even initiated, no matter how badly she is hurt, women being what women are.

In trying to understand violence against women, one must consistently look at how laws work, not at what they say, to see whether they in fact further violence against women, regulate it (for instance, by establishing some conditions under which violence is condoned and others under which it is discouraged), or stop it. Under male domination, law virtually always furthers or regulates violence against women by keeping women subordinate to men, allowing or encouraging violence against at least some women all the time, and holding women responsible for the violence done to us with its doctrinal insistence that we actually provoke violence and get sexual pleasure from it.

The feminist fight against violence against women is also necessarily a fight against male law: because the way the law really works—in rape, battery, prostitution, and incest—women are its victims.

The state, then, keeps women available to men for abuse—that is one of its functions. The dominance of men over women through violence is not an unfortunate series of accidents or mistakes but is instead state policy, backed by police power.

For conceptual clarity, I am going to divide the crimes of violence against women into two categories: simple crimes, which include rape, battery, incest, torture, and murder; and complex crimes, which include sexual harassment, prostitution, and pornography. These acts are the primary violent abuses of women in the West. In other societies, other acts may have the same mainstream cultural significance—for instance, clitoridectomy or infibulation or dowry burnings.

The simple crimes are acts of violation that are relatively easy to comprehend as discrete events once the violation is made known. The act is usually committed in privacy or in secret, but if a victim tells about it, one can see what happened, how, when, where, for how long, by whom, to whom, even why. Even though these acts are committed so frequently that they are commonplace, they are usually committed in private, done to women as individuals. Each time a rape happens, it happens to a particular woman, a particular child. There is no sense of public contagion: rape is not experienced as spreading through the community like cholera. There is also no sense of public enjoyment of the crime, public complicity, public enthusiasm.

In complex crimes, there is contagion. The community knows that there is a public dimension to the abuse, that there is mass complicity, mass involvement. The crimes are in the public air, they happen outside the privacy of the home, they happen to many nameless, faceless women, who are moving through public space: many men are doing these things to many women, all at once, not in private at all. There is a sense of "everyone does it—so what?" with many of the elements that distinguish sexual harassment; prostitution and pornography are widely taken to be things men need and things men use—lots of men, most men.

The violence itself in a complex crime is a convoluted mass of violations involving many kinds of sexual abuse; it is hard to pull them apart. There is a machine-like quality to the abuse, as if women's bodies were on an assembly line, getting processed, getting used: getting drilled, getting screwed, getting hammered, getting checked over, poked, passed on.

The complex crimes are done to the already disappeared: the women are anonymous; they have no personal histories that matter and no personal qualities that can change the course of events. Sexual harassment, for instance, makes women vagabonds in the labor market: cheap labor, immediately replaceable, moving out of low paid job after low paid job. Prostitution and pornography erase all personality.

In complex crimes, there is ongoing intimidation and intricate coercion that exists on many levels. There is a profit motive as well as a pleasure/power motive: big business, one way or another, stands behind the abuser. The simple crimes are most often done in secret, but the complex crimes have real social visibility. Sexual harassment happens in a society of fellow workers; prostitutes have a social presence on the streets; the point of pornography is that it is on view.

All the simple and complex crimes of violence are also acts of sex. Under male domination, there is no phenomenological division between sex and violence. Every crime of violence committed against a woman is sexual: sex is central to the targeting of the victim, the way in which she is hurt, why she is hurt, the sense of entitlement the man has to do what he wants to her, the satisfaction the act gives him, the social support for the exploitation or injury. The social support can be mainstream or subterranean, fully sanctioned by the system or implicit in how it works.

In most crimes of violence against women, a sex act involving penetration of the woman, not always vaginally, not always with a penis, is intrinsic to the violence or the reason for it. In some crimes of violence, for instance, battery, while rape is part of the long-term configuration of the abuse, sex is more frequently exhausted, brutalized compliance; it occurs as if in the eye of the hurricane—after the last beating and to try to forestall the next one. Sometimes the beating is the sexual event for the man.

When feminists say *rape is violence, not sex*, we mean to say that from our perspective as victims of forced sex, we do not get sexual pleasure from rape; contrary to the rapist's view, the pornographer's view, and the law's view, rape is not a good time for us. This is a valiant effort at crosscultural communication, but it is only half the story: because for men, rape and sex are not different species of event. Domination is sexual for most men, and rape, battery, incest, use of prostitutes and pornography, and sexual harassment are modes of domination imbued with sexual meaning. Domination is power over others and also hostility toward and dehumanization of the powerless. The domination of men over women is both expressed and achieved through sex *as men experience sex*, not as women wish it would be. This means that we have to recognize that sex and violence are fused for men into dominance; and that not only is violence sexual* but also sex is consistently used to assert dominance.

This is a desperate and tragic reality. Those closest to us—those inside us—cannot separate sex and violence, because for them they are not separate: the fusion of sex and violence is the dominance that gives them pleasure. Our lives are held hostage to this pleasure they want. Rape, battery, incest, torture, murder, sexual harassment, prostitution, and pornography are acts of real violence against us enjoyed by our husbands, fathers, sons, brothers, lovers, teachers, and friends. They call these acts by different names when they do them.

Pornography especially shows how dominance and abuse are pleasure and entertainment. In the United States, pornography saturates the environment, private and public. In Ireland, access to it is more restricted at this time; and yet, videos showing the torture of women, allowable under Irish censorship laws because video is not covered, have reached an avid population of male consumers. No time to develop an appetite for the violence was required. Normal men, having rights of sexual dominance, took to torture videos like ducks to water. Pornography is central to male dominance, even when

---

* New experimental research in the United States shows that films showing extreme and horrific violence against women that are not sexually explicit sexually stimulated nearly a third of the men who watched them. The films are called "splatter" films. They are made from the point of view of the killer as he stalks a female victim. She ends up splattered. The researchers told me that they could not construct a film scenario of violence against women that did not sexually stimulate a significant percentage of male viewers.

access to it is limited, because every form of sexual abuse is implicated in it and it is implicated in every form of sexual abuse; and it is apprehended by men as pure pleasure.

In the United States, perhaps three-quarters of the women in pornography are incest victims. Women are recruited through being raped and beaten. Forced sex is filmed; so is torture, gang rape, battery; and the films are used (as blackmail, sexual humiliation, and threat) to keep new women in prostitution. Once seasoned,* prostitutes are used in films as their pimps determine. Rapes of women who are not prostitutes, not runaway children, not on the streets to stay, are filmed and sold on the commercial pornography market. Pornography has actually introduced a profit motive into rape. Women in pornography are penetrated by animals and objects. Women are urinated on and defecated on. All of these things are done to real women in pornography; then the pornography is used so that these acts are committed against other real women.

The worthlessness of women as human beings is entirely clear when it is understood that pornography is a form of mass entertainment, in the United States now grossing an estimated eight billion dollars a year. Men, the primary consumers of pornography, are entertained by these acts of sexual abuse.

The lives of women are circumscribed by the terrorism of pornography, because it is the distilled yet entirely trivialized terror of rape, battery, incest, torture, and murder—women are objects, not human, assaulted and hurt, used in sex, because men want and like sexual dominance. Pornography is the prostitution of the women in it, and it is a metaphysical definition of all women as whores by nature; so it is also the terror of being born to be used, traded, and sold. The substance of this terror—its details, its ambiance—is the pleasure, is the entertainment, for the men who watch. It is hard to imagine how much they hate us.

It is also difficult to understand how absolutely, resolutely indifferent to our rights they are. Yet these men who like to see us

---

* "Seasoning" is the process of making a woman or a girl into a compliant prostitute. It usually involves raping her, having her gang-raped, drugging her, beating her, repeated and purposeful humiliation. It often involves filming these acts, showing her the film (making her watch herself), and threatening to send the pictures to her family or school.

being used or hurt are not indifferent to rights as such: they guard their own. They claim, for instance, that in being entertained by pornography they are exercising rights of theirs, especially rights of expression or speech. How is it possible that in watching rape—or, frankly, in watching female genitals, women's legs splayed— they are exercising rights of speech? It must be that our pain is what they want to say. Perhaps our genitals are words they use. Incomprehensible as it may be to us, their enjoyment in our abuse is articulated as a civil liberty of theirs. The logic of the argument is that if their rights to pornography (to possession, exploitation, and abuse of us) are abrogated, they will be unable to say what they want to say. They must have "freedom of speech."

Also, the sexual exploitation of women is held to be "sexual liberation." The uses of women in pornography are considered "liberating." What is done to us is called "sexual freedom."

Our abuse has become a standard of freedom—the meaning of freedom—the requisite for freedom—throughout much of the Western world.

Being hurt, being threatened with physical injury as a condition of life, being systematically exploited, has profoundly disturbing effects on people. They get numb; they despair; they are often ignoble, becoming indifferent to the suffering of others in their same situation. People are also known to fight oppression and to hate cruelties they are forced to endure; but women are supposed to enjoy being hurt, being used, being made inferior. The remedies historically used by oppressed peoples to fight domination and terror are not supposed to be available to women: because what is done to us is supposed to be appropriate to what we are—*women*. God, nature, and men concur.

But sometimes we dissent. We see the violence done to us as violence, not love, not romance, not inevitable and natural, not our fate, not to be endured and suffered through, not what we are for because of what we are.

Feminists call this often painful process of learning to see with our own eyes *consciousness-raising*. We discard the eyes of men, which had become our eyes. We break the isolation that violence creates; we find out from each other how much we are treated the same, how much we have in common in how we are used, the acts of insult and injury committed against us because we are women.

Consciousness means that we have developed an acute awareness of both our suffering and our humanity: what happens to us and what we have a right to. We know we are human and so the suffering (inferior status, exploitation, sexual abuse) is an intolerable series of violations that must be stopped. Experiencing suffering as such—instead of becoming numb—forces us to act human: to resist oppression, to demand fairness, to create new social arrangements that include us as human. When humans rebel against suffering, the heroes of history, known and unknown, are born.

So even though women are expected to enjoy being used and being hurt, women resist; women fight back; women organize; women are brave; women go up against male power and stop it in its tracks; women fight institutions of male dominance and weaken them; women create social and political conflict, so that male power is challenged and hurt; women retaliate against rapists and batterers and pimps; women infiltrate male systems of power; women change laws to benefit women and increase our rights; women provide secret refuge for battered women and above-ground advocacy for rape victims and abortions for pregnant women who need help; women create work and wealth for other women to subvert the economic hold men have over women; sometimes women kill; women sit-in and picket and commit civil disobedience to destroy pornographers and militarists; women sue to stop sex discrimination; women claim more and more public space to change the configurations of public power; feminists keep refining the targets, so that we attack male power where it is most vulnerable and where we can best amass collective strength in our respective countries; feminists go at male power where it is most dangerous, so heavy on top that it must topple over if we push hard enough; feminists keep thinking, writing, talking, organizing, marching, demonstrating, with militance and patience and a rebelliousness that burns. The fight is hard and ugly and deadly serious. Sometimes women are killed. Often, women are hurt. Vengeance against women is real, physical, economic, psychological: swift and cruel. Still: women resist, women fight back, women want to win.

What we want to win is called freedom or justice when those being systematically hurt are not women. We call it equality, because our enemies are family. No violent reform will work for us, no bloody coup followed by another regime of illegitimate power: because our enemy is family; and we cannot simply wipe him out and kill him dead.

The burden is very great. Because the enemy is family, and because he is so cruel and so arrogant and so intimate and so close, because he smiles when we hurt and pays money to be entertained by our abuse, we know we have to go to the roots of violence, the roots of domination, the roots of why power gives pleasure and how hierarchy creates exploitation. We know we have to level social hierarchies. We know we have to destroy the pleasure and possibility of sexual domination. We know we have to raise ourselves up and pull men down, not tenderly. We know we have to end the violence against us by ending the rights of men over us. There is no friendly domination, no self-respecting submission.

Violence against women hurts the heart, also the bones. Feminists are unnatural women who do not like being hurt at all.

Preface to the British Edition of
Right-wing Women
1983

Someone at The Women's Press in London, a publishing company I esteem, wrote me a fairly condescending letter (in apparent response to Right-wing Women, *which The Women's Press was publishing) in which she explained to me that in England right-wing women were women who wore hats and were prudes and fascists and left-wing women, in England, didn't and weren't. In these terms (honest) she tried to explain right-wing and left-wing to me, the simple-minded colonial. I had been asked to write an introduction to* Right-wing Women *for England so I wrote this essay on Left and Right, the origins and meaning of each. I thought my correspondent could use the information. This essay has never been published in the United States.*

"RIGHT" AND "LEFT" as meaningful political designations originated in the complicated course of the French Revolution. Most probably, the first physical arrangement from right to left of parliamentary representatives occurred on September 11, 1789, when the National Assembly, the parliamentary body of revolutionary France, was arranged physically to reflect political ideology and class loyalty. Royalists were seated on the right; presumably Jacobins were on the far left. Those on the right, who mostly favored a bicameral legislative system in the grip of a monarch's absolute veto power, were called Anglomaniacs or Monarchicals or just plain "Englishmen." Those on the left got much of their inspiration from the recent American Revolution of 1776.

By 1815, the Second Restoration under Louis XVIII, "Right" and

"Left" were accepted, commonly understood political terms rooted in French legislative practice. France finally had its English-like parliament and a new monarch to go with it. Members of the legislature sat in a semi-circle. On the right sat the ultra-royalists, called the Ultras, "more royalist than the king and more catholic than the pope" according to one pundit. They represented the interests of the land-owning aristocracy, former emigrés, and clergy. They were the party of victorious counter-revolution. On the left sat the Independents, a mixture of Bonapartists, Liberals, and Republicans, all antipathetic to the current monarch but with varying degrees of commitment to the egalitarian goals of the Revolution. In the center sat the Constitutionalists, those who wanted a little of this and a little of that.

Political ideas and political values were explicitly characterized as "Right" or "Left" or "Centrist." "Right" was the term with the absolute meaning. It really did mean "more royalist than the king": "Long live the king, despite himself" was one Ultra slogan. All other political positions were in some sense defined relative to the Right. With the Jacobins purged from French politics, the Left was a shadow Left. Not wanting a king (or a particular king) was not the same as demanding an egalitarian social order by any means necessary. The values of the Right were fixed and clear. The values of the Left were subject to negotiation and convenience. This led, in part, to the rise of the Emperor Bonaparte.

The terms "Right" and "Left" are genuinely modern referents. They do not travel back in time very well, especially in England or the United States. In England the modern party system began to develop after 1783, but political parties as such did not become strong until after 1830. The vaguer, less programmatic word "conservative" did not come into use until 1824, when a coalition of Whigs and Tories used it to indicate their antagonism to revolutionary France. The Tories adopted it for themselves in 1830. It is perhaps a reasonable convenience to think of Tories and Whigs compared with each other as conservatives and liberals respectively, but both were monarchists with all the loyalties to class and property therein implied; and so both were, in the original French sense, rightists. The French were not being facetious when they called their own royalists Anglomaniacs or "Englishmen."

The new Americans, on the other hand, were all resolute republicans. None of the founding fathers was willing to tolerate monarchy or any institution that resembled monarchy. And yet many were what we would call conservative. They wanted to replicate the stability of the English system. They wanted a social order that protected property and wealth. They were republicans but they certainly were not democrats. The idea of egalitarian democracy repelled them. Alexander Hamilton, for instance, insisted on "a government wholly and purely republican" and yet he considered the French Revolution a "disgusting spectacle." He, like other American conservatives, was an Anglophile. Thomas Jefferson, by contrast, was a liberal, a democrat. For him, a function of government was to promote equality. He, typical of the egalitarians, was a Francophile. But in the new political geography of the new United States there was no Right or Left in the French sense because there were no monarchists at all.

The political concepts of "Right" and "Left" could not have originated in England or the United States: they come out of the specificity of the French experience. They were born in the chaos of the first fully modern revolution, the French Revolution, in reaction to which all Europe subsequently redefined itself. As a direct result of the French Revolution, the political face of Europe changed and so did the political discourse of Europeans. One fundamental change was the formal division of values, parties, and programs into "Right" and "Left"—modern alliances and allegiances emerged, heralded by new, modern categories of organized political thought. What had started in France's National Assembly as perhaps an expedient seating arrangement from right to left became a nearly metaphysical political construction that swept Western political consciousness and practice.

In part this astonishing development was accomplished through the extreme reaction against the French Revolution embodied especially in vitriolic denunciations of it by politicians in England and elsewhere committed to monarchy, the class system, and the values implicit in feudalism. Their arguments against the French Revolution and in behalf of monarchy form the basis for modern right-wing politics, or conservatism. The principles of organized conservatism, its social, economic, and moral values, were enunciated in a great body of reactionary polemic, most instrumentally in the English Whig

Edmund Burke's *Reflections on the Revolution in France*. Written in 1789 before the ascendancy of the Jacobins—and therefore not in response to the Terror or to Jacobin ideological absolutism—Burke's *Reflections* is suffused with fury at the audacity of the Revolution itself because this revolution uniquely insisted that political freedom *required* some measure of civil, economic, and social equality. The linking of freedom with equality philosophically or programmatically remains anathema to conservatives today. Freedom, according to Burke, required hierarchy and order. That was his enduring theme.

"I flatter myself," Burke wrote,* "that I love a manly, moral, regulated liberty." "Manly" liberty is bold, resolute, not effeminate or timorous (following a dictionary definition of the adjective "manly"). "Manly" liberty (following Burke) has a king. "Manly" liberty is authoritarian: the authority of the king—his sovereignty—presumably guarantees the liberty of everyone else by arcane analogy. "Moral" liberty is the worship of God and property, especially as they merge in the institutional church. "Moral" liberty means respect for the authority of God and king, especially as it manifests in feudal hierarchy. "Regulated" liberty is limited liberty: whatever is left over once the king is obeyed, God is worshipped, property is respected, hierarchy is honored, and the taxes or tributes that support all these institutions are paid. The liberty Burke loved particularly depended on the willingness of persons not just to accept but to *love* the social circumstances into which they were born: "To be attached to the subdivision, to love the little platoon we belong to in society, is the first principle (the germ as it were) of public affections. It is the first link in the series by which we proceed towards a love to our country and to mankind." The French rabble had noticeably violated this first principle of public affections.

To Burke, history showed that monarchy and the rights of Englishmen were completely intertwined so that the one required the other. Because certain rights had been exercised under monarchy, Burke held that monarchy was essential to the exercise of those rights. England had no proof, according to Burke, that rights could exist and be exercised without monarchy. Burke indicted political theorists who claimed that there were natural rights of men that

---

* All quotes from Burke are from *Reflections on the Revolution in France* (1789).

superseded in importance the rights of existing governments. These theorists "have wrought under-ground a mine that will blow up, at one grand explosion, all examples of antiquity, all precedents, charters, and acts of parliament. They have 'rights of men.' Against these there can be no prescription: against these no argument is binding... I have nothing to say to the clumsy subtilty of their political metaphysicks." In Burke's more agile metaphysics, hereditary rights were transmitted through a hereditary crown because they had been before and so would continue to be. Burke provided no basis for evaluating the quality or fairness of the rights of "the little platoon we belong to in society" as opposed to the rights of other little platoons: to admit such a necessity would not be loving our little platoon enough. The hereditary crown, Burke suggests, restrains dictatorship because it gives the king obeisance without making him fight for it. It also inhibits civil conflict over who the ruler will be. This is as close as Burke gets to a substantive explanation of *why* rights and monarchy are inextricably linked.

Liberties are described as property: "an *entailed inheritance*," "an estate specially belonging to the people of this kingdom, without any reference whatever to any other more general or prior right." The feudal right to property is in fact the unimpeachable right, and liberties are seen to depend on the security of property. Along with property, appropriate liberties are passed from generation to generation: liberties apportioned by one's relationship to property. This is the essence of a stable social order. Any freedom that would challenge or destroy the primacy and sanctity of inherited property was freedom outside the bounds of "manly, moral, regulated liberty." Burke noted that in the National Assembly "liberty is always to be estimated perfect as property is rendered insecure." His own view was the opposite.

Religion was instrumental in keeping a society civilized, well-ordered, moral. Morality was in fact an acceptance of the social order as God-given. The atheism of the French revolutionaries and natural rights philosophers was perverse, an aberration: "We know, and it is our pride to know, that man is by his constitution a religious animal; that atheism is against, not only our reason but our instincts; and that it cannot prevail long." The institutional church provided occasions for somber expressions of acquiescence: and the institutional church was the vehicle of a morality that was both absolute and congruent with the existing social order. Burke's religion had nothing to do with the compassionate side of morality; it had to do with power and money. In a special frenzy of repugnance he insisted that the Jews—through the French Revolution—were attempting to destroy the Church of England. More commonly, he likened the despised French rabble to Jews. The religion Burke upheld was the religion of Anglo-Saxon power, the religion of king and property.

Implicit in all the above positions and explicitly articulated as such was Burke's contempt for democracy. Democracy, he held, was synonymous with tyranny or led inevitably to it. In democracy he discerned true oppression. "Of this I am certain," he wrote, "that in a democracy the majority of citizens is capable of exercising the most cruel oppressions upon the minority." Cruel oppressions did not trouble him if they were exercised on a majority by a well-dressed, elegant minority ("To make us love our country, our country ought to be lovely"). He objected to the majority itself, not its numbers so much as its nature: "what sort of a thing must be a nation of gross, stupid, ferocious, and, at the same time, poor and sordid barbarians, destitute of religion, honour, or manly pride, possessing nothing at present, and hoping for nothing hereafter?" His view of Marie Antoinette had a different tone: "I thought ten thousand swords must have leaped from the scabbards to avenge even a look that threatened her with insult." Equality meant that "a king is but a man, a queen is but a woman," which was even more degrading than it would seem on the surface because "a woman is but an animal; and an animal not of the highest order." Equality then was particularly bad luck for a queen. Equality also meant that "the murder of a king, or a queen, or a bishop, or a father, are only common homicide." Equality meant the end of the world as Burke knew it, the end of king, church, property, and *entailed* liberties, the end of "manly" pride and "manly" liberty. But Burke was a shade too pessimistic. "Manly" pride and "manly" liberty have survived every revolution so far. Equality has not yet destroyed all Burke's world.

The Right has not changed much since Burke wrote. It still defends authority, hierarchy, property, and religion. It still abhors egalitarian political ideas and movements. It still doesn't like Jews.

In the United States there never was a king, but there were many obvious surrogates in whom imperial power was vested: from slaveholder to husband. Today the authority the Right defends is the "manly" authority of the President, the Pentagon, the FBI and CIA, police power in general, the male religious leader, and the husband in the male-dominated family. The Old Right was content to defend the "manly" authority of the military, the police, oligarchal racist legislators, a strong (even if corrupt) chief executive, and the USA as a superpower. It took more privatized expressions of "manly" authority entirely for granted. The New Right, which arose in reaction to the Women's Movement, is distinguished from the Old Right by its political militancy on so-called social issues—women's rights, abortion, and homosexuality, for instance. The New Right has particularly emphasized the importance of the authority of the husband and the androcentric church. Authority itself is seen as male, and the rebellion of women threatens authority as such with dissolution. In New Right logic, any weakening of the husband's authority over the wife is a weakening of authority per se, a weakening of the authority of the nation and the institutions that properly govern it.

In the United States, the hierarchy the Right defends is rich over poor, white over black, man over woman. There is a frequently articulated belief that social inequality simply expresses natural or God-given differences; that hierarchy is unchangeable. It is frequently argued that those who want equality want to change "the nature of man." Stalin's mass murders are frequently pointed to as the logical consequence of trying to forge a classless society, a society that repudiates hierarchy.

Class as such functions differently in the United States than it does in England. In the United States there is no feudal history. There are no aristocrats. One cannot be titled in the United States and also be a citizen. There is great mobility from class to class: both upward and downward. Change of class can occur in a generation. Money and property determine class, individual to individual: it is not a status passed on from generation to generation; it is not necessarily familial. Money and property change hands with more fluidity and frequency than in countries with a feudal history. The ruling class in the United States, the small number of families who control most of the real wealth, has no relationship at all to kings or landed aristocracy: these people are ruthless, self-made merchants who are powerful because they control capital; they have no cultural, emotional, genetic, or historical claim to being élite or noble. In the United States people do not habitually become what their parents were. People move frequently, so there is little sense of influence being handed down.

In the United States race fixes one's "class" status more certainly than any other factor. Virulent white supremacy determines that black unemployment passes from generation to generation: also inherited are illiteracy, poverty, isolation in ghettos, and life lived on the margins of survival. The white middle class is huge, encompassing about eighty percent of whites. Movement into it is not difficult (compared with any analogous movement in England or Europe) for whites. "Middle class" is determined by money more than by kind of labor—though this could be argued. One could say that many working-class men (especially skilled laborers) tend to have middle-class children (monied, educated). Blacks do not have this same mobility: and there is a black *lumpen*, at a dead end of possibility, who inherit despair in an otherwise vigorous society. It is not possible to overstate how racist the so-called class structure in the United States actually is.

In the United States, the Right's defense of property includes, for instance, the recent campaign to keep the Panama Canal as United States property. The Right sees United States economic and military imperialism as a necessary defense of United States property interests—whether the property is Viet Nam or El Salvador. The United States has property where the United States does business, wherever that is. Oil that the United States needs rests on United States property wherever it happens to be. Europe is United States property if the United States wants to base missiles there. Any place the Soviets are—including any barren rock in Afghanistan—is United States property waiting to be rescued from foreign invasion. United States property includes the multinational corporation, the factory, and the sweatshop. Women and children are also property: fenced in, guarded, frequently invaded.

Religion is fundamentalist, orthodox, essential to the Right's political agenda. The moral order and the social order are supposed to mirror each other: authority, hierarchy, and property are God-given values, not to be compromised by secular humanists, atheists, or liberals who have perverse ideas about equality. In the United States, religion is a political arm of the New Right. Antiabortion political action is organized in churches; gay rights legislation is defeated by religious leaders organizing against sin; equal rights legislation for women is opposed on theological grounds. The husband is likened to Christ, and legislation is introduced in the United States Congress to see that the simile becomes enforceable public policy. Battered women are called "runaway wives" when they do get away and are denounced for being insufficiently submissive: escape is immoral. Sexually harassed women are faulted for not being "virtuous." Depictions of men and women in school books are supposed to conform to fundamentalist dicta for men and women: the wife is to be shown in the full splendor of her domesticity. The family is intended to be a feudal unit in this political passion play: and religion is a fundamental and politically effective tool in this program of domestic repression and social control.

In the United States, the Right is especially concerned with opposing equality as a social goal. It stands against what Margaret Papandreou has called "the democratic family," a family not based on the subordination of women but instead on equality, cooperation, and reciprocity. It stands against all programmatic efforts to achieve racial and economic equality. It stands against sex equality as idea and as practice. It seeks to destroy any movement, program, law, discourse, or sentiment that would end, injure, or undermine male dominance over women.

The contemporary Right in the United States is Burke through and through: authority, hierarchy, property, and religion are what it is for; democracy is what it is against. It is eighteenth-century conservatism almost without revision. Except. Except that it has mobilized women, which Burke did not do in the eighteenth century. Except that it has succeeded in organizing women into right-wing activists. Except that it has succeeded in getting *women as women* (women who claim to be acting in the interests of women as a group) to act effectively in behalf of male authority over women, in behalf of a hierarchy in which women are subservient to men, in behalf of women as the rightful property of men, in behalf of religion as an expression of transcendent male supremacy. It has succeeded in

193

getting women to act effectively against their own democratic inclusion in the political process, against their own civil equality, against any egalitarian conception of their own worth. This book accepts a fairly orthodox definition of right-wing values and ideas (as outlined in this preface) and asks why women are promoting those values and ideas, since the authority they are defending consistently degrades them, the hierarchy they are defending puts them on the bottom, the right to property they are defending deprives them of full human standing, the religion they are defending insists that they must subject themselves to petty and often violent tyranny, and the equality they oppose is the only remedy. Why do right-wing women agitate for their own subordination? How does the Right, controlled by men, enlist their participation and loyalty? And why do right-wing women truly hate the feminist struggle for equality?

One feminist writer has called this book "a subtle discourse on complicity." The complicity is not limited to women on the organized Right. A premise of this book is that right-wing women are women who accept the legitimacy of sex hierarchy, male authority, and women as property in any way no matter what they call themselves. The same definition of "right-wing" obtains for men. The question then may well be: can anyone find the Left?

Andrea Dworkin
New York City
February 1983

IV

THE NEW
TERRORISM

If you can't stand the heat,
step down from the stake.
> Robin Morgan, "Jottings of a
> Feminist Activist"
> in *Lady of the Beasts*

Pornography:
The New Terrorism

1977

This is the first speech I ever gave that dealt exclusively with the subject of pornography. Maybe seventy-five students heard it at the University of Massachusetts at Amherst in the dead of winter, early 1977. They mobilized on the spot to demonstrate against the pornography being shown on campus: a film advertised in the school newspaper (see The Power of Words *for more information about this newspaper) that had been brought on campus by a man who had just been arrested for beating the woman he lived with. Do you know how badly she had to be hurt for him to be arrested back in 1977? I gave this speech on lots of college campuses and in every case students organized to do something about pornography after hearing it. In December 1978, I gave it at a conference at the New York University Law School. A news story in* The New York Times *noted that people rose to their feet, many crying, and that one famous civil liberties lawyer walked out, refusing to listen. After that, within the month,* The New York Times *published two editorials quoting from this speech and denouncing feminists for being "overwrought" and "strident." I wrote a response (see* For Men, Freedom of Speech; For Women, Silence Please) *but* The New York Times *refused to publish it. According to the reporter who wrote the news story, it became* Times *policy not to cover newsworthy events involving feminists opposing pornography because such coverage would "hurt the First Amendment." We were pretty effectively boycotted by the* Times, *the so-called newspaper of record. We know a lot more now about how pornography hurts women, why it is so pernicious; but this speech was a conceptual breakthrough that helped change the terms of the argument. The new terms mobilized women to action.*

ALL THROUGH HUMAN history, there have been terrible, cruel wrongs. These wrongs were not committed on a small scale. These wrongs were not rarities or oddities. These wrongs have raged over the earth like wind-swept fires, maiming, destroying, leaving humans turned to ash. Slavery, rape, torture, extermination have been the substance of life for billions of human beings since the beginning of patriarchal time. Some have battened on atrocity while others have suffered from it until they died.

In any given time, most people have accepted the cruellest wrongs as right. Whether through indifference, ignorance, or brutality, most people, oppressor and oppressed, have apologized for atrocity, defended it, justified it, excused it, laughed at it, or ignored it.

The oppressor, the one who perpetrates the wrongs for his own pleasure or profit, is the master inventor of justification. He is the magician who, out of thin air, fabricates wondrous, imposing, seemingly irrefutable intellectual reasons which explain why one group must be degraded at the hands of another. He is the conjurer who takes the smoking ash of real death and turns it into stories, poems, pictures, which celebrate degradation as life's central truth. He is the illusionist who paints mutilated bodies in chains on the interior canvas of the imagination so that, asleep or awake, we can only hallucinate indignity and outrage. He is the manipulator of psychological reality, the framer of law, the engineer of social necessity, the architect of perception and being.

The oppressed are encapsulated by the culture, laws, and values of the oppressor. Their behaviors are controlled by laws and traditions based on their presumed inferiority. They are, as a matter of course, called abusive names, presumed to have low or disgusting personal and collective traits. They are always subject to sanctioned assault. They are surrounded on every side by images and echoes of their own worthlessness. Involuntarily, unconsciously, not knowing anything else, they have branded into them, burned into their brains, a festering self-hatred, a virulent self-contempt. They have burned out of them the militant dignity on which all self-respect is based.

Oppressed people are not subjugated or controlled by dim warnings or vague threats of harm. Their chains are not made of shadows. Oppressed people are *terrorized*—by raw violence, real violence, unspeakable and pervasive violence. Their bodies are assaulted and despoiled, according to the will of the oppressor.

This violence is always accompanied by cultural assault—propaganda disguised as principle or knowledge. The purity of the "Aryan" or Caucasian race is a favorite principle. Genetic inferiority is a favorite field of knowledge. Libraries are full of erudite texts that prove, beyond a shadow of a doubt, that Jews, the Irish, Mexicans, blacks, homosexuals, women are slime. These eloquent and resourceful proofs are classified as psychology, theology, economics, philosophy, history, sociology, the so-called science of biology. Sometimes, often, they are made into stories or poems and called art. Degradation is dignified as biological, economic, or historical necessity; or as the logical consequence of the repulsive traits or inherent limitations of the ones degraded. Out on the streets, the propaganda takes a more vulgar form. Signs read "Whites Only" or "Jews and Dogs Not Allowed." Hisses of kike, nigger, queer, and pussy fill the air. In this propaganda, the victim is marked. In this propaganda, the victim is targeted. This propaganda is the glove that covers the fist in any reign of terror.

This propaganda does not only sanction violence against the designated group; it incites it. This propaganda does not only threaten assault; it promises it.

These are the dreaded images of terror.

—A Jew, emaciated, behind barbed wire, nearly naked, mutilated by the knife of a Nazi doctor: the atrocity is acknowledged.

—A Vietnamese, in a tiger cage, nearly naked, bones twisted and broken, flesh black and blue: the atrocity is acknowledged.

—A black slave on an Amerikan plantation, nearly naked, chained, flesh ripped up from the whip: the atrocity is acknowledged.

—A woman, nearly naked, in a cell, chained, flesh ripped up from the whip, breasts mutilated by a knife: she is entertainment, the boy-next-door's favorite fantasy, every man's precious right, every woman's potential fate.

The woman tortured is sexual entertainment.

The woman tortured is sexually arousing.

The anguish of the woman tortured is sexually exciting.

The degradation of the woman tortured is sexually entrancing.

The humiliation of the woman tortured is sexually pleasing, sexually thrilling, sexually gratifying.

Women are a degraded and terrorized people. Women are degraded and terrorized by men. Rape is terrorism. Wife-beating is terrorism. Medical butchering is terrorism. Sexual abuse in its hundred million forms is terrorism.

Women's bodies are possessed by men. Women are forced into involuntary childbearing because men, not women, control women's reproductive functions. Women are an enslaved population—the crop we harvest is children, the fields we work are houses. Women are forced into committing sexual acts with men that violate integrity because the universal religion—contempt for women—has as its first commandment that women exist purely as sexual fodder for men.

Women are an occupied people. Our very bodies are possessed, taken by others who have an inherent right to take, used or abused by others who have an inherent right to use or abuse. The ideology that energizes and justifies this systematic degradation is a fascist ideology—the ideology of biological inferiority. No matter how it is disguised, no matter what refinements pretty it up, this ideology, reduced to its essence, postulates that women are biologically suited to function only as breeders, pieces of ass, and servants. This fascist ideology of female inferiority is the preeminent ideology on this planet. As Shulamith Firestone put it in *The Dialectic of Sex*, "Sex class is so deep as to be invisible." That women exist to be used by men is, quite simply, the common point of view, and the concommitant of this point of view, inexorably linked to it, is that violence used against women to force us to fulfill our so-called natural functions is not really violence at all. Every act of terror or crime committed against women is justified as sexual necessity and/or is dismissed as utterly unimportant. This extreme callousness passes as normalcy, so that when women, after years or decades or centuries of unspeakable abuse, do raise our voices in outrage at the crimes committed against us, we are accused of stupidity or lunacy, or are ignored as if we were flecks of dust instead of flesh and blood.

We women are raising our voices now, because all over this country a new campaign of terror and vilification is being waged against us. Fascist propaganda celebrating sexual violence against women is sweeping this land. Fascist propaganda celebrating the sexual degradation of women is innundating cities, college campuses, small towns. Pornography is the propaganda of sexual fascism. Pornography is the propaganda of sexual terrorism. Images of women bound, bruised, and maimed on virtually every street corner, on every magazine rack, in every drug store, in movie house after movie house, on billboards, on posters pasted on walls, are death threats to a female population in rebellion. Female rebellion against male sexual despotism, female rebellion against male sexual authority, is now a reality throughout this country. The men, meeting rebellion with an escalation of terror, hang pictures of maimed female bodies in every public place.

We are forced either to capitulate, to be beaten back by those images of abuse into silent acceptance of female degradation as a fact of life, or to develop strategies of resistance derived from a fully conscious will to resist. If we capitulate—smile, be good, pretend that the woman in chains has nothing to do with us, avert our eyes as we pass her image a hundred times a day—we have lost everything. What, after all, does all our work against rape or wife-beating amount to when one of their pictures is worth a thousand of our words?

Strategies of resistance are developing. Women are increasingly refusing to accept the pernicious, debilitating lie that the sexual humiliation of women for fun, pleasure, and profit is the inalienable right of every man. Petitions, leafleting, picketing, boycotts, organized vandalism, speak-outs, teach-ins, letter writing campaigns, intense and militant harassment of distributors and exhibitors of woman-hating films, and an unyielding refusal to give aid and comfort to the politically self-righteous fellow-travelers of the pornographers are increasing, as feminists refuse to cower in the face of this new campaign of annihilation. These are beginning actions. Some are rude and some are civil. Some are short-term actions, spon-taneously ignited by outrage. Others are long-term strategies that require extensive organization and commitment. Some disregard male law, break it with militancy and pride. Others dare to demand that the law must protect women—even women—from brazen terrorization. All of these actions arise out of the true perception that pornography actively promotes violent contempt for the integrity and rightful freedom of women. And, despite male claims to the contrary, feminists, not pornographers, are being arrested and prosecuted by male law enforcers, all suddenly "civil libertarians" when male privilege is confronted on the streets by angry and uppity women. The concept of "civil liberties" in this country has not ever, and does not now, embody principles and behaviors that respect the sexual rights of women. Therefore, when pornographers are challenged by *women*, police, district attorneys, and judges punish the women, all the while ritualistically claiming to be the legal guardians of "free speech." In fact, they are the legal guardians of male profit, male property, and phallic power.

Feminist actions against pornography must blanket the country, so that no pornographer can hide from, ignore, ridicule, or find refuge from the outrage of women who will not be degraded, who will not submit to terror. Wherever women claim any dignity or want any possibility of freedom, we must confront the fascist propaganda that celebrates atrocity against us head on—expose it for what it is, expose those who make it, those who show it, those who defend it, those who consent to it, those who enjoy it.

In the course of this difficult and dangerous struggle, we will be forced, as we experience the intransigence of those who commit and support these crimes against us, to ask the hardest and deepest questions, the ones we so dread:

—what is this male sexuality that requires our humiliation, that literally swells with pride at our anguish;

—what does it mean that yet again—and after years of feminist analysis and activism—the men (gay, leftist, whatever) who proclaim a commitment to social justice are resolute in their refusal to face up to the meaning and significance of their enthusiastic advocacy of yet another woman-hating plague;

—what does it mean that the pornographers, the consumers of pornography, and the apologists for pornography are the men we grew up with, the men we talk with, live with, the men who are familiar to us and often cherished by us as friends, fathers, brothers, sons, and lovers;

—how, surrounded by this flesh of our flesh that despises us, will we defend the worth of our lives, establish our own authentic integrity, and, at last, achieve our freedom?

Why Pornography Matters
to Feminists

1981

The New York Times *struck again in the spring of 1981 when* Pornography: Men Possessing Women *was published. Having ignored* Woman Hating, Our Blood, *and the new womans broken heart (short stories),* The New York Times Book Review *chose a political adversary with a history of tearing down other feminists to review my book on pornography. She trashed it, especially by suggesting that any critique of pornography was necessarily right-wing, strengthened the political Right by giving it aid and comfort, and advocated censorship. Because the woman was a feminist,* The New York Times *(the single most important forum for book reviews in the United States) had what they needed to discredit the book, the integrity of the fight against pornography, and feminism too. Not having access to any mainstream forum, I published this short article in a Boston-based feminist newspaper,* Sojourner, *to say* Why Pornography Matters to Feminists. *I haven't seen any defense of pornography by anyone posturing as a feminist that addresses even one point made in this piece.*

PORNOGRAPHY IS AN essential issue because pornography says that women want to be hurt, forced, and abused; pornography says women want to be raped, battered, kidnapped, maimed; pornography says women want to be humiliated, shamed, defamed; pornography says that women say No but mean Yes—Yes to violence, Yes to pain.

Also: pornography says that women are things; pornography says that being used as things fulfills the erotic nature of women; pornography says that women are the things men use.

Also: in pornography women are used as things; in pornography force is used against women; in pornography women are used.

Also: pornography says that women are sluts, cunts; pornography says that pornographers define women; pornography says that men define women; pornography says that women are what men want women to be.

Also: pornography shows women as body parts, as genitals, as vaginal slits, as nipples, as buttocks, as lips, as open wounds, as pieces.

Also: pornography uses real women.

Also: pornography is an industry that buys and sells women.

Also: pornography sets the standard for female sexuality, for female sexual values, for girls growing up, for boys growing up, and increasingly for advertising, films, video, visual arts, fine art and literature, music with words.

Also: the acceptance of pornography means the decline of feminist ethics and an abandonment of feminist politics; the acceptance of pornography means feminists abandon women.

Also: pornography reinforces the Right's hold on women by making the environment outside the home more dangerous, more threatening; pornography reinforces the husband's hold on the wife by making the domestic environment more dangerous, more threatening.

Also: pornography turns women into objects and commodities; pornography perpetuates the object status of women; pornography perpetuates the self-defeating divisions among women by perpetuating the object status of women; pornography perpetuates the low self-esteem of women by perpetuating the object status of women; pornography perpetuates the distrust of women for women by perpetuating the object status of women; pornography perpetuates the demeaning and degrading of female intelligence and creativity by perpetuating the object status of women.

Also: pornography is violence against the women used in pornography and pornography encourages and promotes violence against women as a class; pornography dehumanizes the women used in pornography and pornography contributes to and promotes the dehumanization of all women; pornography exploits the women used in pornography and accelerates and promotes the sexual and economic exploitation of women as a class.

Also: pornography is made by men who sanction, use, celebrate, and promote violence against women.

Also: pornography exploits children of both sexes, especially girls, and encourages violence against children, and does violence to children.

Also: pornography uses racism and anti-Semitism to promote sexual arousal; pornography promotes racial hatred by promoting racial degradation as "sexy"; pornography romanticizes the concentration camp and the plantation, the Nazi and the slaveholder; pornography exploits demeaning racial stereotypes to promote sexual arousal; pornography celebrates racist sexual obsessions.

Also: pornography numbs the conscience, makes one increasingly callous to cruelty, to the infliction of pain, to violence against persons, to the humiliation or degradation of persons, to the abuse of women and children.

Also: pornography gives us no future; pornography robs us of hope as well as dignity; pornography further lessens our human value in the society at large and our human potential in fact; pornography forbids sexual self-determination to women and to children; pornography uses us up and throws us away; pornography annihilates our chance for freedom.

Pornography's Part in Sexual Violence

1981

It took a year to get this published in eviscerated form in Newsday, *a Long Island, New York, daily newspaper. Nearly four months later,* The Los Angeles Times *published this version, closer to what I wrote. The manuscript is lost, so this is the most complete version existing. In Ohio, Sisters of Justice destroy adult bookstores in lightning attacks. In Minnesota, a few hundred women savage an adult bookstore and destroy the stock. In California, in dozens of supermarkets,* Hustler *is saturated with India ink month after month. In Canada, feminists are jailed for bombing an outlet of a chain that sells video-pornography. In Massachusetts, a woman shoots a bullet through the window of a closed bookstore that sells pornography. A model of nonviolent civil disobedience is the* National Rampage Against Penthouse, *organized by the brilliant activists, Nikki Craft and Melissa Farley. Women invade bookstores, especially B. Dalton, the largest distributor of* Penthouse *in the United States, and tear up magazines until arrested. They tear up* Playboy *and* Hustler *too where they find them. They claim this as protected political speech. They have been arrested in Des Moines, Dubuque, Iowa City, Cedar Rapids, Cedar Falls, and Coralville, Iowa; Lincoln and Omaha, Nebraska; Santa Cruz, Davis, and San José, California; Madison and Beloit, Wisconsin; Minneapolis, Minnesota; St. Joseph, Missouri; Provincetown, Massachusetts; Durham, North Carolina; Rock Island and Chicago, Illinois. One leaflet says: "Next action is pending. We will not be Rehabilitated by jail."*

L AST FEBRUARY THREE women—Linda Hand, Jane Quinn and Shell Wildwomoon—entered a store in Hartford, Conn., and poured human blood on books and films that depicted the sexual abuse of women and children, as well as on an arsenal of metal-studded dildos and whips.

The store, "The Bare Facts," nominally sells lingerie. A "fantasy room" in the back houses the above-mentioned stock. Several times a year, on holidays, there is an open house in the fantasy room. As the men drink champagne provided by the management, female models strut and pose amidst the sexual paraphernalia in lingerie that the male audience selects from the store's stock.

Hand, Quinn and Wildwomoon picketed the Christmas celebration. They tried to stop the Valentine's Day party by spilling blood. They were charged with criminal mischief, a felony that carries a possible five-year sentence and $5000 fine, and criminal trespass, a misdemeanor with a possible one-year sentence.

The three conducted their own defense. They claimed that they had acted to prevent a greater crime—the sexual abuse of women and children; that the materials in question contributed materially to sexual violence against women and children; that society had a greater obligation to protect women's lives than dildos. In the great tradition of civil disobedience, they placed the rights of people above the rights of property. This was the first time ever that such a defense was put forth in behalf of women, against pornography, in a court of law. They were acquitted.

I testified for the defense as an expert witness on pornography. For the first time, I was under oath when asked whether, in my opinion, pornography is a cause of violence against women.

I hate that question, because pornography *is* violence against women: the women used in pornography. Not only is there a precise symmetry of values and behaviors in pornography and in acts of forced sex and battery, but in a sex-polarized society men also learn about women and sex from pornography. The message is conveyed to men that women enjoy being abused. Increasingly, research is proving that sex and violence—and the perception that females take pleasure in being abused, which is the heart of pornography—teach men both ambition and strategy.

But beyond the empirical research, there is the evidence of testimony: women coming forth, at least in the safety of feminist circles, to testify to the role that pornography played in their own experiences of sexual abuse. One nineteen-year-old woman testified at the Hartford trial that her father consistently used pornographic material as he raped and tortured her over a period of years. She also told of a network of her father's friends, including doctors and lawyers, who abused her and other children. One of these doctors treated the children to avoid being exposed.

Stories such as these are not merely bizarre and sensational; they are beginning to appear in feminist literature with increasing frequency. To dismiss them is to dismiss the lives of the victims.

The refusal, especially among liberals, to believe that pornography has any real relationship to sexual violence is astonishing. Liberals have always believed in the value and importance of education. But when it comes to pornography, we are asked to believe that nothing pornographic, whether written or visual, has an educative effect on anyone. A recognition that pornography must teach something does not imply any inevitable conclusion: it does not per se countenance censorship. It does, however, demand that we pay some attention to the quality of life, to the content of pornography.

And it especially demands that when sexual violence against women is epidemic, serious questions be asked about the function and value of material that advocates such violence and makes it synonymous with pleasure.

Is it "prudish," "repressive," "censorious" or "fascistic" to demand that "human rights" include the rights of women, or to insist that women who are being raped, beaten or forced into prostitution are being denied fundamental human rights? Are the advocates of freedom really concerned only for the freedom of the abusers?

We in the United States are so proud of our freedom, but women in the United States have lost ground, not gained it, even in controlling sexual access to our own bodies. This is the system of power in which rape within marriage is considered a crime in only three states (New Jersey, Nebraska and Oregon). This is the same system of power that condones the pornography that exalts rape and gang rape, bondage, whipping and forced sex of all kinds. In this same system of power, there are an estimated twenty-eight million battered wives. Where, after all, do those drunken men go when they leave the porn shop's fantasy room? They go home to women and children.

The women who poured human blood over the material in that

Hartford shop faced the true "bare facts": Pornography is dangerous and effective propaganda that incites violence against easy targets—women and children.

The ACLU:
Bait and Switch

1981

The American Civil Liberties Union claims to protect rights, political dissenters, and the vitality of political and creative discourse. The organization, in my view, is exceptionally corrupt, a handmaiden of the pornographers, the Nazis, and the Ku Klux Klan. Only the pornographers give them lots of money. The Nazis and the Klan they help on principle. It's their form of charity work. I didn't understand this in 1981. I thought something was wrong but I wasn't exactly sure what. I wrote this piece to try to raise a real debate about the values and tactics of the ACLU. Forget it, folks. The ACLU is immune to criticism because virtually none gets published—none on the Left. I couldn't get this piece published but I did get some mean—even handwritten—letters from left, progressive, and libertarian editors expressing their disgust with my "contempt" for free speech. Speech is what I do; it ain't free; it costs a lot. This piece has never been published before.

TOWARDS THE END of 1975, I received several letters asking me to become a member of the ACLU. The stationery was lined with the names of eminent women. The letters were signed by an eminent woman. The plea was a feminist plea: the ACLU was in the forefront of the fight for women's rights. In 1975, I earned $1679. Deeply moved by the wonderful work being done by my sisters in the ACLU, that crusading organization for women's rights, I wrote a check for fifteen dollars and joined. I received a letter thanking me. This letter too had names on it, all male. It was signed by Aryeh Neier, then Executive Director. Verily, a woman's name, a reference to feminist issues, was not to be found. I wrote Mr Neier a letter that said in part: "All of the mail soliciting my membership was exemplary in its civility—that is, female names mingled with male names on letterheads; even men were chairpersons, etc. Now that I am a member, I find that I have been deceived by a bait and switch technique. My form letter welcoming me is replete with 'man's' and men, and nary a woman or a nod to feminist sensibilities is to be found." Of course, being very poor I had missed the fifteen dollars, but not for long. Mr Neier returned it to me immediately. He said that he would rather receive my complaint that old stationery "doesn't use the latest neologism than a complaint about profligacy for discarding it." My membership fee was "cheerfully refunded."

In the intervening years, letters soliciting money continued to arrive at a steady pace. Despite Mr Neier's cavalier attitude, it seemed that my fifteen dollars was sorely needed. As feminists confronted the issue of pornographic assault on women as individuals and as a class, prominent civil libertarians, Mr Neier foremost among them, denounced us for wasting civil libertarian time by speaking about the issue at all. Meanwhile, the ACLU saw to it that Nazis marched in Skokie and that the Klan was defended in California. While we feminists piddled around, the ACLU was doing the serious business of defending freedom.

In January 1981, I received yet another letter claiming that the ACLU needed me, this time from George McGovern. The letter said that the ACLU was fighting the Right, the Moral Majority, the Right to Life Movement, the New Right, and the evangelical Right. The entire thrust of the letter pitted a gargantuan Right against a broadly construed left. Reading it, one could only believe that the passion and purpose of the ACLU was to triumph over the terrible and terrifying Right. And what were the Nazis and the Klan, I asked myself. Chopped liver?

The ACLU, in both philosophy and practice, makes no distinction between Right and Left, or Right and Liberal, or Right and anything else. It does not even make a distinction between those who have genocidal ambitions and those who do not. The ACLU prides itself on refusing to make these distinctions.

Some think that the ACLU would not choose to defend Nazis if Nazis were what is called "a real threat." For some, this supposition gets the ACLU off the hook. But the Klan is "a real threat": count the dead bodies; watch the murderers acquitted; see the military training camps the Klan is establishing. It is time for the ACLU to come clean. Its fight is not against the Right in any form, including the Moral Majority or opponents of the Equal Rights Amendment (as Mr McGovern's letter claims). Its fight is for an absence of distinctions: "kill the Jews" and "rape the women" indistinguishable from all other speech; action mistaken for speech; the victim confounded into honoring the so-called rights of the executioner. In bondage photographs and movies, we are to interpret the bondage itself as speech and protect it as such. The symbol of free speech ACLU-style might well be a woman tied, chained, strung up, and gagged. Needless to say, she will not be on any letterhead. If the ACLU were honest, she would be.

I am tired of the sophistry of the ACLU and also of its good reputation among progressive people. In 1975, it seemed smart to rope in feminists, so eminent women were used to proclaim the ACLU a strong feminist organization, which no doubt they wanted it to become. This year, people are afraid of the so-called Moral Majority, and so the ACLU gets bucks by claiming to be a stalwart enemy of the Right. There is nothing in ACLU philosophy or practice to prohibit the use of those bucks to defend the Right—the Nazis, the Klan, or the Moral Majority.

There is nothing as dangerous as an unembodied principle: no matter what blood flows, the principle comes first. The First Amendment absolutists operate precisely on unembodied principle: consequences do not matter; physical acts are taken to be abstractions; genocidal ambitions and concrete organizing toward genocidal goals are trivialized by male lawyers who are a most protected and privileged group. Meanwhile, those who are targeted as victims are left defenseless. Of course, the ACLU does help the targeted groups sometimes, in some cases, depending on the resources available, resources depleted by defenses of the violent Right.

It is time for the ACLU to stop working both sides of the street. Some groups exist in order to hurt other groups. Some groups are socially constructed for the purpose of hurting other groups. The Klan is such a group. Some people are born into groups that others want to hurt. The distinction is fundamental: so fundamental that even the ACLU will have to reckon with it.

Why So-Called Radical Men Love and Need Pornography

1977

This is especially about the boys of the Sixties, boys my age, who fought against the Viet Nam War. The flower children. The peaceniks. The hippies. Students for a democratic society. Weatherboys. Draft resisters. Draft dodgers. Draftcard burners. War resisters. Conscientious objectors. Yippies. We women fought for the lives of these boys against the war machine. They fight now for pornography. In demonstrations we said: "Bring the War Home." The war is home.

I

When they arrived at the place God had pointed out to him, Abraham built an altar there, and arranged the wood. Then he bound his son Isaac and put him on the altar on top of the wood. Abraham stretched out his hand and seized the knife to kill his son.

Genesis, 22:9-10

MEN LOVE DEATH. In everything they make, they hollow out a central place for death, let its rancid smell contaminate every dimension of whatever still survives. Men especially love murder. In art they celebrate it, and in life they commit it. They embrace murder as if life without it would be devoid of passion, meaning, and action, as if murder were solace, stilling their sobs as they mourn the emptiness and alienation of their lives.

Male history, romance, and adventure are stories of murder, literal or mythic. Men of the right justify murder as the instrument of establishing or maintaining order, and men of the left justify murder as the instrument of effecting insurrection, after which they justify it in the same terms as men on the right. In male culture, slow murder is the heart of eros, fast murder is the heart of action, and systematized murder is the heart of history. It is as if, long, long ago, men made a covenant with murder: I will worship and serve you if you will spare *me*; I will murder so as not to be murdered; I will not betray you, no matter what else I must betray. Murder promised: to the victor go the spoils. This covenant, sealed in blood, has been renewed in every generation.

Among men, the fear of being murdered causes men to murder. The fathers, who wanted their own likeness lifted from the thighs of laboring women, who wanted sons, not daughters, at some point recognize that, like wretched King Midas, they have gotten their way. There before them are the sons who are the same as they, sons who will kill for power, sons who will take everything from them, sons who will replace them. The sons, clay sculpted but not yet fired in the kiln, must kill or be killed, depose the tyrant or be ground to dust, on a battlefield or under his feet. The fathers are the divine architects of war and business; the sons are a sacrifice of flesh, bodies slaughtered to redeem the diminishing virility of the aging owners of the earth.

In Amerika, the most recent sacrifice of the sons was called Viet Nam. As Abraham obeyed the God created to serve his own deepest psychosexual needs, raised the knife to kill Isaac with his own hand, so the fathers of Amerika, in obedience to the State created to serve them, sated themselves on a blood feast of male young.

The sons who went were obedient apprentices to the fathers. War had for them its most ancient meaning: it would initiate them into the covenant with murder. They would appease their terrible fathers by substituting the dead bodies of other sons for their own. Each son of another race that they killed would strengthen their alliance with the fathers of their own. And if they could also murder without being murdered and kill in themselves whatever still shunned murder, then they might have the father's blessing, be heir to his dominion, change in midlife from son to father, become one of the powerful ones who choreograph war and manipulate death.

The sons who did not go declared outright a war of rebellion. They would rout the father, vanquish him, humiliate him, destroy him.

Over the grave of the fresh killed father, feeding on the new cadaver, would flower a brotherhood of young virility, sensual, without constraint, and there would be war no more.

Still, this innocence knew terror. These rebels had terror marked indelibly in their flesh—terror at the treachery of the father, who had had them sanctified, adored, and fattened, not to crown them king of the world, but instead to make them ripe for slaughter. These rebels had seen themselves bound on the altar, knife in the father's hand coming toward them. The father's cruelty was awesome, as was his mammoth power.

II

> Noah, a tiller of the soil, was the first to plant the vine. He drank some of the wine, and while he was drunk he uncovered himself inside his tent. Ham, Canaan's ancestor, saw his father's nakedness, and told his two brothers outside. Shem and Japheth took a cloak and they both put it over their shoulders, and walking backwards, covered their father's nakedness; they kept their faces turned away, and did not see their father's nakedness. When Noah awoke from his stupor he learned what his youngest son had done to him. And he said: "Accursed be Canaan. He shall be his brothers' meanest slave."
>
> Genesis, 9:20-25

The fathers hoard power. They use power to amass more power. They are not sentimental about power. In every area of life, they act to take or to consolidate power.

The rebellious sons, born in the image of the father, are born to power, but they do not value it in terms the father can recognize. These sons renounce the fathers' cold love of power. These sons claim that the purpose of power is pleasure. These sons want power to keep them warm between the thighs.

The fathers know that taboo is the essence of power: keep the source of power hidden, mysterious, sacred, so that those without power can never find it, understand it, or take it away.

The rebellious sons think that power is like youth—theirs forever. They think that power can never be used up, thrown away, or taken

216

away. They think that power can be spent in the pursuit of pleasure without being diminished, that pleasure replenishes power.

The fathers know that either power is used to make more power, or it is lost forever.

In Amerika, during the Viet Nam war, the argument took this form: the fathers maintained, as they always have, that the power of manhood is in the phallus: keep it covered, hidden; shroud it in religious taboo; use it in secret; on it build an empire, but never expose it to the powerless, those who do not have it, those who would, if they could but see its true, naked, unarmed dimensions, have contempt for it, grind it to nothing under their thumbs. The fathers wanted to maintain the *sacred character* of the phallus; as Yahweh's name must not be pronounced, so the phallus must be omnipresent in its power, but in itself concealed, never profaned.

The rebel sons wanted phallic power to be secular and "democratic" in the male sense of the word; that is, they wanted to fuck at will, as a birthright. With a princely arrogance that belied their egalitarian pretensions, they wanted to wield penises, not guns, as emblems of manhood. They did not repudiate the illegitimate power of the phallus: they repudiated the authority of the father that put limits of law and convention on their lust. They did not argue against the power of the phallus; they argued for pleasure as the purest use to which it could be put.

The fathers used the institutions of their authority—law, religion, etc.—to forbid the hedonism of the rebel sons because they understood that these sons, in their reckless promiscuity, would undermine male hegemony: not the power of the fathers over the sons, exercised with raw malice in Viet Nam, but the power of all men over all women. In vulgarizing the penis, the rebels would uncover it; in uncovering it, they would expose it to women, from whom it had been hidden by carefully cultivated and enforced ignorance, myth, and taboo for hundreds of centuries. The fathers knew that the romance of boys enchanted by their own virility could not take the place of taboo in protecting the penis from the wrath, buried but festering, of those who had been colonialized by it.

III

You must not uncover the nakedness of your father or mother.

Leviticus, 18:7

You must not uncover the nakedness of your father's wife; it is your father's nakedness.

Leviticus, 18:8

You must not uncover the nakedness of your father's sister; for it is your father's flesh.

Leviticus, 18:12

According to the editors of *The Jerusalem Bible*, "uncovering nakedness" is a "pejorative phrase for sexual intercourse." The above prohibitions in Leviticus, written to delineate lawful male behavior, all forbid incest—incest with the father. In vulgar English, they might all read: you must not fuck your father.

Abraham binds Isaac on the altar, to penetrate him with a phallic substitute, a knife. In male mythology, knife or sword is a primary metaphor for the penis; the word vagina literally means sheath. The scenario itself, devoid of any symbolism, is stark homoerotic sadomasochism.

Noah is violated when Ham sees him naked. The offense of the youngest son is so vile to Noah that he exiles that son's descendants into eternal slavery.

Father-son incest, repressed, veiled in a thousand veils, too secret even to be denied, is an invisible specter that haunts men, stalks them, shames them. This erotic repression is the silent pulse of institutionalized phallic power. The fathers, wombless perpetuators of their own image, know themselves; that is, they know that they are dangerous, purveyors of raw violence and constant death. They know that male desire is the stuff of murder, not love. They know that male eroticism, atrophied in the mummified penis, is sadistic; that the penis itself is as they have named it, a knife, a sword, a weapon. They know too that the sexual aggression of men against each other, especially sons against fathers, once let loose would destroy them.

The fathers do not fuck the sons, not because they have never wanted to, but because they know the necessity of subordinating eroticism to the purposes of power: they know that this desire, above all others, must be buried, left to rot under the ground of male experience to feed the vermin that crawl there. To take the son would suggest to the son another possibility—that he might turn on the aging father, subdue him through sexual assault.

The fathers must destroy in the sons the very capacity to violate them. They must turn this impulse to paralysis, impotence, dead nerve endings, memory numbed in ice. For if father and son were naked, face to face, the male weapon that is aggression mortified into what men call passion would rend the father, conquer and disgrace him.

In war, the fathers castrate the sons by killing them. In war, the fathers overwhelm the penises of the surviving sons by having terrorized them, having tried to drown them in blood.

But this is not enough, for the fathers truly fear the potency of the sons. Knowing fully the torture chambers of male imagination, they see themselves, legs splayed, rectum split, torn, shredded by the saber they have enshrined.

Do it to her, they whisper; do it to her, they command.

IV

In Amerika, after the Viet Nam war, this happened.

The rebellious sons were no longer carefree boys, wildly flushed by the discovery of their penises as instruments of pleasure. They had seen the murder spawned by the fathers coming toward them, pursuing them, encompassing them. They had been chastened and hardened, stunned and fixed in the memory of a single horror: the father had bound them on the altar; the father's hand, clutching the knife, was coming toward them.

The rebellious sons had gotten older. Their penises too had aged, experienced impotence, failure. The capacity of the nineteen-year-old boy to fuck at will was no longer theirs.

The rebellious sons, as the fathers might have prophesied, had experienced another loss, a consequence of their prideful sacrilege: they had profaned the penis by uncovering it, ripping from it the effective protection of mystery and taboo; those colonialized by it had seen it without mystification, experienced it raw, and they had organized to destroy its power over them. The sons, vain and narcissistic, did not recognize or respect the revolutionary militance of the women: they knew only that the women had left them, abandoned them, and that without the supine bodies of women to firm up the earth under them, they had nowhere to put their feet. The very earth beneath them betrayed them, turned to quicksand or dust.

The sons, dispossessed, did have a choice: to bond with the fathers to crush the women or to ally themselves with the women against the tyranny of all phallic power, including their own.

The sons, faithful to the penis, bonded with the fathers who had tried to kill them. Only in this alliance could they make certain that they would not again be bound on the altar for sacrifice. Only in this alliance could they find the social and political power that could compensate them for their waning virility. Only in this alliance could they gain access to the institutionalized brute force necessary to revenge themselves on the women who had left them.

The perfect vehicle for forging this alliance was pornography.

The fathers, no strangers to pornography, used it as secret ritual. In it they intoned chants of worship to their own virility, sometimes only a memory. These chants conjured up a promised land where male virility never waned, where the penis in and of itself embodied pure power. The fathers also used pornography to make money. In their system, secret vice was the alchemist's gold.

Using the rhetoric of the youths they no longer were, the sons claimed that pornography was pleasure, all the while turning it to profit. Proclaiming a creed of freedom the sons made and sold images of women bound and shackled. Proclaiming the necessity and dignity of freedom, the sons made and sold images of women humiliated and mutilated. Proclaiming the urgent honor of free speech, the sons used images of rape and torture to terrorize women into silence. Proclaiming the absolute integrity of the First Amendment, the sons used it to browbeat women into silence.

The sons want their share of the father's empire. In return, they offer the father this: new avenues of making money; new means of terrorizing women into submission; new masks to protect the penis. This time, the sons will make the masks. The cloth will be liberal jargon about censorship; the thread will be such pure violence that women will avert their eyes.

The sons have already allied themselves with one sector of fathers—organized crime. Still spouting anticapitalist, liberationist platitudes, they have not hesitated to become the filth they denounce.

The other fathers will follow suit. The secret fear of incestuous rape is still with them, and it is intensified by the recognition that these sons have learned to turn pleasure to profit, profligacy to power.

In pornography, the rebellious sons have discovered the keys to the kingdom. Soon they will be sitting on the throne.

For Men, Freedom of Speech;
For Women, Silence Please

1979

I wrote this to answer two editorials in The New York Times *that quoted from* Pornography: The New Terrorism *and denounced feminists for undermining the First Amendment (freedom of speech) by speaking out against pornography.* The New York Times *would not publish it; neither would* The Washington Post, Newsweek, Mother Jones, The Village Voice, The Nation, The Real Paper, *or anywhere else one could think to send it. It was first published in 1980 in the anthology* Take Back the Night, *edited by Laura Lederer. I had been named in one of the* Times *editorials and thought that ethically I was entitled to some right of response. No. I thought the other places—very big on free speech—should publish it because they were very big on free speech. No.*

A GREAT MANY men, no small number of them leftist lawyers, are apparently afraid that feminists are going to take their dirty pictures away from them. Anticipating the distress of forced withdrawal, they argue that feminists really must shut up about pornography—what it is, what it means, what to do about it—to protect what they call "freedom of speech." Our "strident" and "overwrought" antagonism to pictures that show women sexually violated and humiliated, bound, gagged, sliced up, tortured in a multiplicity of ways, "offends" the First Amendment. The enforced silence of women through the centuries has not. Some elementary observations are in order.

The Constitution of the United States was written exclusively by white men who owned land. Some owned black slaves, male and female. Many more owned white women who were also chattel.

The Bill of Rights was never intended to protect the civil or sexual rights of women and it has not, except occasionally by accident.

The Equal Rights Amendment, which would, as a polite afterthought, extend equal protection under the law such as it is to women, is not yet part of the Constitution. There is good reason to doubt that it will be in the foreseeable future.

The government in all its aspects—legislative, executive, judicial, enforcement—has been composed almost exclusively of men. Even juries, until very recently, were composed almost entirely of men. Women have had virtually nothing to do with either formulating or applying laws on obscenity or anything else. In the arena of political power, women have been effectively silenced.

Both law and pornography express male contempt for women: they have in the past and they do now. Both express enduring male social and sexual values; each attempts to fix male behavior so that the supremacy of the male over the female will be maintained. The social and sexual values of women are barely discernible in the culture in which we live. In most instances, women have been deprived of the opportunity even to formulate, let alone articulate or spread, values that contradict those of the male. The attempts that we make are both punished and ridiculed. Women of supreme strength who have lived in creative opposition to the male cultural values of their day have been written out of history—silenced.

Rape is widespread. One characteristic of rape is that it silences women. Laws against rape have not functioned to protect the bodily integrity of women; instead, they have punished some men for using women who belong to some other men.

Battery is widespread. One characteristic of battery is that it silences women. Laws against battery have been, in their application, a malicious joke.

There is not a feminist alive who could possibly look to the male legal system for real protection from the systematized sadism of men. Women fight to reform male law, in the areas of rape and battery for instance, because something is better than nothing. In general, we fight to force the law to recognize *us* as the victims of the crimes committed against us, but the results so far have been paltry and pathetic. Meanwhile, the men are there to counsel us. We must not demand the conviction of rapists or turn to the police when raped because then we are "prosecutorial" and racist. Since white men have used the rape laws to imprison black men, we are on the side of the racist when we (women of any color) turn to the law. The fact that most rape is intraracial, and more prosecution will inevitably mean the greater prosecution of white men for the crimes they commit, is supposedly irrelevant. (It is, of course, suddenly very relevant when one recognizes that this argument was invented and is being promoted by white men, significantly endangered for perhaps the first time by the anti-rape militancy of women.) We are also counselled that it is wrong to demand that the police enforce already existing laws against battery because then we "sanction" police entry into the home, which the police can then use for other purposes. Better that rape and battery should continue unchallenged, and the law be used by some men against other men with no reference to the rightful protection of women. The counsel of men is consistent: maintain a proper—and respectful—silence.

Male counsel on pornography, especially from leftist lawyers, has also been abundant. We have been told that pornography is a trivial issue and that we must stop wasting the valuable time of those guarding "freedom of speech" by talking about it. We have been accused of trivializing feminism by our fury at the hatred of women expressed in pornography. We have been told that we must not use existing laws even where they might serve us or invent new ones because we will inevitably erode "freedom of speech"—but that the use of violence against purveyors of pornography or property would not involve the same hazards. Others, less hypocritical, have explained that we must not use law; we must not use secondary boycotts, a civil liberties No-No (since women do not, with rare exceptions, consume pornography, women cannot boycott it by not buying it; other strategies, constituting secondary boycotts, would have to be used); we must not, of course, damage property, nor do we have the right to insult or harass. We have even been criticized for picketing, the logic being that an exhibitor of pornography might cave in under the pressure which would constitute a dangerous precedent. The men have counselled us to be silent so that "freedom of speech" will survive. The only limitation on it will be that women simply will not have it—no loss, since women have not had it. Such a limitation does not "offend" the First Amendment or male civil libertarians.

The First Amendment, it should be noted, belongs to those who can buy it. Men have the economic clout. Pornographers have empires. Women are economically disadvantaged and barely have token access to the media. A defense of pornography is a defense of the brute use of money to encourage violence against a class of persons who do not have—and have never had—the civil rights vouchsafed to men as a class. The growing power of the pornographers significantly diminishes the likelihood that women will ever experience freedom of anything— certainly not sexual self-determination, certainly not freedom of speech.

The fact of the matter is that if the First Amendment does not work for women, it does not work. With that premise as principle, perhaps the good lawyers might voluntarily put away the dirty pictures and figure out a way to make freedom of speech the reality for women that it already is for the literary and visual pimps. Yes, they might, they could; but they will not. They have their priorities set. They know who counts and who does not. They know, too, what attracts and what really offends.

Pornography and Male Supremacy
1981

This was written as a speech, my part of a debate on pornography with civil liberties lawyer and Harvard professor Alan Dershowitz, who recently went on the Penthouse *payroll but had no direct ties with the pornographers that I know of at the time of the debate. The debate was sponsored by The Schlesinger Library for Women at Radcliffe College, Cambridge, Massachusetts. In his autobiography,* The Best Defense, *Mr Dershowitz claims that he was threatened during the course of the debate by lesbians with bicycle chains. He wasn't; there were no bicycle chains and no threats. He continuously insulted the audience of mostly women and they talked back to him with loud and angry eloquence. The ACLU defends the "heckler's veto"—the right of hecklers to shout a speaker down; but when women answer misogynist insults with cogent, self-respecting speech, Mr Dershowitz doesn't like speech so much anymore. Even though he has spent years defending the pornographers in the name of principled free speech, he suppressed the tape of the debate by refusing to give permission for its distribution. This piece has never been published before.*

W E LIVE IN a system of power that is male-supremacist. This means that society is organized on the assumption that men are superior to women and that women are inferior to men. Male supremacy is regarded as being either divine or natural, depending on the proclivities of the apologist for it. Theologically, God is the supreme male, the Father, and the men of flesh and blood one might meet on the streets or in the corridors of universities are created in His image. There is also a divine though human though divine Son, and a phallic Holy Ghost who penetrates women as light penetrates a window. In both Jewish and Christian tradition, women are dirty, inclined to evil, not fit for the responsibilities of religious or civil citizenship, should be seen and not heard, are destined, or predestined as it were, for sexual use and reproduction and have no other value. Also, in both traditions (which are Father and Son respectively), the sexuality of women is seen as intrinsically seductive and sluttish, by its nature a provocation to which men respond. In theological terms, men are superior and women are inferior because God/He made it so, giving women a nature appropriate to their animal functions and men a nature with capacities that raise them above all other creatures.

The biological argument is even sillier, but because it is secular and university-sponsored, it has more credibility among intellectuals. Throughout patriarchal history, not just now, biological determinists have made two essential claims: first, that male superiority to women resides in an organ or a fluid or a secretion or a not-yet-discovered but urgently anticipated speck on a gene; and second, that we should study primates, fish, and insects to see how they manage, especially with their women. Sociobiologists and ethologists, the latest kinds of biological determinists, are selective in the species they study and the conclusions they draw because their argument is political, not scientific. The male, they say, regardless of what bug they are observing, is naturally superior because he is naturally dominant because he is naturally aggressive and so are his sperm; the female is naturally compliant and naturally submissive and exists in order to be fucked and bear babies. Now, fish do not reproduce through fucking; but that did not stop Konrad Lorenz's followers from holding up the cichlid as an example to the human woman. The cichlid is a prehistoric fish, and according to Lorenz the male cichlids could not mate unless the female cichlids demonstrated awe. Kate Millett wonders in *Sexual Politics* how one measures awe in a fish. But biological determinists do not wait around to answer such silly questions: they jump from species to species as suits their political purposes. And of course there are species they do avoid: spiders, praying mantises, and camels, for instance, since the females of these species kill or maim the male after intercourse. Biological determinists do not find such behaviors instructive. They love the gall wasp, which they have affectionately nicknamed the "killer wasp"—so one gets an idea of its character— and they do not pay much attention to the bee, what with its queen. There are also relatively egalitarian primates who never get a mention, and male penguins that care for the young, and so forth. And of course, no biological determinist has yet found the bug, fish, fowl, or even baboon who had managed to write *Middlemarch*. Humans create culture; even women create culture. "Sociobiology" or "ethology" may be new words, but biological arguments for the superiority of one group over another are not new. They are as old as genocide and slave labor. If women are held to be a natural class that exists to be fucked and to bear babies, then any method used to get women to do what they exist to do is also natural. And—to add insult to injury—they dare to call it Mother Nature.

The biological determinists believe precisely what the theologians believe: that women exist to be sexually used by men, to reproduce, to keep the cave clean, and to obey; failing which both men of religion and men of nature hypothesize that hitting the female might solve her problem. In theological terms, God raised man above all other creatures; in biological terms, man raised himself. In both systems of thought, man is at the top, where he belongs; woman is under him, literally and figuratively, where she belongs.

Every area of conflict regarding the rights of women ultimately boils down to the same issue: what are women for; to what use should women be put—sexually and reproductively. A society will be concerned that the birth rate is not high enough, but not that there is a paucity of books produced by women. For women as a class, sex and reproduction are presumed to be the very essence of life, which means that our fate unfolds in the opening of our thighs and the phallic penetration of our bodies and the introjection of sperm into our vaginas and the appropriation of our uteruses. In *The Dialectic of Sex*, Shulamith Firestone wrote: "Sex class is so deep as to be invisible." That is because sex class is seen as the work of God or nature, not men; and so the possession of women's bodies by men is considered to be the correct and proper use of women.

In male-supremacist terms, sex is phallic sex; it is often called possession or conquest or taking. A woman's body is taken or conquered or possessed or—to use another supposedly sexy synonym—violated; and the means of the taking or possessing or violating is penile penetration.

The sexual colonialization of women's bodies is a material reality: men control the sexual and reproductive uses of women's bodies. In this system of male power, rape is the paradigmatic sexual act. The word "rape" comes from the Latin *rapere*, which means to steal, seize, or carry away. The first dictionary definition of rape is still "the act of seizing and carrying off by force." A second meaning of rape is "the act of physically forcing a woman to have sexual intercourse." Rape is first abduction, kidnapping, the taking of a woman by force. Kidnapping, or rape, is also the first known form of marriage—called "marriage by capture." The second known form of marriage is basically prostitution: a father, rather than allow the theft of his daughter, sells her. Most social arrangements for the exchange of women operate on one ancient model or the other: stealing, which is rape; or buying and selling, which is prostitution.

The relationship of prostitution to rape is simple and direct: whatever can be stolen can be sold. This means that women were both stolen and sold and in both cases were sexual commodities; and when practices were codified into laws, women were defined as sexual chattel. Women are still basically viewed as sexual chattel—socially, legally, culturally, and in practice. Rape and prostitution are central contemporary female experiences; women as a class are seen as belonging to men as a class and are systematically kept subservient to men; married women in most instances have lost sexual and reproductive control of their own bodies, which is what it means to be sexual chattel.

The principle that whatever can be stolen can be sold applies not only to women as such, but also to the sexuality of women. The sexuality of women has been stolen outright, appropriated by men—conquered, possessed, taken, violated; women have been systematically and absolutely denied the right to sexual self-determination and to sexual integrity; and because the sexuality of women has been stolen, this sexuality itself, *it*—as distinguished from an individual woman as a sentient being—*it* can be sold. It can be represented pictorially and sold; the idea or suggestion of it can be sold; representations of it in words can be sold; signs and gestures that denote it can be sold. Men can take this sexuality—steal it, rape it—and men can pimp it.

We do not know when in history pornography as such first appeared. We do know that it is a product of culture, specifically male-supremacist culture, and that it comes after both rape and prostitution. Pornography can only develop in a society that is viciously male-supremacist, one in which rape and prostitution are not only well-established but systematically practiced and ideologically endorsed. Feminists are often asked whether pornography causes rape. The fact is that rape and prostitution caused and continue to cause pornography. Politically, culturally, socially, sexually, and economically, rape and prostitution generated pornography; and pornography depends for its continued existence on the rape and prostitution of women.

The word *pornography* comes from the ancient Greek *pornē* and *graphos*: it means "the graphic depiction of whores." *Pornē* means "whore," specifically the lowest class of whore, which in ancient Greece was the brothel slut available to all male citizens. There were distinct classes of prostitutes in ancient Greece: the *pornē* was the sexual cow. She was, simply and clearly and absolutely, a sexual slave. *Graphos* means "writing, etching, or drawing."

The whores called *porneia* were captive in brothels, which were designated as such by huge phalluses painted on or constructed near the door. They were not allowed out, were never educated, were barely dressed, and in general were miserably treated; they were the sexual garbage of Greek society. Wives were kept in nearly absolute isolation, allowed the company of slaves and young children only. High-class prostitutes, a class distinct from the *porneia* and from wives both, had the only freedom of movement accorded women, and were the only educated women.

Two very significant words originated in the ancient Greece many of us revere: *democracy* and *pornography*. Democracy from its beginnings excluded all women and some men. Pornography from its beginnings justified and promoted this exclusion of all women by presenting the sexuality of all women as the sexuality of the brothel slut. The brothel slut and the sexuality of the brothel slut had been stolen and sold—raped and prostituted; and the rape and prostitution of that captive and degraded being with her captive and degraded sexuality is precisely the sexual content of pornography. In pornography, the will of the chattel whore is synonymous with her function: she is purely for sex and her function is defined as her nature and her will. The isolation of wives was based on the conviction that women were so sexually voracious on male terms that wives could not be let out—or they would naturally turn whorish. The chattel whore was the natural woman, the woman without the civilizing discipline of marriage. The chattel whore, of course, as we know, was the product of the civilizing discipline of slavery, but men did not then and do not now see it that way.

Pornography illustrated and expressed this valuation of women and women's sexuality, and that is why it was named *pornography*— "the graphic depiction of whores." Depicting women as whores and the sexuality of women as sluttish is what pornography does. Its job in the politically coercive and cruel system of male supremacy is to justify and perpetuate the rape and prostitution from which it springs. This is its function, which makes it incompatible with any notion of freedom, unless one sees freedom as the right of men to rape and to prostitute women. Pornography as a genre says that the stealing and buying and selling of women are not acts of force or abuse because women want to be raped and prostituted because that is the nature of women and the nature of female sexuality. Gloria Steinem has said that culture is successful politics. As a cultural phenomenon, pornography *is* the political triumph of rape and prostitution over all female rebellion and resistance.

A piece of Greek pornography may have been a drawing on a vase or an etching. No live model was required to make it; no specific sexual act had to be committed in order for it to exist. Rape, prostitution, battery, pornography, and other sex-based abuse could be conceptualized as separate phenomena. In real life, of course, they were all mixed together: a woman was beaten, then raped; raped, then beaten, then prostituted; prostituted, then beaten, then raped; and so on. As far back as we know, whorehouses have provided live sex shows in which, necessarily, pornography and prostitution were one and the same thing. We know that the world's foremost pornographer, the Marquis de Sade, tortured, raped, imprisoned, beat, and bought women and girls. We know that influential male thinkers and artists who enthused about rape or prostitution or battery had, in many cases, raped or bought or battered women or girls and were also users and often devotees of pornography. We know that when the technical means of graphic depiction were limited to writing, etching, and drawing, pornography was mostly an indulgence of upper-class men, who were literate and who had money to spend on the almost always expensive etchings, drawings, and writings. We know that pornography flourished as an upper-class male pleasure when the power of upper-class men knew virtually no limitation, certainly with regard to women: in feudal societies, for instance. But in societies that did not find much to oppose in the rape and prostitution of women, there were certainly no inquiries, no investigations, no political or philosophical or scientific searches, into the role pornography played in acts of forced sex or battery. When pornography was in fact writing, etching, or drawing, it was possible to consider it something exclusively cultural, something on paper not in life, and even partly esthetic or intellectual. Such a view was not accurate, but it was possible. Since the invention of the camera, any such view of pornography is completely despicable and corrupt. Those are real women being tied and hung, gutted and trounced on, whipped and pissed on, gang-banged and hit, penetrated by dangerous objects and by animals. It is important to note that men have not found it necessary—not legally, not morally, not sexually—to make distinctions between drawing and writing on the one hand and the use of live women on the other. Where is the visceral outcry, the famous *humanist* outcry, against the tying and hanging and chaining and bruising and beating of women? Where is the visceral recognition, the *humanist* recognition, that it is impossible and inconceivable to tolerate—let alone to sanction or to apologize for—the tying and hanging and chaining and bruising and beating of women? I am saying what no one should have to say, which is simply that one does not do to human beings what is done to women in pornography. And why are these things done to women in pornography? The reasons men give are these: entertainment, fun, expression, sex, sexual pleasure, and because the women want it.

Instead of any so-called humanist outcry against the inhumanity of the use of women in pornography—an outcry that we might expect if dogs or cats were being treated the same way—there has been the pervasive, self-congratulatory, indolent, male-supremacist assumption that the use of women in pornography is the sexual will of the woman, expresses her sexuality, her character, her nature, and appropriately demonstrates a legitimate sexual function of hers. This is the same assumption about the nature of women and the nature of female sexuality that men have always used to justify the raping and prostituting of women. It is no less believed today than when Greek men imprisoned chattel whores in the fifth century BC. Almost without exception, the main premise of pornography is that women want to be forced, hurt, and cruelly used. The main proof of the power of this belief is when the female victim of rape, battery, or incest is blamed for the crime. But the proof is also in the size and growth of the pornography industry; the ever-increasing viciousness of the material itself; the greater acceptance of pornography as part of the social and the domestic environment; the ever-expanding alliances between pornographers and lawyers, pornographers and journalists, pornographers and politicians. Pornography is now used in increasing numbers of medical schools and other institutions of higher learning that teach "human sexuality." The pornography is everywhere, and its apologists are everywhere, and its users are everywhere, and its pimps are rich, and surely if we assumed that the women in the photographs and films were really human beings and not by nature chattel whores we would not have been able to stand it, to acquiesce, to collaborate through silence or cowardice or, as some in this room have done, to collaborate actively. If we assumed that these women were human, not chattel whores by nature, we would destroy that industry—with our bare hands if we could—because it steals and buys and sells women; it rapes and prostitutes women. In 1978, *Forbes* magazine reported that the pornography industry was a $4-billion-a-year business, larger than the conventional film and record industries combined. A big part of the pornography business is cash-and-carry: for instance, the film loops, where one deposits quarters for a minute or so of a woman being fucked by Nazis or the like. A huge part of the pornography business is mail-order. Here one finds the especially scurrilous material, including both magazines and films of women being tortured, tied, hung, and fucked by large animals, especially dogs. Child pornography—still photographs and films—is obtained under the counter or through mail-order. Books of child pornography that are print with drawings and some magazines with photographs can be obtained in drug stores as well as sex shops in urban areas. The above-ground slick so-called men's entertainment magazines are flourishing, and every indication is that the *Forbes* figure of a $4-billion industry was low to begin with and is now completely outdated. *Playboy*, *Penthouse*, and *Hustler* together sell fifteen million copies a month. According to *Folio*, a magazine for professionals in magazine management, United States magazines with the greatest overseas newsstand dollar sales were (1) *Playboy* with well over ten million dollars in foreign newsstand sales; (2) *Penthouse* with well over nine million dollars in foreign newsstand sales; (3) *Oui*; (4) *Gallery*, owned by F. Lee Bailey who surprisingly could not convince a jury that Patricia Hearst had been raped; (5) *Scientific American*; and (6) *Hustler*. Also in the top ten are *Vogue*, which consistently publishes the work of S and M photographer Helmut Newton, and *Easy Riders*, a motorcycle, gang-bang, fuck-the-bitch-with-your-Iron-Cross kind of magazine. This was as of October 1980. According to *Mother Jones* magazine, also in 1980, there are three to four times as many adult bookstores in the United States as there are McDonald's Restaurants. And the live exhibition of women displaying genitals or being used in sex of various descriptions or being tied and whipped is increasing. And there is cable television and the home video market, both potentially huge and currently expanding markets for pornographers who use live women. Women. Real women. Live women. Chattel whores.

Now, some people are afraid that the world will be turned into a nuclear charnel house; and so they fight the nuclear industries and lobbies; and they do not spend significant amounts of their time debating whether the nuclear industries have the right to threaten human life or not. Some people fear that the world is turning, place by place, into a concentration camp; and so they fight for those who are hounded, persecuted, tortured, and they do not suggest that the rights of those who persecute supersede the rights of the persecuted in importance—unless, of course, the persecuted are only women and the torture is called "sex." Some feminists see the world turning into a whorehouse—how frivolous we always are—a whorehouse, in French *maison d'abattage*, which literally means "house of slaughter." Whorehouses have been concentration camps for women. Women have been kept in them like caged animals to do slave labor, sex labor, labor appropriate to the nature, function, and sexuality of the chattel whore and her kind. The spread of pornography that uses live women, real women, is the spread of the whorehouse, the concentration camp for women, the house of sexual slaughter. Now I ask you: what are we going to do?

Women Lawyers and Pornography
1980

This speech was given at a conference of women law students and lawyers held at Yale University Law School in March 1980. In it I discuss throat rape briefly, for the first time. Gloria Steinem and I each had independent sources that had seen women dead in hospital emergency rooms from this kind of rape. They would not come forward. I agonized about whether to talk about throat rape at all. Gloria had written an article that said women were being raped this way, but it hadn't been published yet. I did say it, citing it to Gloria's forthcoming article. I can't tell you how horrible it was—the night before—to try to figure out whether in discussing this new rape one somehow had a role in spreading it. One has to tell women. Otherwise only the rapists know about it. But in an exploitative society, to bring a new form of rape into the spotlight is a sickening responsibility. I had been raped this way, and so I felt especially responsible and especially sick. This piece has never been published before.

I AM HONORED to have been invited here today, but I must tell you that it is strange for me to be speaking at Yale Law School to lawyers. I once wanted to be a lawyer, but, fortunately or unfortunately, became a criminal first—when I was eighteen, in a demonstration against the Viet Nam War. My visions of myself as Clarence Darrow or Perry Mason were supplanted by the reality of being brutalized in jail and in court both. For a long time after that experience, it did not seem possible to me that one could be a lawyer (for either side) and a decent human being also. The invention of the feminist lawyer in the last several years has changed my mind—a little.

I have to start out by telling you frankly that I cannot speak to you as a lawyer might on any of the issues involved in the discussion of pornography. I am mostly a self-educated writer, a resolute street activist, someone who is both contemptuous of the law and afraid of it. Nothing in my own experiences—with male lawyers of the Left, for instance—has made me either less contemptuous or less afraid.

The ways in which feminists have learned to use the law—to fight for economic dignity, to fight for reproductive freedom, to fight against sexual harassment, to initiate some reforms with respect to rape, to fight for the protection of battered women—have very much earned my respect. But the real progress of women has been minuscule; and the legal system in which feminists struggle for change is still rotten to the core. The law was built on the subjection of women, and that subjection is unendingly perpetuated in both the application and the spirit of the law, with the result that feminist lawyers and legal workers spill blood for rewards that are both too little and too late.

And yet, the survival of women day to day and year to year depends on these small advances, these victories that, however big, are never big enough. Without them, we would have no hope, no future, and a present impossible to endure. Whenever you secure for any woman—be she prostitute, wife, lesbian, or all of those and more—one shred of real justice, you have given her and the rest of us a little more time, a little more dignity: and time and dignity give us the chance to organize, to speak out, to fight back.

But without basic structural changes in this society—changes that would radically transform this system of law—you cannot do more than rescue some of us momentarily from the assaults that constitute a female life—the petty assaults and the grand assaults, the bone-breaking assaults and the mind-destroying assaults. Temporary rescue will not stop the rape, the battery, the sexual harassment, the economic indignities, the tyranny of male or state control of reproduction. Temporary rescue will not stop the violence. Temporary rescue will not protect women from tomorrow.

If we begin—as I think we must—with the premise that each and every woman has an absolute right to sexual and reproductive self-determination, then we have begun outside the law: outside its intention, its purpose, its practice, and its effect. We do not begin outside the law in the Nietzschean sense of being above and beyond the law, superior to it because we are great and the law is pitiful. We begin outside the law because we are below the law, despised by it, denied by it, condemned by it to sexual, reproductive, and economic servility. We are outside the law because we are pitiful and the law is great.

No issue concerning women can be discussed *as if* women had contributed to the development of the law as an institution, to the enforcement of the law, to the interpretation of the law, or to the ethics of the law. No issue concerning women can be discussed *as if* the law worked in the interests of women—in behalf of our rights. No issue concerning women can be discussed *as if* women were truly participants in culture, in power, in the creation of values. No issue concerning women can be discussed *as if* women were sexually self-determining or intellectually self-respecting or economically self-sustaining. Certainly, the issue of pornography cannot be discussed *as if* women had basic human rights of bodily integrity or inviolability, or freedom of movement or speech, or even simple, prosaic equality before the law. Pornography originates in a real social system in which women are sexually colonialized and have been for hundreds of centuries. Pornography—whether as genre or as industry or as aid to masturbation—originates in that system, flourishes in that system, and has no meaning or existence outside that system. Pornography is inseparable from the undeniable brutality of commonplace male usage of the female.

The word *pornography* means "the graphic depiction of whores." Whores exist to serve men sexually. Whores exist only within a framework of male sexual domination. Indeed, outside that framework the notion of whores would be absurd. The word *whore* is incomprehensible unless one is immersed, as we all are, in the lexicon of male domination. Men have created the group, the type, the concept, the epithet, the insult, the industry, the trade, the commodity, the reality of woman as whore. But even the word *whore* does not convey the whole spirit of this valuation of women because we commonly use it as a synonym for the word *prostitute*, the woman who is paid to serve men sexually. The word that really connotes the pornographic ethos is *slut*. The idea at the base of all pornography is that women are insatiable sluts who crave abuse. In pornography—if you can believe it—even prostitutes are sluts.

The basic action of pornography is rape: rape of the vagina, rape of the rectum, and now, after the phenomenal success of *Deep Throat*, rape of the throat. Yes, the throat. According to Gloria Steinem in the May issue of *Ms.* magazine, some emergency room doctors believe that real victims of suffocation from rape of the throat may be on the increase. Did women die from throat rape before *Deep Throat*? I do not know. With the popularity of throat rape in current pornography, will the number of deaths from it increase? I think so.

Here is a typical passage from a pornographic novel (so-called) that celebrates rape of the throat. In this scene, the woman is on her knees with the Super Stud Hero's cock in her mouth. He has a gun pointed at her head.

He could kill me with [his cock], she thought. He didn't need a gun in his hand.

As his hot organ filled her mouth and throat, Sandy felt him beginning to thrust his hips forward. The shiny cockhead crammed into the back of her throat. She tried to take as much of his cock into her mouth as possible, but it filled her throat so full that she couldn't [sic] at first get it down. She swallowed and swallowed at each of his forward thrusts, but her throat wouldn't stretch large enough to accommodate him. It wasn't until he grabbed her hair with his left fist and held her head against the force of his tool that she was able to relax her throat muscles enough that his cock raped its way over her tongue and throat and buried itself in the passage to her stomach.

Pain seared through her throat like she had swallowed a hot branding iron as her throat stretched to its maximum capacity. At first she thought she would be unable to breathe as his erection pumped lustfully and lewdly in and out of her mouth, but as she relaxed her throat more and more, she discovered that she could suck in air during his out strokes and be set to enjoy his painfully delicious forward thrusts. She nursed greedily at his body. (*The Ravished Girlfriend*, pp. 60–61)

Note that the female quickly learns to love what is done to her: in fact, she becomes greedy. This theme is important. In pornography, a woman is forced, she is horribly hurt; and the greater the force and the more terrible the pain, the greater is her sexual desire and gratification. She becomes greedy for more pain, more force, more abuse, because that is her true nature. Any behavior or attitude on her part that is not greed for pain and force is presented as pretense or sexual ignorance.

Neil Malamuth and James Check, two psychologists at the University of Manitoba in Canada, have isolated what they call "the belief in victim pleasure" as an essential factor in the arousal of the male. ("Penile Tumescence and Perceptual Responses to Rape as a Function of Victim's Perceived Reactions," June 1979, p. 21. Manuscript.) Their study is but one of a host of new and conscientious studies that *do* demonstrate a significant connection between exposure to pornography and aggression against women. According to Malamuth and Check, "[the male] subjects were considerably more sexually aroused to a rape depiction in which the victim was perceived by the rapist to become involuntarily sexually aroused than when she continuously abhorred the assault." (pp. 20–21) Also, men who believed in victim pleasure were more likely to want to rape, to report that they would rape if they could be certain of not being caught or punished. Malamuth and Check point out that this information is especially significant because numerous studies have shown that many actual rapists believe that their victims did experience pleasure no matter how badly they were hurt.

In all pornography, the "belief in victim pleasure" is fundamental and overwhelming. Pornography effectively encourages and promotes rape by encouraging and promoting this belief, this lie, about the pleasure of the victim in being forced and hurt. The pin-ups are foreplay; they show the woman with the open invitation. The rest of pornography shows what she invites: bondage, pain, and acts of forced sex inseparable from acts of extreme brutality. Now pornography shows women loving and adoring throat rape; now increasing numbers of real women may be dying from it.

Women mistakenly think that pornography is largely built on the good girl/bad girl or the Madonna/whore theme. With rare exceptions, it is not. It is built on the whore/whore theme. No posturing of the female ultimately contradicts her greedy desire to be used and hurt. The sexual insatiability of the female means that she cannot really be abused, no matter what is done to or with her. Abuse means the misuse of someone. The abused person is credited with having a will, an ethic, or rights that have been violated. The female cannot be abused so long as the use made of her is sexual within the male value system, because her purpose on this earth is to be used sexually and her fundamental nature as defined by men requires rape, bondage, and pain. This sexual insatiability also means that the male must use, and is always justified in using, any form of domination in order to control the female. Otherwise her sexuality will devour him.

There is pornography in which the woman is sadistic. This type of pornography illustrates for men the consequences of losing control over women. In such pornography, a male falls prey to a sadistic woman—who has whip in hand and spiked heels planted firmly in his scrotum—because of a failure of masculinity on his part. The text often suggests that perhaps he is a faggot, or, even worse, that in a weak moment he has simply failed to be cruel enough. Such a failure makes him vulnerable in the literal sense of the word, meaning subject to assault. The sadistic woman punishes him for not being sufficiently male. In the end, a really masculine man inevitably manages to rape and beat the heretofore uppity woman, and he does so with such stunning brutality that she finally learns her proper place. The sadistic woman is often labeled a feminist, an Amazon, or a Women's Libber. She, too, in the end, loves being raped and humiliated and hurt. The independent woman, the feminist woman, the professional woman, and, of course, the lesbian woman, are all shown to be shrews who are truly happy only in captivity and who are sexually fulfilled only through force, pain, and unrelenting penile penetration.

Which brings me, rather reluctantly, to the politics of the penis. Women cannot discuss pornography *as if* we are all just plain folks, *as if* a sex caste system based on the centrality and superiority of the penis did not exist.

In pornography, the penis is characterized as a weapon: sword, knife, scissor, gun, pistol, rifle, tank, various instruments of torture, steel rod, cattle prod; and all these weapons are used in place of the penis or in conjunction with the penis. Anything is used as a penile weapon that can be used, including telephones, pistol hair dryers, bottles, dildos, live snakes, and so forth. The woman's sex organs are characterized as dirty and smelly and treacherous, which apparently justifies the disgust and contempt implicit in ramming all these things into her. While male poets and psychologists obsessively conjure up a sentimental return to the womb, men's pornography suggests a military assault, the worst excesses of police brutality, or the kind of annihilation associated with racist and imperialist programs of extermination.

Men, not feminists, have assigned this value to the penis. They control the language and the pornography, and this valuation of the penis is evident in every area of male culture, not only in pornography. In the commonplace vocabulary of both romance and sex, conquest and possession are central. The penis conquers and possesses; the penis distinguishes the male conqueror from the female conquered.

Pornography does not exist to effect something as vague as so-called erotic interest or sexual arousal; it exists specifically to provoke penile tumescence or erection. In male-supremacist culture and in male-supremacist sexuality, the penis is a carrier of aggression, a weapon, the standard-bearer of male identity, the proof and the measure of masculinity.

The use of the penis to conquer is its normal use. In the male system, rape is a matter of degree. The wise men of the culture posit that the male, properly developed, is essentially sadistic in his sexuality, the female masochistic in hers. So-called normal sex occurs when the normal sexual aggression of the male meets the normal masochism of the female *not* in an alley. Male conquest of the female is construed to be normal and properly commonplace. In this context, pornography does not express a deviant value system. On the contrary, it both expresses and promotes the values and ethics of male supremacy—that system based on the primacy of the imperial penis. The penis in pornography is the penis in rape is the penis in sex is the penis in history.

Women cannot discuss pornography *as if* the photographs of female genitalia exist for some other purpose than to enable men to experience the power of the penis. Women cannot discuss pornography *as if* antagonism, hostility, aggression, and a conviction of superiority were absent from the penile power experienced by men on viewing depictions of female genitalia. Women cannot discuss pornography *as if* the penile power experienced by men on viewing depictions of women splayed, tied up, being fucked, being hurt, meant nothing. Women cannot discuss pornography *as if* it existed apart from male supremacy, in which the penis is the determinant of superiority. Women cannot discuss pornography *as if* it existed apart

241

from the sexual colonization of the female, in which the penis is the primary instrument of conquest and aggression. Women cannot discuss pornography *as if* the penis were not still being used on a massive scale as a weapon against women.

For centuries women as a class have remained basically unresponsive to the penis as a purveyor of sexual pleasure. Those unpoliticized women—more often called frigid or prudes—you know the litany of epithets—understand that the issue is not their pleasure but their conquest. He takes her; he takes a wife.

I said that I was somewhat reluctant to address this issue at all. It is not an easy thing to do. Feminists have been vilified for introducing the subject of the penis as a necessary political issue. An example of the kind of insult that greets our raising of this issue is this unsigned passage from the March *Playboy*—you know *Playboy*, that pro-woman, pro-feminist magazine:

> For the past decade, the penis has been getting a lot of bad press. One feminist wrote derisively: "We can stimulate ourselves or be stimulated by other women as well as men can stimulate us, because that unique male offering, the phallus, is of peripheral importance, or may even be irrelevant to our sexual satisfaction." Well, sit on my face, bitch. (*Playboy*, "Books," vol. 27, no. 3, March 1980, p. 41)

I also call your attention to *Playboy*'s statement on freedom of speech in the same issue. A man asks the *Playboy* "Advisor":

> I have sex with my girlfriend often and we both enjoy it. However, something is missing. I want her to talk dirty. I want her to say things like: "I want to feel your giant cock in my pussy!" or "Cram your prick in and screw me!" We love each other very much and I've tried talking to her. I know she would do it if she could, and she wants to talk dirty, but when she tries, nothing comes out of her mouth and she gets upset with herself. What can we do?

Playboy's answer is this:

> Obviously, your girlfriend thinks that love means never having to say "Cram your prick in and screw me!" She should be reminded of her civic duty. The First Amendment guarantees freedom of expression—verbal, if not physical. (We have a hard time separating the two.) ("The Playboy Advisor," *Playboy*, vol. 27, no. 3, March 1980, p. 51)

These two passages from *Playboy*—"Well, sit on my face, bitch" and "Cram your prick in and screw me!"—provide an anatomy of the situation. The coercion of the female is centered on getting her to have phallocentric sex. Feminists challenge the politics, the ethics, even the efficacy of this sexual institution, and the answer is "Well, sit on my face, bitch." In this same value system, the First Amendment means that the woman, any woman, had better be prepared to say whatever the male wants to hear, especially that which enables him to heighten his sense of penile power. And most important, *his* First Amendment means that his right to determine her verbal expression is inseparable from his right to determine her physical expression.

As might be expected, pornographers also manipulate the image of the feminist: she is the sadistic woman who must be tamed, the expendable woman who can be viciously insulted even as the men's magazine professes its advocacy of women's rights, the vicious prude who is castrating in her hatred of men and sex. She is also, by implication, the lesbian woman who arrogantly believes that sexual gratification does not depend on the penis. In pornography, women have sex together to excite and please the male. Forcing women to have sex together is one means of humiliating women. The real lesbian, who has sex with women without reference to the male or to the penis, is viewed by the pornographers as an implacable enemy.

The goal of pornography, finally, is to uphold and strengthen male sexual prerogatives; to perpetuate and energize male sexual values and practices based on the supremacy of the penis, based on sexualized aggression and hostility to the female.

What we learn from pornography is that this is the very value system we must destroy if we are to be free. And as the *Playboy* advisor makes clear, women will never have freedom of physical or verbal expression so long as love or sex means having to say "Cram your prick in and screw me!" We will never have freedom of speech so long as it means having to say "Cram your prick in and screw me!" Right now, "Cram your prick in and screw me!" represents the summit of sexual and verbal freedom for women. Feminists are the dissenters from this male-supremacist value system. We are the ones with different ideas, political ideas, subversive ideas. Yet the energy of the civil liberties lawyers as well as the pornographers in these last few years has gone into shutting us up. Their argument is that when we address male sexual hegemony as expressed in and perpetuated by pornography—whether we do it through speaking or demonstrating or writing—we are endangering the speech of others. Their suggested solution is that we shut up. But our survival depends on untangling this knot of forced sex, of male pleasure, of rape as entertainment and delight, of sex as hostility, of abuse as normalcy. The necessity is to end the sexual colonialization of women.

Now I come back to the fact that you are lawyers and legal workers. What can you do?

First, every single victory gained for women in the areas of rape, battery, sexual harassment, lesbian rights, and reproductive rights works to establish some expression of female sexual integrity. Every single advance in these areas works to lessen the power of pornographers, who thrive in an environment where the sexual victimization of women is commonplace and utterly mainstream.

Second, every legal victory that results in the economic empowerment of women also diminishes the sexual stranglehold that men have on women. Economic dependence on men means sexual exploitation by men. Economic empowerment means that women do not have to barter in sex. Economic empowerment would mean that poor and desperate women would not be forced to turn to the pornographers for work.

Third, women must gain real access to the media in this country, to communication, to the *means* of speech. We do not have a cultural dialogue on sexual or social values: we have a perpetual male monologue. The very existence of pornography derives from the male monopoly on speech: the centuries-old monopoly on literature, philosophy, science, social science, the unmitigated male control of ideas and of sexual ideology. Pornography as such could not exist in an egalitarian society; it would not have developed as a quasi-sexual institution if women had been real participants in the formulation of values, if women had had the power to express ideas. Every area of culture and communication is male-dominated and male-controlled. Make no mistake: power and wealth are required to exercise freedom of speech. In simpler days, before films and television and multinational communications networks, women were kept illiterate. Women are still three-quarters of the world's illiterates. But women are also silenced by being kept poor and being kept out. The pornographers thrive on female intellectual and creative silence and insignificance. To fight the influence and to challenge the very existence of the pornographers, you must find ways to destroy the male monopoly on communications media.

Fourth, in the next several years, feminist activists will be on the streets demonstrating against pornographers. Unaccountably, there will be widespread vandalism against pornography—against displays of pornography and at points of distribution. Defend these activists.

Fifth, in the next several years, feminist writers and activists are likely to experience severe police harassment— conspiracy charges, police brutality, and the like. The police do not go after pornographers when it is women who are protesting; they go after the women. Defend the women.

Sixth, speak out. Do not be silent or passive on the issue of pornography. Confront, challenge. If necessary walk out of forums in which you are insulted or threatened or treated like dirt. Especially do not allow your male peers in your profession to define the issues for you, to browbeat you, to talk you down, to treat you as if you are stupid because you refuse to accept the depiction of sexual violence against women as cute or meaningless or exciting or necessary. Keep track of the relationship of your male colleagues to cases of rape and battery in particular: do they understand the crimes? do they abuse the victims to defend the criminals? do they systematically defend accused rapists whom they know to be guilty? are they active, not passive, in using their resources and talents in the interests of women or do they systematically make sure to be on the other side? Do not allow these issues to go undiscussed or undefined. In your own work for women, dare to take cases that make your male colleagues sick to death.

Seventh, defend prostitutes, but do not allow yourself to be used to defend prostitution as an inevitable social institution, one that must exist in perpetuity because, after all, that's how people are, especially that's how women are.

Eighth, do not take money from the Playboy Foundation. *Playboy* magazine has launched one of the most sophisticated antifeminist campaigns ever devised. Each monthly issue mounts a new attack on feminists who challenge the sexual supremacy of the male. The

Playboy Foundation hands out pimp's money. Pimps do not give away anything out of the goodness of their hearts. The Playboy empire is raw male power, pimp power. Other feminists will pay for what you take.

Ninth, in the next decade, along with the rapid spread of pornography, violence against women will increase. Do not allow those who commit or endorse that violence to get away with it—be they individuals, organized crime, police, or lawyers.

Tenth, if a way does not exist, invent one.

As lawyers, perhaps right now you cannot do more. But you are also, after all, women. I hope to see you out on the streets getting your asses busted with the rest of us.

Silence Means Dissent

1984

This was a speech, given in Toronto at a symposium on pornography and media violence. The audience was mostly right-wing. The speakers were almost all experimental researchers who had studied the relationship between pornography and violence against women: all were persuaded that there was one. I am happy to say that the audience responded with a very long, loud, standing ovation. I believe that this speech was a breakthrough in reaching right-wing women. Healthsharing, a Canadian feminist magazine, published it; 60 Minutes (CBS) broadcast some short excerpts from it. Shortly before speaking, I had seen, for the first time, one of Hustler's *sexually explicit cartoons of me projected on a big screen in front of the 800 people in the auditorium. It was an exhibit in a slide show by a woman researcher whose purpose was not to hurt me but to show what pornographers do to women. I got through the speech; I managed to get off the stage, just, before becoming unconscious. There was nothing left, no light or sound or hope, nothing. Many minutes are blanked out. I have never gotten them back. A cartoon like that says, bang, you're dead, and one way or another you are, a little.*

As A FEMINIST I have been organizing against pornography for a long time. I am very grateful to the research community, which has taken feminist theory seriously enough to try to see if in fact pornography does harm to women. I say that because I am entirely outraged that someone has to study whether hanging a woman from a meat hook causes harm or not. We are grateful to the research community out of our despair and our devastation, because mostly we are silent, and because when we speak up, nobody listens. We know how to quantify, we know how to count, we can show you the dead; yet it doesn't matter if it comes from us. Objectivity, as I understand it, means that it doesn't happen to you.

There are women researchers who are trying very hard to bring what they know as women into their research. There are male researchers who have paid attention to what we have said. I am not dismissing them, but I am saying that we are living in a society where you can maim and kill a woman, and there is a question as to whether or not there is a social harm. Somebody has to study it to find out.

We know that men like hurting us. We know it because they do it and we watch them liking it. We know that men like dominating us because they do it and we watch them enjoying it. We know that men like using us because they do it, and they do it, and they do it, and they do it, and they do it. And men don't do things that they don't like, generally speaking. They like doing it and they like watching it and they like watching other men do it and it is entertainment and men pay money to see it and that is one of the reasons that men make pornography. It's *fun*.

Now, what we know is—the "we" being women—that there are people that it is fun for, and there are people that it is not fun for, and that women are the people it is not fun for.

Pornography is the sexualized subordination of women. It means being put down through sex, by sex, in sex, and around sex, so that somebody can use you as sex and have sex and have a good time. And subordination consists of a hierarchy that means one person is on the top and one person is on the bottom. And while hierarchy has been described in beautiful ideological terms over thousands and thousands of years, for us it is not an abstract idea because we know who is on top. We usually know his name and address. Often we do. So we understand hierarchy, and this is a hierarchy that has men on the top and women on the bottom.

Subordination also consists of objectification. Objectification is when a human being is turned into a thing, a commodity, an object—someone who is no longer a human being. They're used, because they're not human like the other people around; and that frequently happens on the basis of their race or it happens on the basis of their sex. It happens to women on the basis of both.

And subordination also consists of violence, overt violence—and it's not just violence against people. It's violence against women. It's violence against children who are very closely connected to women in powerlessness. It's violence that isn't such a mystery. Crazy maniacs don't do it. People who have power over other people do it. Men do it to women.

Now, if you take hierarchy and if you take sex and if you understand that hierarchy is very sexy, then what you have is a situation in which people are exploited systematically; and they are exploited in such a way that everyone thinks it's normal. The people who are doing it think it's normal. The people to whom it's done think it's normal. The people who report about it think it's normal. The people who study it think it's normal. And it is normal. That's the thing about it—it's actually normal. It doesn't make a difference if it happens in private or if it happens in public, because women are primarily hurt in private. Now that pornography is out in the world, where it is an officially established form of public terrorism against women, we think we are dealing with something that is qualitatively different from anything we have ever dealt with before. This is, in fact, not true, because the pornography gets acted out on women whether women see the pornography or not. This is because men use the pornography when it's criminal, when it's illegal—they still have access to it, they still use it, and it still has all the consequences that you heard about today and those consequences are acted out on the bodies of women.

I want to talk about social subordination, because women are not equal in this society and one of the ways that you can tell is the quality of our silence. The Three Marias of Portugal said (and they were put in jail for saying this) silence does not mean consent: silence means dissent. Women are the population that dissents most, through silence. The so-called speech of women in pornography is silence. Splayed legs on a page are silence. Being beaver, pussy, cunt, bunnies, pets, whatever, that is silence. The words that women say in pornography: that is silence. "Give it to me," "do it to me," "hurt me," "I want it bad," "do it more": that is silence. And those who think that is speech have never heard a woman's voice. I want to tell you that even those screams, even the screams of women tortured in pornography, are silence. Men pay money and watch, but no one hears a *human* scream. They hear silence. And that's what it means to be born female. No one hears you scream as if you are a human being.

Catharine MacKinnon and I wrote a civil rights bill that makes pornography a form of discrimination based on sex and a violation of the civil rights of women. We hallucinated those rights in a frenzy of hope, in a delirium of dreaming. We hallucinated that women could be recognized as human beings in this social system. Human enough even to have civil rights. Human enough to be able to assert those rights in the face of systematic sexual exploitation, brutality and malice.

So human, in fact, that one would not have to study it to see if any harm is done when a woman is tortured. So human that no one would have to study it to see if harm is done by long-term pervasive systematic exploitation, dehumanization, objectification. So human that one could actually assume as a premise throughout life—not just today but seven days a week all year long, forever—that when a woman is being tortured, or even only exploited or even only used and used up, that a human being is being tortured, exploited, used and used up, and that that constitutes harm to a human being. You don't have to study it. It's happening to a human being so it constitutes harm to a human being.

We dreamed that women might be taken to be so extremely human that one would know, even without laboratory evidence, that when a woman is diminished in her integrity, in her rights, humankind is diminished because of it. And we thought that it might even be possible that a woman could be so human that even the law, which is not big on recognizing human beings, might recognize her as being human enough to deserve equal protection under the law. Just that human, not a smidgen more, just that.

That's not even equality; that's not as human as men, not really, not entirely. That's not asking for much, is it? So human that when the pimps, the parasites sell her and coerce her and rape her and destroy her and abuse her and insult her—so that men can be entertained by her exploitation and abuse—that those pimps and those users will have to face her in court for violating her human rights because she is a human being.

Pornography is at the heart of male supremacy and that is true whether the pornography is in public or in private. When you see pornography, you see male supremacy; and if you look around you and you see male supremacy, you had better believe that you're seeing pornography even if you don't know where it is in the room. The goal of feminists who are fighting pornography is to end the hierarchy, the objectification, the exploitation: the dominance of men over women and children.

And we *are* going to do it. I want to tell you this: if you love male supremacy but you abhor pornography, then you do not abhor pornography enough to do anything about it. Some people don't want pornography to be seen in public because it shows some very true things about what men want from women; for instance: dominance, power over women, women's inequality, the use of women as sexual objects. It also shows what men do not want women to have: humanity, integrity, self-determination and complete and total control over our own bodies. We need these so we are not used, so that we are not forced into sex, forced into pregnancy, forced into any sexual relationship that is not our choice.*

It's important to understand that the feminist movement against pornography is a grassroots movement against male supremacy. We are going to settle for nothing less than full social and sexual equality of the sexes. We are going to get whatever institutional changes have to be made to accomplish that. We are going to get self-determination for women. We're even going to get something that people call justice.

I am wondering, and I think it is worth thinking about, what justice would look like for the raped and the prostituted, and I would like to know how afraid men really are of what that justice would look like. For instance, would it look like *Snuff*? Would it look like *Deep Throat*? It might. Study that.

We are going to stop the pornography in the shops and in our lives, when it's written down and when it's acted out, and we're going to do it one way or another. Before I came here on Thursday night, another victim story reached me—another one in twelve years of listening to women who have been hurt by pornography—from a woman who had been tied up, raped, photographed. The man had made hundreds of pictures of her, he had made hundreds of pictures of other women, he had a list of names of the other women he was going to assault.

---

* Feminists took over the stage at the conference to demonstrate for reproductive rights and lesbian rights, the denial of those rights being (in common with pornography) sexual colonization.

She went to the police; they didn't do anything. She went to some people who knew the man; they didn't do anything. Nothing, nothing, nothing. That is typical. What he said to her when he tied her up, after having raped her and having started photographing her was, "Smile or I'll kill you. I can get lots of money for pictures of women who smile when they're tied up like you."

I want you to think about the way women smile. I want you to think about it every minute of every day, and I want to suggest to the men in this audience, in particular, that you had better be afraid of women who learn to smile at you that way.

Against the Male Flood: Censorship, Pornography, and Equality

1985

Early in 1984, I was asked to write an essay on the civil rights law recognizing pornography as sex discrimination that Catharine A. MacKinnon and I had conceived and the Minneapolis City Council had passed on December 30, 1983. A chief-editor, a student (all law school reviews are edited by students), went to considerable effort to persuade me to do this, especially promising no interference, his quid pro quo for no money and a tiny circulation. I worked for many months on my essay and then the boy-editor, who had lost his manners in the interim, refused to publish it unless I took out points, themes, connections, insights, sentences, and paragraphs. I had a screaming fight with this boy in his early twenties who told me what I could and couldn't say as a writer. I refused to change it; he refused to publish it. Women law students at Harvard took pity on me, and this essay was published in the Harvard Women's Law Journal late spring 1985. They were pretty intrusive too. I made changes I regret. Why did I have to run this gauntlet to get this essay into print? Misogyny, stupidity, and the arrogance of children aside, this editing business has gotten out of hand; it has become police work for liberals.

To say what one thought—that was my little problem—against the prodigious Current; to find a sentence that could hold its own against the male flood.

Virginia Woolf

I want to say right here, that those well-meaning friends on the outside who say that we have suffered these horrors of prison, of hunger strikes

253

and forcible feeding, because we desired to martyrise ourselves for the cause, are absolutely and entirely mistaken. We never went to prison in order to be martyrs. We went there in order that we might obtain the rights of citizenship. We were willing to break laws that we might force men to give us the right to make laws.

Emmeline Pankhurst

1. Censorship

CENSORSHIP IS A real thing, not an abstract idea or a word that can be used to mean anything at all.

In ancient Rome, a censor was a magistrate who took the census (a count of the male population and an evaluation of property for the purpose of taxation done every fifth year), assessed taxes, and inspected morals and conduct. His power over conduct came from his power to tax. For instance, in 403 BC, the censors Camillus and Postimius heavily fined elderly bachelors for not marrying. The power to tax, then as now, was the power to destroy. The censor, using the police and judicial powers of the state, regulated social behavior.

At its origins, then, censorship had nothing to do with striking down ideas as such; it had to do with acts. In my view, real state censorship still does. In South Africa and the Soviet Union, for instance, writing is treated entirely as an act, and writers are viewed as persons who engage in an act (writing) that by its very nature is dangerous to the continued existence of the state. The police in these countries do not try to suppress ideas. They are more specific, more concrete, more realistic. They go after books and manuscripts (writing) and destroy them. They go after writers as persons who have done something that they will do again and they persecute, punish, or kill them. They do not worry about what people think—not, at least, as we use the word *think*: a mental event, entirely internal, abstract. They worry about what people do: and writing, speaking, even as evidence that thinking is going on, are seen as things people *do*. There is a quality of immediacy and reality in what writing is taken to be. Where police power is used against writers systematically, writers are seen as people who by writing do something socially real and significant, not contemplative or dithering. Therefore, writing is never peripheral or beside the point.

It is serious and easily seditious. I am offering no brief for police states when I say that virtually all great writers, crossculturally and transhistorically, share this view of what writing is. In countries like ours, controlled by a bourgeoisie to whom the police are accountable, writing is easier to do and valued less. It has less impact. It is more abundant and cheaper. Less is at stake for reader and writer both. The writer may hold writing to be a life-or-death matter, but the police and society do not. Writing is seen to be a personal choice, not a social, political, or esthetic necessity fraught with danger and meaning. The general view in these pleasant places* is that writers think up ideas or words and then other people read them and all this happens in the head, a vast cavern somewhere north of the eyes. It is all air, except for the paper and ink, which are simply banal. Nothing happens.

Police in police states and most great writers throughout time see writing as act, not air—as act, not idea; concrete, specific, real, not insubstantial blather on a dead page. Censorship goes after the act and the actor: the book and the writer. It needs to destroy both. The cost in human lives is staggering, and it is perhaps essential to say that human lives destroyed must count more in the weighing of horror than books burned. This is my personal view, and I love books more than I love people.

Censorship is deeply misunderstood in the United States, because the fairly spoiled, privileged, frivolous people who are the literate citizens of this country think that censorship is some foggy effort to suppress ideas. For them, censorship is not something in itself—an act of police power with discernible consequences to hunted people; instead, it is about something abstract—the suppressing or controlling of ideas. Censorship, like writing itself, is no longer an act. Because it is no longer the blatant exercise of police power against writers and books because of what they do, what they accomplish in the real world, it becomes vague, hard to find, except perhaps as an attitude. It gets used to mean unpleasant, even angry frowns of

---

* "Well, you know, it amazes me...," says dissident South African writer Nadine Gordimer in an interview. "I come to America, I go to England, I go to France... nobody's at risk. They're afraid of getting cancer, losing a lover, losing their jobs, being insecure.... It's only in my own country that I find people who voluntarily choose to put everything at risk—in their personal life." Nadine Gordimer, *Writers at Work*, Sixth Series, edited by George Plimpton (New York: Viking Penguin Inc., 1984), p. 261.

disapproval or critiques delivered in harsh tones; it means social disapproval or small retaliations by outraged citizens where the book is still available and the writer is entirely unharmed, even if insulted. It hangs in the air, ominous, like the threat of drizzle. It gets to be, in silly countries like this one, whatever people say it is, separate from any material definition, separate from police power, separate from state repression (jail, banning, exile, death), separate from devastating consequences to real people (jail, banning, exile, death). It is something that people who eat fine food and wear fine clothes worry about frenetically, trying to find it, anticipating it with great anxiety, arguing it down as if—if it were real—an argument would make it go away; not knowing that it has a clear, simple, unavoidable momentum and meaning in a cruel world of police power that their privilege cannot comprehend.

2.   Obscenity

In the nineteenth and twentieth centuries, in most of Western Europe, England, and the United States, more often than not (time-out for Franco, for instance), writing has been most consistently viewed as an act warranting prosecution when the writing is construed to be obscene.

The republics, democracies, and constitutional monarchies of the West, now and then, do not smother writers in police violence; they prefer to pick off writers who annoy and irritate selectively with fairly token prosecutions. The list of writers so harassed is elegant, white, male (therefore the pronoun "he" is used throughout this discussion), and remarkably small. Being among them is more than a ceremonial honor. As Flaubert wrote his brother in 1857: "My persecution has brought me widespread sympathy. If my book is bad, that will serve to make it seem better. If, on the other hand, it has lasting qualities, that will build a foundation for it. There you are! I am hourly awaiting the official document which will name the day when I am to take my seat (for the crime of having written in French) in the dock in the company of thieves and homosexuals."[1] A few months later that same year, Baudelaire was fined 300 francs for publishing six obscene poems. They also had to be removed from future editions of his book. In harder, earlier days, Jean-Jacques Rousseau spent eight years as a fugitive after his *Émile* was banned and a warrant was issued for his arrest. English censors criminally prosecuted Swinburne's *Poems and Ballads* in 1866. They were particularly piqued at Zola, even in translation, so his English publisher, seventy years old, went to jail for three months. In 1898, a bookseller was arrested for selling Havelock Ellis' work and received a suspended sentence. This list is representative, not exhaustive. While prosecutions of writers under obscenity laws have created great difficulties for writers already plagued with them (as most writers are), criminal prosecutions under obscenity law in Europe and the United States are notable for how narrowly they reach writers, how sanguine writers tend to be about the consequences to themselves, and how little is paid in the writer's lifeblood to what D. H. Lawrence (who paid more than most modern Western writers) called "the censor-moron."[2] In South Africa, one would hardly be so flip. In our world, the writer gets harassed, as Lawrence did; the writer may be poor or not—the injury is considerably worse if he is; but the writer is not terrorized or tortured, and writers do not live under a reign of terror as writers, because of what they *do*. The potshot application of criminal law for writing is not good, nice, or right; but it is important to recognize the relatively narrow scope and marginal character of criminal prosecution under obscenity law in particular—especially compared with the scope and character of police-state censorship. Resisting obscenity law does not require hyperbolic renderings of what it is and how it has been used. It can be fought or repudiated on its own terms.

The use of obscenity laws against writers, however haphazard or insistent, is censorship and it does hold writing to be an act. This is a unique perception of what writing is, taking place, as it does, in a liberal context in which writing is held to be ideas. It is the obscene quality of the writing, the obscenity itself, that is seen to turn writing from idea into act. Writing of any kind or quality is idea, except for obscene writing, which is act. Writing is censored, even in our own happy little land of Oz, as act, not idea.

What is obscenity, such that it turns writing, when obscene, into something that actually happens—changes it from internal wind somewhere in the elevated mind into a genuinely offensive and utterly real fart, noticed, rude, occasioning pinched fingers on the nose?

There is the legal answer and the artistic answer. Artists have been consistently pushing on the boundaries of obscenity because great writers see writing as an act, and in liberal culture only obscene writing has that social standing, that quality of dynamism and heroism. Great writers tend to experience writing as an intense and disruptive act; in the West, it is only recognized as such when the writing itself is experienced as obscene. In liberal culture, the writer has needed obscenity to be perceived as socially real.

What is it that obscenity does? The writer uses what the society deems to be obscene because the society then reacts to the writing the way the writer values the writing: as if it does something. But obscenity itself is socially constructed; the writer does not invent it or in any sense originate it. He finds it, knowing that it is what society hides. He looks under rocks and in dark corners.

There are two possible derivations of the word *obscenity*: the discredited one, *what is concealed*; and the accepted one, *filth*. Animals bury their filth, hide it, cover it, leave it behind, separate it from themselves: so do we, going way way back. Filth is excrement: from down there. We bury it or hide it; also, we hide where it comes from. Under male rule, menstrual blood is also filth, so women are twice dirty. Filth is where the sexual organs are and because women are seen primarily as sex, existing to provide sex, women have to be covered: our naked bodies being obscene.

Obscenity law uses both possible root meanings of obscene intertwined: it typically condemns nudity, public display, lewd exhibition, exposed genitals or buttocks or pubic areas, sodomy, masturbation, sexual intercourse, excretion. Obscenity law is applied to pictures and words: the artifact itself exposes what should be hidden; it shows dirt. The human body, all sex acts and excretory acts, are the domain of obscenity law.

But being in the domain of obscenity law is not enough. One must feel alive there. To be obscene, the representations must arouse prurient interest. *Prurient* means *itching* or *itch*; it is related to the Sanskrit for *he burns*. It means sexual arousal. Judges, lawmakers, and juries have been, until very recently, entirely male: empirically, prurient means *causes erection*. Theologians have called this same quality of obscenity "venereal pleasure," holding that "if a work is to be called obscene it must, of its nature, be such as actually to arouse or calculated to arouse in the viewer or reader such venereal pleasure. If the work is *not* of such a kind, it may, indeed, be vulgar, disgusting, crude, unpleasant, what you will—but it will *not* be, in the strict sense which Canon Law obliges us to apply, obscene."[3] A secular philosopher of pornography isolated the same quality when he wrote: "Obscenity is our name for the uneasiness which upsets the physical state associated with self-possession..."[4]

Throughout history, the male has been the standard for obscenity law: erection is his venereal pleasure or the uneasiness which upsets the physical state associated with his self-possession. It is not surprising, then, that in the same period when women became jurors, lawyers, and judges—but especially jurors, women having been summarily excluded from most juries until perhaps a decade ago—obscenity law fell into disuse and disregard. In order for obscenity law to have retained social and legal coherence, it would have had to recognize as part of its standard women's sexual arousal, a more subjective standard than erection. It would also have had to use the standard of penile erection in a social environment that was no longer sex-segregated, an environment in which male sexual arousal would be subjected to female scrutiny. In my view, the presence of women in the public sphere of legal decision-making has done more to undermine the efficacy of obscenity law than any self-conscious movement against it.

The act that obscenity recognizes is erection, and whatever produces erection is seen to be obscene—act, not idea—because of what it makes happen. The male sexual response is seen to be involuntary, so there is no experientially explicable division between the material that causes erection and the erection itself. That is the logic of obscenity law used against important writers who have pushed against the borders of the socially-defined obscene, because they wanted writing to have that very quality of being a socially recognized act. They wanted the inevitability of the response—the social response. The erection makes the writing socially real from the society's point of view, not from the writer's. What the writer needs is to be taken seriously, by any means necessary. In liberal societies, only obscenity law comprehends writing as an act. It defines the nature and quality of the act narrowly—not writing itself, but producing erections. Flaubert apparently did produce them; so did Baudelaire,

Zola, Rousseau, Lawrence, Joyce, and Nabokov. It's that simple.

What is at stake in obscenity law is always erection: under what conditions, in what circumstances, how, by whom, by what materials men want it produced in themselves. Men have made this public policy. Why they want to regulate their own erections through law is a question of endless interest and importance to feminists. Nevertheless, that they do persist in this regulation is simple fact. There are civil and social conflicts over how best to regulate erection through law, especially when caused by words or pictures. Arguments among men notwithstanding, high culture is phallocentric. It is also, using the civilized criteria of jurisprudence, not infrequently obscene.

Most important writers have insisted that their own uses of the obscene as socially defined are not pornography. As D. H. Lawrence wrote: "But even I would censor genuine pornography, rigorously. It would not be difficult. . . . [Y]ou can recognize it by the insult it offers, invariably, to sex, and to the human spirit."[5] It was also, he pointed out, produced by the underworld. Nabokov saw in pornography "mediocrity, commercialism, and certain strict rules of narration. . . . [A]ction has to be limited to the copulation of clichés. Style, structure, imagery should never distract the reader from his tepid lust."[6] They knew that what they did was different from pornography, but they did not entirely know what the difference was. They missed the heart of an empirical distinction because writing was indeed real to them but women were not.

The insult that pornography offers, invariably, to sex is accomplished in the active subordination of women: the creation of a sexual dynamic in which the putting-down of women, the suppression of women, and ultimately the brutalization of women, *is* what sex is taken to be. Obscenity in law, and in what it does socially, is erection. Law recognizes the act in this. Pornography, however, is a broader, more comprehensive act, because it crushes a whole class of people through violence and subjugation: and sex is the vehicle that does the crushing. The penis is not the test, as it is in obscenity. Instead, the status of women is the issue. Erection is implicated in the subordinating, but who it reaches and how are the pressing legal and social questions. Pornography, unlike obscenity, is a discrete, identifiable system of sexual exploitation that hurts women as a class by creating inequality and abuse. This is a new legal idea, but it is the recognition and naming of an old and cruel injury to a dispossessed and coerced underclass. It is the sound of women's words breaking the longest silence.

3. Pornography

In the United States, it is an $8-billion trade in sexual exploitation.

It is women turned into subhumans, beaver, pussy, body parts, genitals exposed, buttocks, breasts, mouths open and throats penetrated, covered in semen, pissed on, shitted on, hung from light fixtures, tortured, maimed, bleeding, disemboweled, killed.

It is some creature called female, used.

It is scissors poised at the vagina and objects stuck in it, a smile on the woman's face, her tongue hanging out.

It is a woman being fucked by dogs, horses, snakes.

It is every torture in every prison cell in the world, done to women and sold as sexual entertainment.

It is rape and gang rape and anal rape and throat rape: and it is the woman raped, asking for more.

It is the woman in the picture to whom it is really happening and the women against whom the picture is used, to make them do what the woman in the picture is doing.

It is the power men have over women turned into sexual acts men do to women, because pornography is the power and the act.

It is the conditioning of erection and orgasm in men to the powerlessness of women: our inferiority, humiliation, pain, torment; to us as objects, things, or commodities for use in sex as servants.

It sexualizes inequality and in doing so creates discrimination as a sex-based practice.

It permeates the political condition of women in society by being the substance of our inequality however located—in jobs, in education, in marriage, *in life*.

It is women, kept a sexual underclass, kept available for rape and battery and incest and prostitution.

It is what we are under male domination; it is what we are *for* under male domination.

LETTERS FROM A WAR ZONE

It is the heretofore hidden (from us) system of subordination that women have been told is just life.

Under male supremacy, it is the synonym for what being a woman is.

It is access to our bodies as a birthright to men: the grant, the gift, the permission, the license, the proof, the promise, the method, how-to; it is us accessible, no matter what the law pretends to say, no matter what we pretend to say.

It is physical injury and physical humiliation and physical pain: to the women against whom it is used after it is made; to the women used to make it.

As words alone, or words and pictures, moving or still, it creates systematic harm to women in the form of discrimination and physical hurt. It creates harm inevitably by its nature because of what it is and what it does. The harm will occur as long as it is made and used. The name of the next victim is unknown, but everything else is known.

Because of it—because it is the subordination of women perfectly achieved—the abuse done to us by any human standard is perceived as using us for what we are by nature: women are whores; women want to be raped; she provoked it; women like to be hurt; she says no but means yes because she wants to be taken against her will which is not really her will because what she wants underneath is to have anything done to her that violates or humiliates or hurts her; she wants it, because she is a woman, no matter what it is, because she is a woman; that is how women are, what women are, what women are for. This view is institutionally expressed in law. So much for equal protection.

If it were being done to human beings, it would be reckoned an atrocity. It is being done to women. It is reckoned fun, pleasure, entertainment, sex, somebody's (not something's) civil liberty no less.

What do you want to be when you grow up? *Doggie Girl? Gestapo Sex Slave? Black Bitch in Bondage?* Pet, bunny, beaver? In dreams begin responsibilities,[7] whether one is the dreamer or the dreamed.

4. Pornographers

Most of them are small-time pimps or big-time pimps. They sell women: the real flesh-and-blood women in the pictures. They like the excitement of domination; they are greedy for profit; they are sadistic in their exploitation of women; they hate women, and the pornography they make is the distillation of that hate. The photographs are what they have created live, for themselves, for their own enjoyment. The exchanges of women among them are part of the fun, too: so that the fictional creature "Linda Lovelace," who was the real woman Linda Marchiano, was forced to "deep-throat" every pornographer her owner-pornographer wanted to impress. Of course, it was the woman, not the fiction, who had to be hypnotized so that the men could penetrate to the bottom of her throat, and who had to be beaten and terrorized to get her compliance at all. The finding of new and terrible things to do to women is part of the challenge of the vocation: so the inventor of "Linda Lovelace" and "deep-throating" is a genius in the field, a pioneer. Or, as Al Goldstein, a colleague, referred to him in an interview with him in *Screw* several years ago: a pimp's pimp.

Even with written pornography, there has never been the distinction between making pornography and the sexual abuse of live women that is taken as a truism by those who approach pornography as if it were an intellectual phenomenon. The Marquis de Sade, as the world's foremost literary pornographer, is archetypal. His sexual practice was the persistent sexual abuse of women and girls, with occasional excursions into the abuse of boys. As an aristocrat in a feudal society, he preyed with near impunity on prostitutes and servants. The pornography he wrote was an urgent part of the sexual abuse he practiced: not only because he did what he wrote, but also because the intense hatred of women that fuelled the one also fuelled the other: not two separate engines, but one engine running on the same tank. The acts of pornography and the acts of rape were waves on the same sea: that sea becoming for its victims, however it reached them, a tidal wave of destruction. Pornographers who use words know that what they are doing is both aggressive and destructive: sometimes they philosophize about how sex inevitably ends in death, the death of a woman being a thing of sexual beauty as well as excitement. Pornography, even when written, is sex because of the dynamism of the sexual hatred in it; and for pornographers, the sexual abuse of women as commonly understood and pornography are both acts of sexual predation, which is how they live.

One reason that stopping pornographers and pornography is not censorship is that pornographers are more like the police in police states than they are like the writers in police states. They are the instruments of terror, not its victims. What police do to the powerless in police states is what pornographers do to women, except that it is entertainment for the masses, not dignified as political. Writers do not do what pornographers do. Secret police do. Torturers do. What pornographers do to women is more like what police do to political prisoners than it is like anything else: except for the fact that it is watched with so much pleasure by so many. Intervening in a system of terror where it is vulnerable to public scrutiny to stop it is not censorship; it is the system of terror that stops speech and creates abuse and despair. The pornographers are the secret police of male supremacy: keeping women subordinate through intimidation and assault.

5. Subordination

In the amendment to the Human Rights Ordinance of the City of Minneapolis written by Catharine A. MacKinnon and myself, pornography is defined as the graphic, sexually explicit subordination of women whether in pictures or in words that also includes one or more of the following: women are presented dehumanized as sexual objects, things, or commodities; or women are presented as sexual objects who enjoy pain or humiliation; or women are presented as sexual objects who experience sexual pleasure in being raped; or women are presented as sexual objects tied up or cut up or mutilated or bruised or physically hurt; or women are presented in postures of sexual submission; or women's body parts are exhibited, such that women are reduced to those parts; or women are presented being penetrated by objects or animals; or women are presented in scenarios of degradation, injury, abasement, torture, shown as filthy or inferior, bleeding, bruised, or hurt in a context that makes these conditions sexual.

This statutory definition is an objectively accurate definition of what pornography is, based on an analysis of the material produced by the $8-billion-a-year industry, and also on extensive study of the whole range of pornography extant from other eras and other cultures. Given the fact that women's oppression has an ahistorical character—a sameness across time and cultures expressed in rape, battery, incest, and prostitution—it is no surprise that pornography, a central phenomenon in that oppression, has precisely that quality of sameness. It does not significantly change in what it is, what it does, what is in it, or how it works, whether it is, for instance, classical or feudal or modern, Western or Asian; whether the method of manufacture is words, photographs, or video. What has changed is the public availability of pornography and the numbers of live women used in it because of new technologies: not its nature. Many people note what seems to them a qualitative change in pornography—that it has gotten more violent, even grotesquely violent, over the last two decades. The change is only in what is publicly visible: not in the range or preponderance of violent pornography (e.g., the place of rape in pornography stays constant and central, no matter where, when, or how the pornography is produced); not in the character, quality, or content of what the pornographers actually produce; not in the harm caused; not in the valuation of women in it, or the metaphysical definition of what women are; not in the sexual abuse promoted, including rape, battery, and incest; not in the centrality of its role in subordinating women. Until recently, pornography operated in private, where most abuse of women takes place.

The oppression of women occurs through sexual subordination. It is the use of sex as the medium of oppression that makes the subordination of women so distinct from racism or prejudice against a group based on religion or national origin. Social inequality is created in many different ways. In my view, the radical responsibility is to isolate the material means of creating the inequality so that material remedies can be found for it.

This is particularly difficult with respect to women's inequality because that inequality is achieved through sex. Sex as desired by the class that dominates women is held by that class to be elemental, urgent, necessary, even if or even though it appears to *require* the repudiation of any claim women might have to full human standing. In the subordination of women, inequality itself is sexualized: made into the experience of sexual pleasure, essential to sexual desire.

Pornography is the material means of sexualizing inequality; and that is why pornography is a central practice in the subordination of women.

Subordination itself is a broad, deep, systematic dynamic discernible in any persecution based on race or sex. Social subordination has four main parts. First, there is *hierarchy*, a group on top and a group on the bottom. For women, this hierarchy is experienced both socially and sexually, publicly and privately. Women are physically integrated into the society in which we are held to be inferior, and our low status is both put in place and maintained by the sexual usage of us by men; and so women's experience of hierarchy is incredibly intimate and wounding.

Second, subordination is *objectification*. Objectification occurs when a human being, through social means, is made less than human, turned into a thing or commodity, bought and sold. When objectification occurs, a person is de-personalized, so that no individuality or integrity is available socially or in what is an extremely circumscribed privacy (because those who dominate determine its boundaries). Objecification is an injury right at the heart of discrimination: those who can be used as if they are not fully human are no longer fully human in social terms; their humanity is hurt by being diminished.

Third, subordination is *submission*. A person is at the bottom of a hierarchy because of a condition of birth; a person on the bottom is dehumanized, an object or commodity; inevitably, the situation of that person requires obedience and compliance. That diminished person is expected to be submissive; there is no longer any right to self-determination, because there is no basis in equality for any such right to exist. In a condition of inferiority and objectification, submission is usually essential for survival. Oppressed groups are known for their abilities to anticipate the orders and desires of those who have power over them, to comply with an obsequiousness that is then used by the dominant group to justify its own dominance: the master, not able to imagine a human like himself in such degrading servility, thinks the servility is proof that the hierarchy is natural and that objectification simply amounts to seeing these lesser creatures for what they are. The submission forced on inferior, objectified groups precisely by hierarchy and objectification is taken to be the proof of inherent inferiority and subhuman capacities.

Fourth, subordination is *violence*. The violence is systematic, endemic enough to be unremarkable and normative, usually taken as an implicit right of the one committing the violence. In my view, hierarchy, objectification, and submission are the preconditions for systematic social violence against any group targeted because of a condition of birth. If violence against a group is both socially pervasive and socially normal, then hierarchy, objectification, and submission are already solidly in place.

The role of violence in subordinating women has one special characteristic congruent with sex as the instrumentality of subordination: the violence is supposed to be sex for the woman too—what women want and like as part of our sexual nature; it is supposed to give women pleasure (as in rape); it is supposed to mean love to a woman from her point of view (as in battery). The violence against women is seen to be done not just in accord with something compliant in women, but in response to something active in and basic to women's nature.

Pornography uses each component of social subordination. Its particular medium is sex. Hierarchy, objectification, submission, and violence all become alive with sexual energy and sexual meaning. A hierarchy, for instance, can have a static quality; but pornography, by sexualizing it, makes it dynamic, almost carnivorous, so that men keep imposing it for the sake of their own sexual pleasure—for the sexual pleasure it gives them to impose it. In pornography, each element of subordination is conveyed through the sexually explicit usage of women: pornography in fact is what women are and what women are for and how women are used in a society premised on the inferiority of women. It is a metaphysics of women's subjugation: our existence delineated in a definition of our nature; our status in society predetermined by the uses to which we are put. The woman's body is what is materially subordinated. Sex is the material means through which the subordination is accomplished. Pornography is the institution of male dominance that sexualizes hierarchy, objectification, submission, and violence. As such, pornography creates inequality, not as artifact but as a system of social reality; it creates the necessity for and the actual behaviors that constitute sex inequality.

6. Speech

Subordination can be so deep that those who are hurt by it are utterly silent. Subordination can create a silence quieter than death. The women flattened out on the page are deathly still, except for *hurt me*. *Hurt me* is not women's speech. It is the speech imposed on women by pimps to cover the awful, condemning silence. The Three Marias of Portugal went to jail for writing this: "Let no one tell me that silence gives consent, because whoever is silent dissents."[8] The women say the pimp's words: the language is another element of the rape; the language is part of the humiliation; the language is part of the forced sex. Real silence might signify dissent, for those reared to understand its sad discourse. The pimps cannot tolerate literal silence—it is too eloquent as testimony—so they force the words out of the woman's mouth. The women say pimp's words: which is worse than silence. The silence of the women not in the picture, outside the pages, hurt but silent, used but silent, is staggering in how deep and wide it goes. It is a silence over centuries: an exile into speechlessness. One is shut up by the inferiority and the abuse. One is shut up by the threat and the injury. In her memoir of the Stalin period, *Hope Against Hope*, Nadezhda Mandelstam wrote that screaming "is a man's way of leaving a trace, of telling people how he lived and died. By his screams he asserts his right to live, sends a message to the outside world demanding help and calling for resistance. If nothing else is left, one must scream. Silence is the real crime against humanity."[9] Screaming is a man's way of leaving a trace. The scream of a man is never misunderstood as a scream of pleasure by passers-by or politicians or historians, nor by the tormentor. A man's scream is a call for resistance. A man's scream asserts his right to live, sends a message; he leaves a trace. A woman's scream is the sound of her female will and her female pleasure in doing what the pornographers say she is for. Her scream is a sound of celebration to those who overhear. Women's way of leaving a trace is the silence, centuries' worth: the entirely inhuman silence that surely one day will be noticed, someone will say that something is wrong, some sound is missing, some voice is lost; the entirely inhuman silence that will be a clue to human hope denied, a shard of evidence that a crime has occurred, the crime that created the silence; the entirely inhuman silence that is a cold, cold condemnation of what those who speak have done to those who do not.

But there is more than the *hurt me* forced out of us, and the silence in which it lies. The pornographers actually use our bodies as their language. We are their speech. Our bodies are the building blocks of their sentences. What they do to us, called speech, is not unlike what Kafka's Harrow machine—"The needles are set in like the teeth of a harrow and the whole thing works something like a harrow, although its action is limited to one place and contrived with much more artistic skill"[10]—did to the condemned in "In the Penal Colony":

> "Our sentence does not sound severe. Whatever commandment the prisoner has disobeyed is written upon his body by the Harrow. This prisoner, for instance"—the officer indicated the man—"will have written on his body: HONOR THY SUPERIORS!"[11]

> "... The Harrow is beginning to write; when it finishes the first draft of the inscription on the man's back, the layer of cotton wool begins to roll and slowly turns the body over, to give the Harrow fresh space for writing.... So it keeps on writing deeper and deeper ..."[12]

Asked if the prisoner knows his sentence, the officer replies: "'There would be no point in telling him. He'll learn it on his body.'"[13]

This is the so-called speech of the pornographers, protected now by law.

Protecting what they "say" means protecting what they do to us, how they do it. It means protecting their sadism on our bodies, because that is how they write: not like a writer at all; like a torturer. Protecting what they "say" means protecting sexual exploitation, because they cannot "say" anything without diminishing, hurting, or destroying us. Their rights of speech express their rights over us. Their rights of speech require our inferiority: and that we be powerless in relation to them. Their rights of speech mean that *hurt me* is accepted as the real speech of women, not speech forced on us as part of the sex forced on us but originating with us because we are what the pornographers "say" we are.

If what we want to say is not *hurt me*, we have the real social power only to use silence as eloquent dissent. Silence is what women have instead of speech. Silence is our dissent during rape unless the rapist, like the pornographer, prefers *hurt me*, in which case we have no dissent. Silence is our moving, persuasive dissent during battery unless the batterer, like the pornographer, prefers *hurt me*. Silence is a fine dissent during incest and for all the long years after.

Silence is not speech. We have silence, not speech. We fight rape, battery, incest, and prostitution with it. We lose. But someday someone will notice: that people called women were buried in a long silence that meant dissent and that the pornographers—with needles set in like the teeth of a harrow—chattered on.

7. Equality

To get that word, male, out of the Constitution, cost the women of this country fifty-two years of pauseless campaign; 56 state referendum campaigns; 480 legislative campaigns to get state suffrage amendments submitted; 47 state constitutional convention campaigns; 277 state party convention campaigns to get suffrage planks in the party platforms; 19 campaigns with 19 successive Congresses to get the federal amendment submitted, and the final ratification campaign.

Millions of dollars were raised, mostly in small sums, and spent with economic care. Hundreds of women gave the accumulated possibilities of an entire lifetime, thousands gave years of their lives, hundreds of thousands gave constant interest and such aid as they could. It was a continuous and seemingly endless chain of activity. Young suffragists who helped forge the last links of that chain were not born when it began. Old suffragists who helped forge the first links were dead when it ended.

Carrie Chapman Catt

Feminists have wanted equality. Radicals and reformists have different ideas of what equality would be, but it has been the wisdom of feminism to value equality as a political goal with social integrity and complex meaning. The Jacobins also wanted equality, and the French Revolution was the first war fought to accomplish it. Conservatism as a modern political movement actually developed to resist social and political movements for equality, beginning with the egalitarian imperatives of the French Revolution.

Women have had to prove human status, before having any claim to equality. But equality has been impossible to achieve, perhaps because, really, women have not been able to prove human status. The burden of proof is on the victim.

Not one inch of change has been easy or cheap. We have fought so hard and so long for so little. The vote did not change the status of women. The changes in women's lives that we can see on the surface do not change the status of women. By the year 2000, women and their children are expected to be one hundred percent of this nation's poor.* We are raped, battered, and prostituted: these acts against us are in the fabric of social life. As children, we are raped, physically abused, and prostituted. The country enjoys the injuries done to us, and spends $8 billion a year on the pleasure of watching us being hurt (exploitation as well as torture constituting substantive harm). The subordination gets deeper: we keep getting pushed down further. Rape is an entertainment. The contempt for us in that fact is immeasurable; yet we live under the weight of it. Discrimination is a euphemism for what happens to us.

It has plagued us to try to understand why the status of women does not change. Those who hate the politics of equality say they know: we are biologically destined for rape; God made us to be submissive unto our husbands. We change, but our status does not change. Laws change, but our status stays fixed. We move into the market place, only to face there classic sexual exploitation, now called sexual harassment. Rape, battery, prostitution, and incest stay the same in that they keep happening to us as part of what life is: even though we name the crimes against us as such and try to keep the victims from being destroyed by what we cannot stop from happening to them. And the silence stays in place too, however much we try to dislodge it with our truths. We say what has happened to us, but newspapers, governments, the culture that excludes us as fully human participants, wipe us out, wipe out our speech: by refusing to hear it. We are the tree falling in the desert. Should it matter: they are the desert.

The cost of trying to shatter the silence is astonishing to those who do it: the women, raped, battered, prostituted, who have something

* For a comprehensive analysis of how the feminization of poverty brutally impacts on people of color in the United States, see *Right-wing Women*, The Women's Press, 1983, "The Coming Gynocide," especially pp. 162–173.

to say and say it. They stand there, even as they are erased. Governments turn from them; courts ignore them; this country disavows and dispossesses them. Men ridicule, threaten, or hurt them. Women jeopardized by them—silence being safer than speech—betray them. It is ugly to watch the complacent destroy the brave. It is horrible to watch power win.

Still, equality is what we want, and we are going to get it. What we understand about it now is that it cannot be proclaimed; it must be created. It has to take the place of subordination in human experience: physically replace it. Equality does not coexist with subordination, as if it were a little pocket located somewhere within it. Equality has to win. Subordination has to lose. The subordination of women has not even been knocked loose, and equality has not materially advanced, at least in part because the pornography has been creating sexualized inequality in hiding, in private, where the abuses occur on a massive scale.

Equality for women requires material remedies for pornography, whether pornography is central to the inequality of women or only one cause of it. Pornography's antagonism to civil equality, integrity, and self-determination for women is absolute; and it is effective in making that antagonism socially real and socially determining.

The law that Catharine A. MacKinnon and I wrote making pornography a violation of women's civil rights recognizes the injury that pornography does: how it hurts women's rights of citizenship through sexual exploitation and sexual torture both.

The civil rights law empowers women by allowing women to civilly sue those who hurt us through pornography by trafficking in it, coercing people into it, forcing it on people, and assaulting people directly because of a specific piece of it.

The civil rights law does not force the pornography back underground. There is no prior restraint or police power to make arrests, which would then result in a revivified black market. This respects the reach of the First Amendment, but it also keeps the pornography from getting sexier—hidden, forbidden, dirty, happily back in the land of the obscene, sexy slime oozing on great books. Wanting to cover pornography up, hide it, is the first response of those who need pornography to the civil rights law. If pornography is hidden, it is still accessible to men as a male right of access to women;

its injuries to the status of women are safe and secure in those hidden rooms, behind those opaque covers; the abuses of women are sustained as a private right supported by public policy. The civil rights law puts a flood of light on the pornography, what it is, how it is used, what it does, those who are hurt by it.

The civil rights law changes the power relationship between the pornographers and women: it stops the pornographers from producing discrimination with the total impunity they now enjoy, and gives women a legal standing resembling equality from which to repudiate the subordination itself. The secret-police power of the pornographers suddenly has to confront a modest amount of due process.

The civil rights law undermines the subordination of women in society by confronting the pornography, which is the systematic sexualization of that subordination. Pornography is inequality. The civil rights law would allow women to advance equality by removing this concrete discrimination and hurting economically those who make, sell, distribute, or exhibit it. The pornography, being power, has a right to exist that we are not allowed to challenge under this system of law. After it hurts us by being what it is and doing what it does, the civil rights law would allow us to hurt it back. Women, not being power, do not have a right to exist equal to the right the pornography has. If we did, the pornographers would be precluded from exercising their rights at the expense of ours, and since they cannot exercise them any other way, they would be precluded period. We come to the legal system beggars: though in the public dialogue around the passage of this civil rights law we have the satisfaction of being regarded as thieves.

The civil rights law is women's speech. It defines an injury to us from our point of view. It is premised on a repudiation of sexual subordination which is born of our experience of it. It breaks the silence. It is a sentence that can hold its own against the male flood. It is a sentence on which we can build a paragraph, then a page.

It is my view, learned largely from Catharine MacKinnon, that women have a right to be effective. The pornographers, of course, do not think so, nor do other male supremacists; and it is hard for women to think so. We have been told to educate people on the evils of pornography: before the development of this civil rights law, we

273

were told just to keep quiet about pornography altogether; but now that we have a law we want to use, we are encouraged to educate and stop there. Law educates. This law educates. It also allows women to *do* something. In hurting the pornography back, we gain ground in making equality more likely, more possible—someday it will be real. We have a means to fight the pornographers' trade in women. We have a means to get at the torture and the terror. We have a means with which to challenge the pornography's efficacy in making exploitation and inferiority the bedrock of women's social status. The civil rights law introduces into the public consciousness an analysis: of what pornography is, what sexual subordination is, what equality might be. The civil rights law introduces a new legal standard: these things are not done to citizens of this country. The civil rights law introduces a new political standard: these things are not done to human beings. The civil rights law provides a new mode of action for women through which we can pursue equality and because of which *our* speech will have social meaning. The civil rights law gives us back what the pornographers have taken from us: hope rooted in real possibility.

Notes

1. Gustave Flaubert, *Letters*, trans. J. M. Cohen (London: George Weidenfeld & Nicolson Limited, 1950), p. 94.

2. D. H. Lawrence, *Sex, Literature and Censorship* (New York: Twayne Publishers, 1953), p. 9.

3. Harold Gardiner (S.J.), *Catholic Viewpoint on Censorship* (Garden City: Hanover House, 1958), p. 65.

4. Georges Bataille, *Death and Sensuality* (New York: Ballantine Books, Inc., 1969), p. 12.

5. Lawrence, *Sex, Literature and Censorship*, p. 74.

6. Vladimir Nabokov, "Afterword," *Lolita* (New York: Berkley Publishing Corporation, 1977), p. 284.

7. The actual line is "In dreams begins responsibility," quoted by Yeats as an epigraph to his collection, *Responsibilities*.

8. Maria Isabel Barreno, Maria Teresa Horta, and Maria Velho da Costa,

The Three Marias: New Portuguese Letters, trans. Helen R. Lane (New York: Bantam Books, 1976), p. 291.

9. Nadezhda Mandelstam, *Hope Against Hope*, trans. Max Hayward (New York: Atheneum, 1978), pp. 42–43.

10. Franz Kafka, "In the Penal Colony," pp. 191–227, *The Penal Colony*, trans. Willa and Edwin Muir (New York: Schocken Books, 1965), p. 194.

11. Kafka, "In the Penal Colony," p. 197.

12. Kafka, "In the Penal Colony," p. 203.

13. Kafka, "In the Penal Colony," p. 197.

Pornography Is A Civil Rights Issue

1986

I *testified before the Attorney General's Commission on Pornography on January 22, 1986, in New York City. Numerous civil liberties folks, including pro-pornography "feminists," had already testified in other cities. I spoke to the Commission because my friends, feminists who work against pornography, asked me to. Every effort was made by the pro-pornography lobby to discredit the Commission. A memo dated June 5, 1986, from Gray and Company, the largest public relations firm in Washington D.C., with ties to both the Reagan White House and the old Kennedy White House, outlines a strategy to discredit the Commission. The memo was prepared for the Media Coalition, a bunch of publishing and media trade groups, including distributors, that has been very active for many years in providing legal protection for pornography, including child pornography. A campaign costing nearly one million dollars would effectively discredit the findings of the Commission by smearing those who oppose pornography, creating a hysteria over censorship, and planting news stories to say that there is no proven relationship between pornography and harm to women and children. I had one half-hour and this is my testimony. Then, the members of the Commission asked me questions. Their questions and my answers are published here. Representatives of* Penthouse *sat with* ACLU *lawyers and so-called feminists organized to defend pornography; and they heckled me during this testimony.*

A NDREA DWORKIN CALLED as a witness on behalf of the Attorney General's Commission on Pornography, testified as follows:*

* This text is based on the Justice Department's transcript, prepared by Ace-Federal Reporters, Inc., which was compared against tape recordings and revised for accuracy. The author has also made slight editorial changes for clarity.

MS DWORKIN: Thank you very much. My name is Andrea Dworkin. I am a citizen of the United States, and in this country where I live, every year millions and millions of pictures are being made of women with our legs spread. We are called beaver, we are called pussy, our genitals are tied up, they are pasted, makeup is put on them to make them pop out of a page at a male viewer. Millions and millions of pictures are made of us in postures of submission and sexual access so that our vaginas are exposed for penetration, our anuses are exposed for penetration, our throats are used as if they are genitals for penetration. In this country where I live as a citizen real rapes are on film and are being sold in the marketplace. And the major motif of pornography as a form of entertainment is that women are raped and violated and humiliated until we discover that we like it and at that point we ask for more.

In this country where I live as a citizen, women are penetrated by animals and objects for public entertainment, women are urinated on and defecated on, women and girls are used interchangeably so that grown women are made up to look like five- or six-year-old children surrounded by toys, presented in mainstream pornographic publications for anal penetration. There are magazines in which adult women are presented with their pubic areas shaved so that they resemble children.

In this country where I live, there is a trafficking in pornography that exploits mentally and physically disabled women, women who are maimed; there is amputee pornography, a trade in women who have been maimed in that way, as if that is a sexual fetish for men. In this country where I live, there is a trade in racism as a form of sexual pleasure, so that the plantation is presented as a form of sexual gratification for the black woman slave who asks please to be abused, please to be raped, please to be hurt. Black skin is presented as if it is a female genital, and all the violence and the abuse and the humiliation that is in general directed against female genitals is directed against the black skin of women in pornography.

Asian women in this country where I live are tied from trees and hung from ceilings and hung from doorways as a form of public entertainment. There is a concentration camp pornography in this country where I live, where the concentration camp and the atrocities that occurred there are presented as existing for the sexual pleasure of the victim, of the woman, who orgasms to the real abuses that occurred, not very long ago in history.

In the country where I live as a citizen, there is a pornography of the humiliation of women where every single way of humiliating a human being is taken to be a form of sexual pleasure for the viewer and for the victim; where women are covered in filth, including feces, including mud, including paint, including blood, including semen; where women are tortured for the sexual pleasure of those who watch and those who do the torture, where women are murdered for the sexual pleasure of murdering women, and this material exists because it is fun, because it is entertainment, because it is a form of pleasure, and there are those who say it is a form of freedom.

Certainly it is freedom for those who do it. Certainly it is freedom for those who use it as entertainment, but we are also asked to believe that it is freedom for those to whom it is done.

Then this entertainment is taken, and it is used on other women, women who aren't in the pornography, to force those women into prostitution, to make them imitate the acts in the pornography. The women in the pornography, sixty-five to seventy percent of them we believe are victims of incest or child sexual abuse. They are poor women; they are not women who have opportunities in this society. They are frequently runaways who are picked up by pimps and exploited. They are frequently raped, the rapes are filmed, they are kept in prostitution by blackmail. The pornography is used on prostitutes by johns who expect them to replicate the sexual acts in the pornography, no matter how damaging it is.

Pornography is used in rape—to plan it, to execute it, to choreograph it, to engender the excitement to commit the act. Pornography is used in gang rape against women. We see an increase since the release of *Deep Throat* in throat rape—where women show up in emergency rooms because men believe they can penetrate, deep-thrust, to the bottom of a woman's throat. We see increasing use of all elements of pornography in battery, which is the most commonly committed violent crime in this country, including the rape of women by animals, including maiming, including heavy bondage, including outright torture.

We have seen in the last eight years an increase in the use of cameras in rapes. And those rapes are filmed and then they are put on the marketplace and they are protected speech—they are real rapes.

We see a use of pornography in the harassment of women on jobs, especially in nontraditional jobs, in the harassment of women in education, to create terror and compliance in the home, which as you know is the most dangerous place for women in this society, where more violence is committed against women than anywhere else. We see pornography used to create harassment of women and children in neighborhoods that are saturated with pornography, where people come from other parts of the city and then prey on the populations of people who live in those neighborhoods, and that increases physical attack and verbal assault.

We see pornography having introduced a profit motive into rape. We see that filmed rapes are protected speech. We see the centrality of pornography in serial murders. There *are* snuff films. We see boys imitating pornography. We see the average age of rapists going down. We are beginning to see gang rapes in elementary schools committed by elementary school age boys imitating pornography.

We see sexual assault after death where frequently the pornography is the motive for the murder because the man believes that he will get a particular kind of sexual pleasure having sex with a woman after she is dead.

We see a major trade in women, we see the torture of women as a form of entertainment, and we see women also suffering the injury of objectification—that is to say we are dehumanized. We are treated as if we are subhuman, and that is a precondition for violence against us.

I live in a country where if you film any act of humiliation or torture, and if the victim is a woman, the film is both entertainment and it is protected speech. Now that tells me something about what it means to be a woman citizen in this country, and the meaning of being second class.

When your rape is entertainment, your worthlessness is absolute. You have reached the nadir of social worthlessness. The civil impact of pornography on women is staggering. It keeps us socially silent, it keeps us socially compliant, it keeps us afraid in neighborhoods; and it creates a vast hopelessness for women, a vast despair. One lives inside a nightmare of sexual abuse that is both actual and potential, and you have the great joy of knowing that your nightmare is someone else's freedom and someone else's fun.

Now, a great deal has happened in this country to legitimize pornography in the last ten to fifteen years. There are people who are responsible for the fact that pornography is now a legitimate form of public entertainment.

Number one, the lobby of lawyers who work for the pornographers; the fact that the pornographers pay lawyers big bucks to fight for them, not just in the courts, but in public, in the public dialogue; the fact that lawyers interpret constitutional principles in light of the profit interest of the pornographers.

Number two, the collusion of the American Civil Liberties Union with the pornographers, which includes taking money from them. It includes using buildings that pornographers own and not paying rent, it includes using pornography in benefits to raise money. It includes not only defending them in court but also doing publicity for them, including organizing events for them, as the Hugh Hefner First Amendment Awards is organized by ACLU people for *Playboy*. It includes publishing in their magazines. It includes deriving great pride and economic benefit from working privately for the pornographers, while publicly pretending to be a disinterested advocate of civil liberties and free speech.

I want you to contrast the behavior of the ACLU in relation to the pornographers with their activities in relation to the Klan and the Nazis. The ACLU pretends to understand that they are all equally pernicious. But do ACLU people publish in the Klan newsletter? No. Do they go to Nazi social events? No. Do they go to cocktail parties at Nazi headquarters? No, they don't, at least not yet.

Finally, they have colluded in this sense, that they have convinced many of us that the standard for speech is what I would call a repulsion standard. That is to say we find the most repulsive person in the society and we defend him. I say we find the most powerless people in this society, and we defend *them*. That's the way we increase rights of speech in this society.

A third group that colludes to legitimize pornography are publishers and the so-called legitimate media. They pretend to believe that under this system of law there is a First Amendment that is indivisible and absolute, which it has never been.

As you know, the First Amendment protects speech that has already been expressed from state interference. That means it protects those who own media. There is no affirmative responsibility to open communications to those who are powerless in the society at large.

As a result, the owners of media, the newspapers, the TV networks, are comfortable with having women's bodies defined as the speech of pimps, because they are protecting their rights to profit as owners, and they think that that is what the First Amendment is for.

I am ashamed to say that people in my profession, writers, have also colluded with the pornographers. We provide their so-called socially redeeming value, and they wrap the tortured bodies of women in the work that we do.

Fourth, politicians have colluded with the pornographers in municipalities all over this country. They do it in these ways:

Zoning laws do not keep pornography out of cities. They are an official legal permission to traffic in pornography. And as a result politicians are able to denounce pornography moralistically while protecting it through zoning laws.

Zoning laws impose pornography on poor neighborhoods, on working-class neighborhoods, on neighborhoods where people of color live, and all of those people have to deal with the increase in crime, the terrible harassment, the degradation of the quality of life in their neighborhoods, and the politicians get to protect the property values of the rich. There is an equal protection issue here: why the state makes some people pay so other people can profit.

But that issue has never been raised. We have never been able to sue a city under the equal protection theory, because lawyers are on the other side. Lawyers belong primarily to pornographers, and the people who live in these neighborhoods that are saturated with pornography are powerless people. They don't even have power in their own municipalities.

In addition, what pornographers do in municipalities is that they buy land that is targeted for development by cities. They hold that land hostage. They develop political power through negotiating around that land. They make huge profits, and they get influence in local city governments.

Five, not finally but next to the last, a great colluder with the pornographers was the last presidential Commission on Obscenity and Pornography. They were very effective in legitimizing pornography in this country. They appeared to be looking for a proverbial ax murderer who would watch pornography and within twenty-four or forty-eight hours go out and kill someone in a horrible and clear way. The country is saturated with pornography, and saturated with violence against women, and saturated with the interfacing of the two. And the Commission didn't find it.

None of the scientific research that they relied on to come to their conclusions is worth anything today. It's all invalid. I ask you to take seriously the fact that society does not exist in a laboratory, that we are talking about real things that happen to real people, and that's what we are asking you to take some responsibility for.

Finally, the ultimate colluders in the legitimizing of pornography, of course, are the consumers. In 1979 we had a $4-billion-a-year industry in this country. By 1985 it was an $8-billion-a-year industry. Those consumers include men in all walks of life: lawyers, politicians, writers, professors, owners of media, police, doctors, maybe even commissioners on presidential commissions. No one really knows, do they?

And no matter where we look, we can't find the consumers. But what we learn is the meaning of first-class citizenship, and the meaning of first-class citizenship is that you can use your authority as men and as professionals to protect pornography both by developing arguments to protect it and by using real social and economic power to protect it.

And as a result of all of this, the harm to women remains invisible; even though we have the bodies, the harm to women remains invisible. Underlying the invisibility of this harm is an assumption that what is done to women is natural, that even if a woman is forced to do something, somehow it falls within the sphere of her natural responsibilities as a woman. When the same things are done to boys, those things are perceived as an outrage. They are called unnatural.

But if you force a woman to do something that she was born to do, then the violence to her is not perceived as a real violation of her.

In addition, the harm to women of pornography is invisible because most sexual abuse still occurs in private, even though we have this photographic documentation of it, called the pornography industry.

Women are extremely isolated, women don't have credibility, women are not believed by people who make social policy.

In addition, the harm of pornography remains invisible because women have been historically excluded from the protections of the Constitution; and as a result, the violations of our human rights, when they don't occur the same way violations to men occur, have not been recognized or taken seriously, and we do not have remedies for them under law.

In addition, pornography is invisible in its harm to women because women are poorer than men and many of the women exploited in pornography are very poor, many of them are illiterate, and also because there is a great deal of female compliance with brutality, and the compliance is based on fear, it's based on powerlessness and it is based on a reaction to the very real violence of the pornographers.

Finally, the harm is invisible because of the smile, because women are made to smile, women aren't just made to do the sex acts. We are made to smile while we do them.

So you will find in pornography women penetrating themselves with swords or daggers, and you will see the smile. You will see things that cannot be done to a human being and that are done to men only in political circumstances of torture, and you will see a woman forced to smile.

And this smile will be believed, and the injury to her as a human being, to her body and to her heart and to her soul, will not be believed.

Now, we have been told that we have an argument here about speech, not about women being hurt. And yet the emblem of that argument is a woman bound and gagged and we are supposed to believe that that is speech. Who is that speech for? We have women being tortured and we are told that that is somebody's speech? Whose speech is it? It's the speech of a pimp, it is not the speech of a woman. The only words we hear in pornography from women are that women want to be hurt, ask to be hurt, like to be raped, get sexual pleasure from sexual violence; and even when a woman is covered in filth, we are supposed to believe that her speech is that she likes it and she wants more of it.

The reality for women in this society is that pornography creates silence for women. The pornographers silence women. Our bodies are their language. Their speech is made out of our exploitation, our subservience, our injury and our pain, and they can't say anything without hurting us, and when you protect them, you protect only their right to exploit and hurt us.

Pornography is a civil rights issue for women because pornography sexualizes inequality, because it turns women into subhuman creatures.

Pornography is a civil rights issue for women because it is the systematic exploitation of a group of people because of a condition of birth. Pornography creates bigotry and hostility and aggression towards all women, targets all women, without exception.

Pornography is the suppression of us through sexual exploitation and abuse, so that we have no real means to achieve civil equality; and the issue here is simple, it is not complex. People are being hurt, and you can help them or you can help those who are hurting them. We need civil rights legislation, legislation that recognizes pornography as a violation of the civil rights of women.

We need it because civil rights legislation recognizes the fact that the harm here is to human beings. We need that recognition. We need civil rights legislation because it puts the power to act in the hands of the people who have been forced into pornographized powerlessness, and that's a special kind of powerlessness, that's a powerlessness that is supposed to be a form of sexual pleasure.

We need civil rights legislation because only those to whom it has happened know what has happened. They are the people who are the experts. They have the knowledge. They know what has happened, how it's happened; only they can really articulate, from beginning to end, the reality of pornography as a human rights injury. We need civil rights legislation because it gives us something back after what the pornographers have taken from us.

The motivation to fight back keeps people alive. People need it for their dignity, for their ability to continue to exist as citizens in a country that needs their creativity and needs their presence and needs the existence that has been taken from them by the pornographers. We need civil rights legislation because, as social policy, it says to a population of people that they have human worth, they have human worth, that this society recognizes that they have human worth.

We need it because it's the only legislative remedy thus far that is drawn narrowly enough to confront the human rights issues for people who are being exploited and discriminated against, without becoming an instrument of police power to suppress real expression.

We need the civil rights legislation because the process of civil discovery is a very important one, and it will give us a great deal of information for potential criminal prosecutions, against organized crime, against pornographers, and I ask you to look at the example of the Southern Poverty Law Center and their Klanwatch Project, which has used civil suits to get criminal indictments against the Klan.

Finally, we need civil rights legislation because the only really dirty word in this society is the word "women," and a civil rights approach says that this society repudiates the brutalization of women.

We are against obscenity laws. We don't want them. I want you to understand why, whether you end up agreeing or not.

Number one, the pornographers use obscenity laws as part of their formula for making pornography. All they need to do is to provide some literary, artistic, political or scientific value and they can hang women from the rafters. As long as they manage to meet that formula, it doesn't matter what they do to women.

And in the old days, when obscenity laws were still being enforced, in many places—for instance the most sadomasochistic pornography—the genitals were always covered because if the genitals were always covered, that wouldn't kick off a police prosecution.

Number two, the use of the prurient interest standard—however that standard is construed in this new era, when the Supreme Court has taken two synonyms, "lasciviousness" and "lust," and said that they mean different things, which is mind-boggling in and of itself. Whatever prurient interest is construed to mean, the reaction of jurors to material—whether they are supposed to be aroused or whether they are not allowed to be aroused, whatever the instructions of the court—has nothing to do with the objective reality of what is happening to women in pornography.

The third reason that obscenity law cannot work for us is: what do community standards mean in a society when violence against women is pandemic, when according to the FBI a woman is battered every eighteen seconds and it's the most commonly committed violent crime in the country? What would community standards have meant in the segregated South? What would community standards have meant as we approached the atrocity of Nazi Germany? What are community standards in a society where women are persecuted for being women and pornography is a form of political persecution?

Obscenity laws are also woman-hating in their construction. Their basic presumption is that it's women's bodies that are dirty. The standards of obscenity law don't acknowledge the reality of the technology. They were drawn up in a society where obscenity was construed to be essentially writing and drawing; and now what we have is mass production in a way that real people are being hurt, and the consumption of real people by a real technology, and obscenity laws are not adequate to that reality.

Finally, obscenity laws, at the discretion of police and prosecutors, will keep obscenity out of the public view, but it remains available to men in private. It remains available to individual men, it remains available to all-male groups; and whenever it is used, it still creates bigotry, hostility and aggression towards all women. It's still used in sexual abuse as part of sexual abuse. It's still made through coercion, through blackmail and through exploitation.

I am going to ask you to do several things. The first thing I am going to ask you to do is listen to women who want to talk to you about what has happened to them. Please listen to them. They know, they know how this works. You are asking people to speculate; they know, it has happened to them.

I am going to ask you to make these recommendations. The first recommendation I would like you to make is to have the Justice Department instruct law-enforcement agencies to keep records of the use of pornography in violent crimes, especially in rape and battery, in incest and child abuse, in murder, including sexual assault after death, to take note of those murders that are committed for sexual reasons. They should keep track, for instance, of suicides of teenage boys, and the place of pornography in those suicides. They should keep track of both the use of pornography before and during the commission of a violent crime and the presence of pornography at a violent crime.

I want to say that a lot of the information that we have about this, what we are calling a correlation, doesn't come from law-enforcement officials; it comes from the testimony of sex offenders. That's how we know that pornography is meaningful in the commission of sexual offenses. Have the FBI report that information in the Uniform Crime Reports, so that we begin to get some real standard here.

Number two, get pornography out of all prisons. It's like sending dynamite to terrorists. Those people have committed violent crimes against women. They consume pornography. They come back out on the street. The recidivism rate is unbelievable, not to mention that prison is a rape-saturated society. What about the rights of those men who are being raped in prisons, and the relationship of pornography to the rapes of them?

No one should be sentenced to a life of hell being raped in a prison. You can do something about it by getting the pornography out of prisons.

Number three, enforce laws against pimping and pandering against pornographers. Pandering is paying for sex to make pornography of it. A panderer is any person who procures another person for the purposes of prostitution. This law has been enforced against pornographers in California. Prosecute the makers of pornography under pimping and pandering laws.

Number four, make it a Justice Department priority to enforce RICO [the Racketeer Influenced and Corrupt Organizations Act] against the pornography industry. Racketeering activity means, as you know, any act or even a threat involving murder, kidnapping, extortion, any trafficking in coerced women—which for reasons that are incomprehensible to me is still called white slaving, although the women are Asian, the women are black, all kinds of women are still being trafficked in in this way. This is how pornographers do their business, both in relation to women and in relation to distributing their product.

RICO, if it were enforced against the industry, could do a great deal toward breaking the industry up.

Number five, please recommend that federal civil rights legislation recognizing pornography as a virulent and vicious form of sex discrimination be passed, that it be a civil law. It can be a separate act or it can be amended as a separate title under the 1964 Civil Rights Act. We want the equal protection principle of the Fourteenth Amendment to apply to women. This is the way to do it. We want a definition of pornography that is based on the reality of pornography, which is that it is the act of sexual subordination of women. The causes of action need to include trafficking, coercion, forcing pornography on a person, and assault or physical injury due to a specific piece of pornography.

I also want to ask you to consider, to consider, creating a criminal conspiracy provision under the civil rights law, such that conspiring to deprive a person of their civil rights by coercing them into pornography is a crime, and that conspiring to traffic in pornography is conspiring to deprive women of our civil rights.

Finally, I would like to ask you to think about pornography in the context of international law. We have claims to make. Women have claims to make under international law. Pornographers violate the rights of women under internationally recognized principles of law. The Universal Declaration of Human Rights says that everyone has the right to life, liberty and security of person, that no one shall be subjected to torture or to cruel, inhuman or degrading treatment or punishment, that everyone has the right to recognition everywhere as a person before the law.

It also says that no one shall be held in slavery or servitude, that slavery and the slave trade shall be prohibited in all their forms, and in international law the trafficking in women has long been recognized as a form of slave trading.

President Carter signed, and I am asking you to recommend that Congress ratify, the United Nations Convention on the Elimination of All Forms of Discrimination Against Women, which includes the following article, article 6. "State Parties shall take all appropriate measures, including legislation, to suppress all forms of traffic in women and exploitation and prostitution of women." That gives the United States Government an affirmative obligation to act against the traffic in women. This is an international problem and it requires in part an international solution.

I am also asking you to acknowledge the international reality of this—this is a human rights issue—for a very personal reason, which is that my grandparents came here, Jews fleeing from Russia, Jews fleeing from Hungary. Those who did not come to this country were all killed, either in pogroms or by the Nazis. They came here for me. I live here, and I live in a country where women are tortured as a form of public entertainment and for profit, and that torture is upheld as a state-protected right. Now, that is unbearable.

I am here asking the simplest thing. I am saying hurt people need remedies, not platitudes, not laws that you know already don't work; people excluded from constitutional protections need equality. People silenced by exploitation and brutality need real speech, not to be told that when they are hung from meat hooks, that is their speech. Nobody in this country who has been working to do anything about pornography, no woman who has spoken out against it, is going to go backwards, is going to forget what she has learned, is going to forget that she has rights that aren't being acknowledged in this country. And there are lots of people in this country, I am happy to say, who want to live in a kind world, not a cruel world, and they will not accept the hatred of women as good, wholesome, American fun; they won't accept the hatred of women and the rape of women as anybody's idea of freedom. They won't accept the torture of women as a civil liberty.

I am asking you to help the exploited, not the exploiters. You have a tremendous opportunity here. I am asking you as individuals to have the courage, because I think it's what you will need, to actually be willing yourselves to go and cut that woman down and untie her hands and take the gag out of her mouth, and to do something, to risk something, for her freedom.

Thank you very much for listening to me. I am going to submit into evidence a copy of Linda Marchiano's book *Ordeal*, which I understand you have not seen. She testified before you yesterday. I ask you, when you come to make your recommendations, think of her. The only thing atypical about Linda is that she has had the courage to make a public fight against what has happened to her.

And whatever you come up with, it has to help her or it's not going to help anyone. Thank you very much.

FROM THE FLOOR: You don't speak for all women.

CHAIRMAN HUDSON: We will make that a part of the record. Do Commissioners have questions of Ms Dworkin? Ms Levine.*

MRS LEVINE: Ms Dworkin, do you make any distinction in your definition between erotica and pornography?

MS DWORKIN: There is a recently emerged definition within the feminist movement articulated, for instance, by Gloria Steinem, that says that erotica is sexually explicit material that shows mutuality and reciprocity and equality. I am prepared to accept that definition as something that is not pornography. In the law that I am suggesting, in what I hope will be a federal civil rights law, certainly the law that Catharine MacKinnon and I developed, applies only to sexually explicit material that subordinates women in a way that is detrimental to our civil status, and not to any sexually explicit material.

MRS LEVINE: I am not a lawyer, and I made an attempt to understand the ordinance. Do you think it is possible that one person's vision of subordination is not another's, and by that instance there would be material that Gloria or other people deem erotica that would be attackable under your ordinance, as it is currently drafted?

MS DWORKIN: No, I think that the definition is very specific and very concrete. It's narrowly constructed, an itemized definition, rather than a general definition, so that it would not be subject to that kind of interpretation. And as I think you know, Gloria Steinem has been an active supporter of this law, from the beginning, precisely because from her point of view, it does make that distinction in a way that is clear and concrete.

MRS LEVINE: Do I understand you, then, to think that material that would not be seen—that would be sexually explicit, but mutually agreeable, would not then be considered obscene?

MS DWORKIN: Sexually explicit, sexual equality, sexual reciprocity, and not containing any of the concrete scenarios that are named in

---

* The commissioners present were: Henry Hudson, chair; Judith Becker; Park Dietz; James Dobson; Ellen Levine; Tex Lezar; The Rev. Bruce Ritter; Frederick Schauer; Deanne Tilton.

the definition of the ordinance which are all scenarios of inequality and degradation, mostly violence.

MRS LEVINE: Do you think that for some of the material that is now—could be prosecuted now as obscene, could not be prosecuted as obscene under your definition?

MS DWORKIN: Well, under our definition, there are two corrections I need to make. First of all, obscenity doesn't function in this definition at all.

MRS LEVINE: I understand that. That is the only thing we have now, so I am looking at the distinctions.

MS DWORKIN: Secondly, nothing can be prosecuted; a person brings a civil suit.

MRS LEVINE: I understand that, but to bring people into court for which they would be fined, are there materials now that can be prosecuted as obscene that could not be brought into court in a civil suit?

MS DWORKIN: Yes, I think that there are many, many such materials that right now, it seems to me, that virtually anything can be prosecuted under obscenity law, and about the only thing that isn't, with all respect to the gentleman from North Carolina, whose accomplishments I am not denying, but pornography is precisely what obscenity law has not been used against. Obscenity laws have traditionally been used against works of literature and so on. They are rife for use against sex education programs, because they are so vague, because community standards can be construed in so many ways.

MRS LEVINE: Would there be sexually explicit pictures of intercourse that was mutually agreeable that would therefore not be a civil rights suit, according to your definition?

MS DWORKIN: Yes, there would be.

MRS LEVINE: So in some ways it would be broader?

MS DWORKIN: In some ways it would be broader and in some ways it would be narrower.

291

MRS LEVINE: Let me ask you this—and I know that you are very concerned about violence against women, as are most women—in your opinion, should all pornography be removed, particularly the violent pornography, do you think you would see a direct drop in violent crimes against women?

MS DWORKIN: Of course, I don't know what we would see. My personal answer is I believe that we would see a drop.

MRS LEVINE: Even though so many of these crimes are committed while under the influence of alcohol and other substance abuse?

MS DWORKIN: Yes. I think there is nothing that has the role that pornography does in engendering sexual abuse. I think that's been the case for all the period of time that pornography was used in private, in private sexual abuse, and it's only with the saturation of the public forum that women have in any way found a receptive social structure to listen about the realities of abuse through pornography that have been occurring.

MRS LEVINE: You also think that the rape rates in prisons would drop if the pornography were not in the prisons?

MS DWORKIN: I truly do.

MRS LEVINE: Are there prisons, by the way, where there is no pornography permissible?

MS DWORKIN: As far as I know right now, pornography is absolutely unrestricted in federal and state prisons. There was an injunction recently gotten by a group of women prison guards in the State of California, because *Hustler* did a layout.

MRS LEVINE: I remember that case.

MS DWORKIN: A gang rape of a woman prison guard in a prison that very much resembled the pool table rape that they had done right before the New Bedford gang rape, and those women under their professional association went into court and got an injunction against the distribution of that particular issue, but it didn't apply to any other issue and it didn't happen in every state.

MRS LEVINE: Thank you very much.

CHAIRMAN HUDSON: Dr Dobson, do you have questions?

DR DOBSON: Yes, I do, Mr Chairman. Ms Dworkin, several witnesses have spoken in favor of the civil rights approach, and several have opposed it on the grounds that we already have the laws on the books to accomplish that. Would you speak to those individuals and to that perspective?

MS DWORKIN: Yes. We have laws that deal with a kind of cosmetic social reality. That is to say, who gets to see the pornography that exists, how publicly accessible will it be, will it be hidden under opaque covers, will it be hidden in back rooms, which primarily means: will it be available to men in a segregated all-male world.

How they use it on women remains constant; and only civil rights legislation speaks to the real human injuries, to the people who are being harmed, both in the production of the material, and in its subsequent social effects, on individuals and on women as a class. Obscenity laws don't do that; they were never constructed for that purpose. With the best intentions in the world, they couldn't be used that way.

And the flaws in them now have reached the point where I believe that they are just simply going to implode. The standards that the Supreme Court has constructed are virtually—I understand that many people here have said they understand them. I understand them from moment to moment, but I don't understand them when I am looking at a picture of Asian women being hung from a tree, and the issue is, is the jury aroused or not aroused?

The issue is that the Asian woman is being hung from the tree because somebody thinks that that is sexual somewhere, and it doesn't have to be the people on the jury. It can be the person who took the pictures or the pornographer who prints them.

So obscenity law is in no way responsive to the reality of the pornography industry now.

DR DOBSON: Do you think it could be? Is it possible to write obscenity laws in such a way to redress that problem?

MS DWORKIN: I don't believe that it can be, because I believe that first of all, enforcement by police and prosecutors will always be essentially directed towards the control, not the evisceration, the control of organized crime; and that, therefore, if the production of pornography is not by organized crime—for instance, is not for profit—the abuses to women will not be in any way a top priority for law-enforcement officials. We fight a constant problem in having law-enforcement officials take seriously, as you know, claims of rape, claims of assault, claims of battery.

Once there is a picture that shows the woman smiling while these things are being done to her, that picture, to many men, sadly, is proof of her complicity and proof of her consent.

DR DOBSON: Clarify one final point for me. I thought I saw a contradiction at one point when you recommended that laws against pornographers be enforced, and yet you are opposed to those laws; did I misunderstand you?

MS DWORKIN: I haven't recommended that obscenity laws be enforced. I specifically recommended that laws against pandering be enforced against pornographers and that RICO be used to destroy the pornography industry, which exists through what is defined in RICO as racketeering, that is, acts or threats of murder, extortion, et cetera, kidnapping and so on, and also a trafficking in women—and I think that the use of those criminal laws will be very, very effective.

DR DOBSON: One final question. You have spoken very, very eloquently, to your point. Why do you not have that same fire with regard to children and the abuse of children?

MS DWORKIN: I do. Children have many spokespeople. As I know, when I have done TV shows in behalf of children's rights and against the exploitation of children in pornography, I am stopped on the street by, for instance, many policemen who are happy to talk to me and want to thank me for what I have done, and all kinds of people.

I think that the reality is that the condition of women and children are very tied together; that is a political reality. We both share similar kinds of exploitation and abuse through sex; and unfortunately, the reality is that people at least proclaim to be willing to do something about the abuses of children but remain impervious to the abuses of adult women, and that is why I am here to speak on behalf of adult women.

DR DOBSON: If you equate them in that way, are you opposed to laws against child pornography and the use of children through pornography?

MS DWORKIN: No, what I would have done, had you asked me about laws about child pornography, before the Ferber decision, was to explain to you why I thought obscenity laws could not work in dealing with child pornography, and why there had to be laws against the actual abuse, and that the pornography was proof of the abuse, and, therefore, there had to be laws against the pornography. The Supreme Court has relieved me of that obligation by recognizing that much child pornography, for instance, does not arouse prurient interest, that you can't get a jury to say that it arouses prurient interest, but that that does not mean that the pornography is not violative of human rights; and I believe that the same situation is true with women, that the pornography violates our rights, but we are not asking for a criminal ban.

We are asking for something that is so much less than a criminal ban, it is basically such a modest request for a social remedy, such a modest request for access to the courts to be able to prove our cases; and, therefore, it's very strange to me that we meet with much skepticism and what is the commonplace belief, frequently, that if women are hurt, it is the fault of the women who are hurt, both the women in the pornography and the women who are raped or abused.

DR DOBSON: Thank you.

CHAIRMAN HUDSON: Professor Schauer.

DR SCHAUER: Yes, Ms Dworkin, in your list of items that you concluded your presentation with, I noted the absence of any discussion of economic pressure, boycotts, whether individual or organized or anything of that sort. Was that omitted only in terms of your view of what our Commission should do, or do you have—would you discuss the question generally of boycotts, individual, organized, economic pressure and the like.

MS DWORKIN: I certainly am in favor of the pornography industry being boycotted, but it seems to me that that doesn't speak to the reality of the issue. I grew up in an era when people were prepared not to eat lettuce, not to eat grapes, not to eat tuna fish under certain circumstances when the tunas weren't being caught the right way. And the reality is that that constituency who went so long without lettuce, who went so long without grapes, consumes pornography and defends pornography and has been responsible for some of the most important social defenses, the construction of the most important social defenses of pornography.

I think that with pornography we are dealing with a very peculiar issue, and that is to say men love to denounce it moralistically in public, but do consume it. When we deal with the reality of consumption, in terms of women's rights, it is not women who are consuming pornography; therefore women can't boycott pornography. Men are consuming it, sometimes in secret, sometimes not. Men are using it, and it's not the kind of issue—it's like asking rapists to boycott rape, don't do it.

Well, I agree, they shouldn't do it. But the question is now what to do because they are doing it.

DR SCHAUER: I guess, I mean, we grew up in an era in which the message was "don't buy grapes" rather than "don't shop in the store that sells grapes." Do you think it could be effective to organize a—would your particular problem that you have just referred to be substantially lessened if boycotts and economic pressure were directed against establishments rather than against the particular items?

MS DWORKIN: Well, perhaps you are aware of feminist activism that is directed, for instance—there is a boycott, for instance, against those advertisers who advertise in *Penthouse*. I think that's appropriate; and hopefully that boycott will grow and grow and grow. People should not buy the products of those who support the torture of women. I think that that is appropriate.

As you perhaps know, there is much feminist activism that is involved in sitting in in supermarkets, demonstrating in different places. Certainly I didn't speak about all of the kinds of feminist activism because I didn't think that this Commission would be particularly interested in it.

But we try to make it a habit to exercise our rights of political speech at every opportunity, including during pornography movies, when men actually would prefer that we keep quiet, and through picket lines and through sit-ins; and the first feminist action against pornography was, in fact, an act of civil disobedience in 1970.

So that the history of activism of feminists against pornography is virtually as old as the women's movement.

DR SCHAUER: Thank you.

CHAIRMAN HUDSON: Father Ritter, do you have a question of Ms Dworkin?

FATHER RITTER: Yes. Ms Dworkin, thank you for your extraordinary and very moving testimony. My question doesn't really imply any disagreement with what you said, although I think in some ways I would differ with you on certain issues.

My question is merely my effort to understand one of the central thrusts of your argument. Is the issue with you mostly the nonconsensual aspect of pornography as it relates to the degradation of women, or is it rather the degradation itself with regards to women? Let me illustrate.

If we could find a man and a woman who totally and freely agree to sadomasochistic activities, would you think that should be prohibited, even though in itself it is a very degrading thing to occur to a woman and to a man also?

MS DWORKIN: My answer to your question is I do object to the degradation intrinsic to the acts. That is why I think that a definition of pornography based on sex inequality is a definition that honors human dignity and sexuality.

I think that I certainly would want to see remedies against that pornography. But the reality for women isn't put in that hypothetical question. The forms of coercion— including the reality of poverty, the vulnerability of child sexual abuse in a society where that is commonplace, as you well know—is such that it's very hard to understand what this word consent means. If you look at the way the word consent is used in rape statutes, a woman could be dead and have met the standard for consent.

I mean, it's very hard to know, in a society in which women have been chattel, what consent is, and mostly it's passive acquiescence.

And feminists have to fight for a society in which we go way beyond consent as a standard for freedom, and we are talking about self-determination in a world with real choices; and right now for women, that world of real choices does not really exist.

So my answer to your question is, that material would be actionable under our law, under our civil rights law; in my view it should be, it is appropriate that it be. I think that it is intrinsically degrading, and I also think that it is demonstrable that the material itself in its social consequences causes the acting out on women of the same dimension of sadomasochistic activity. There is simply no reality to the notion that women consent to it, because women don't.

FR RITTER: Thank you.

CHAIRMAN HUDSON: Mrs Levine, do you have another question?

MRS LEVINE: I know Park wanted to go first.

CHAIRMAN HUDSON: Dr Dietz.

DR DIETZ: I know that many people would be interested to hear some specifics about what kinds of depictions would constitute subordination of women, because this is often discussed with some bewilderment. I would like to pose some hypotheticals, some specific images and ask you whether there is enough information here to tell me if that is subordination; and if there is, is it or isn't it? Is it subordination of women to depict naked—a woman on her knees, naked, a man standing, while the woman fellates the man, she on her knees, he standing.

MS DWORKIN: I need to explain something to you about our law, which deserves a little more credit than you are giving it, which is that the definition itself isn't actionable. All right. There is nothing actionable about something meeting the definition. It has to be trafficked in, somebody has to be forced into it, it has to be forced on somebody or it has to be used in a specific kind of assault; so that the hypothetical question about whether I think that is subordination or not depends a great deal—has the women been forced into it? I want to know. What is the sociology around it, is it being used on people, are women being forced to watch it and then do it; and those are the kinds of issues, that is what is required to trigger this law.

DR DIETZ: So if the players truly were voluntary, and if those exposed to it voluntarily chose exposure, then it wouldn't be subordination no matter what was depicted?

MS DWORKIN: No, that is not the case. If it meets the definition, if it meets the definition, and it's trafficked in, the idea is that it creates bigotry and hostility and aggression towards all women. The Indianapolis definition—which I have here if you want me to read it at any point, I know you are all familiar with it—the Indianapolis definition would probably not include the scenario that you describe, because it's all violence-oriented. The definition is oriented toward the violation of women, violence against women, the commission of rape, the creation of pain and pleasure; and as a result, because it's violence-oriented, none of those particular scenarios fall under its reach. Now, in some cases, that is extremely unfortunate, because if you look at a film like *Deep Throat*, it is very hard to find in the film the kind of sexual violence that allows this law to be triggered. Yet somebody was coerced into making that film through the most reprehensible and extreme violence, so some choices have got to be made here about what are our priorities.

Dorothy Stratton was coerced and raped in the *Playboy* system. There is a history of the exploitation of women through sexual harassment, through coercion in the *Playboy* system. Do you want that material to be covered or not? I do. Because I think the women who have been hurt are more important than the existence of Bunnies in society for men. All right? But when we are talking about the prototype for this legislation, when we are talking about the Indianapolis definition, it focuses on sexually violent material.

DR DIETZ: I take it from your response to other questions that you believe it does not occur that a woman voluntarily poses for pictures for *Penthouse* or *Playboy*.

MS DWORKIN: No, that is not true. I believe that it does voluntarily occur. *Playboy* is the top of the ladder and it's all downhill from there. It's the highest amount of money that a woman gets paid for posing in pornography; it consistently involves the exploitation of extremely young women who have very few options in society, although *Playboy* has certainly made it part of its major publicity goal to do everything that they can to target professional and working women for sexual exploitation and sexual harassment; and it's not that I don't think that women ever voluntarily are part of pornography. I think that the fact that women sometimes voluntarily are part of pornography should not stop us from doing something about the women who are coerced.

I think the fact that most women who are in pornography are victims of child sexual abuse is probably the most telling point about what the pornography system is all about.

DR DIETZ: I have a question on that one.

MS DWORKIN: Okay. I think if you look at the pornography, what you see is the slick stuff; you see *Playboy* has pictures of Asian women with needles in them throughout their body. There is plenty of violence in *Playboy*. So you see that kind of violence legitimized.

DR DIETZ: I think we have just slipped off the topic of consent.

MS DWORKIN: Part of what I want to say is a lot of the pornography you see in the market if you go and you buy it, not in the supermarket but in the adult bookstores, are women who are so at the bottom of the social ladder, they are so scooped up off the street and stood up and photographed before they nod out. They are so totally at the end of their ropes as human beings, at the end of their lives, that that is the main population of women that we are talking about, not the cosmeticized *Playboy* Bunny.

DR DIETZ: I think you may have some information that may be very helpful to us. I am going to try to elicit that.

One is, how do you know about the proportion of women who have, in fact, been victimized in other settings, such as incestuous relationships, before coming to pornography? What is the population from which you know that?

MS DWORKIN: All right. First of all there are several studies, because unfortunately if one is a feminist, one is not allowed out in public without studies. No matter how many women have come to one and told one about what has happened, that doesn't count, it doesn't matter. So there are several studies that pretty much consistently show a sixty-five to seventy-five percentage of women who are in prostitution or pornography who have had experiences in child sexual abuse.

DR DIETZ: These are studies of prostitutes?

MS DWORKIN: Studies of prostitutes.

DR DIETZ: Are there any studies of women—you may not think it's possible. Is there such a thing in your view as a woman engaging in hard-core pornography who is not a prostitute?

MS DWORKIN: No, in my view there is no such thing.

DR DIETZ: So the studies of prostitutes would include women whose pictures have not been taken?

MS DWORKIN: Yes.

DR DIETZ: But you don't have studies of women exclusively of whom pictures are taken?

MS DWORKIN: No, the studies are in fact just being generated by a lot of the political work that we've been doing. The most we have right now is something that is not so much a study, although it was printed as such, by the Delancy Street Foundation on Divisadero Street in San Francisco, where they did a study of 200 prostitutes and asked no questions about pornography at all, and were given so much information about it, that they published their findings, even though they are not scientifically valid. Of those 200 women, I believe there were 193 cases of rape, 178 cases of child sexual abuse. This is in a population of 200 women, and a very large number of them had been put into pornography as children. I don't have it with me and I don't remember the percentages, but I'll get it for you if you want it. ["Pornography and Sexual Abuse of Women," by Mimi H. Silber and Ayala M. Pines in *Sex Roles*, Vol. 10, Nos. 11/12, 1984, pp. 857–868]

I hope now that the studies are going to be done. We are asking rape crisis centers all over the country to begin intake information on all of this. We are doing what we can to get the information, but we have had no help.

DR DIETZ: Would it be correct to say that it is your view that of the women who have their pictures taken in a manner that is disseminated for the sexual pleasure of men, that some proportion of those women have been criminally coerced at the very moment of the photographs being taken?

MS DWORKIN: Yes.

DR DIETZ: That is, they have a gun to their head. Or someone has just beaten them.

MS DWORKIN: Yes.

DR DIETZ: That there is another proportion whose coercion is more like that of battered women who for two years have been kept captive and this day seems to be going smoothly, but they know perfectly well they have no choice that day but to behave, though there is no gun that day; and that there is yet another group who come to this with neither of those happening to them at the moment but in the past have been abused in some way that leads them to act as if they were currently being battered by those dealing with them. That is, former incest victims—

MS DWORKIN: Yes. I don't know that those categories are as discrete as you're making them.

DR DIETZ: That's right. They are not mutually exclusive, certainly. Is there still, after all of that, a group of women whose coercion is occurring only in the sense that they live in a society in which it is expected that women who wish to pose this way if they get paid enough and are—treated the right way; would you call that group coercion?

MS DWORKIN: I would say that the existence of that group, contrary to popular opinion, is the most hypothetical, that we don't know, that we can't find that group, that we can find the women who are coerced by the pimps, we can find the women who are battered, we can find the women who are sexually abused, but women who have a series of choices that make sense, and choose pornography, those women are not easy to find.

DR DIETZ: If a woman chose to come to this Commission and say I chose to pose and I enjoyed it and it's the best thing I ever did, would you think she's lying to us?

MS DWORKIN: Having talked to many women who have come before many groups saying that, and having talked to them in private, it has never yet happened that there hasn't been some form of sexual abuse that has been major in what pushed her one way or another into the industry. I have never encountered it. That certainly doesn't mean that it doesn't exist, but my question is, I know William Blake found all the world in a grain of sand, but I think when you look at this situation, we have to deal with pornography as a real system of coercion that operates both in terms of physical coercion and economic vulnerability.

DR DIETZ: One last question. You have talked to us a lot about women and the exploitation and torture of women. What about pornography depicting men? What do you think about that?

MS DWORKIN: I have also talked to you about the rape of men in prisons. I think feminists are very concerned about rape wherever we find it, and I think that the exploitation of men in pornography is a serious problem for young men, for men who are runaways, for men who are dispossessed in some sense from society; but men who don't die in it get out of it, usually.

It doesn't become a way of life for men in the same way that it does for women. It's not a total dead end with no other options ever; and for women that is what it tends to be.

I think that in Minneapolis, in our hearings that we had there around the civil rights legislation, we had a great deal of testimony about the use of all-male pornography in homosexual battery; I believe that that is real, that that is true, that under civil rights legislation, men who are battered in that way must have a right to sue.

I think that pornography also has tremendous implications for the civil status of black men in this country, whose constant, constant use as rapists in the pornography is very tied to their low civil status historically in this country. I think that that matters. So I think the implications for men are very important.

CHAIRMAN HUDSON: Mrs Tilton.

MS TILTON: Let me also ask Dr Dietz's question. You mentioned that there are snuff films. Are you aware of specific snuff films? Have you seen them? Can you give us more information?

MS DWORKIN: I will give you the information that I can give you on them.

No, I have never seen them. I hope never to. We know of a conviction in California; it's the Douglas and Hernandez case of two men who were making a snuff film. Of course they were convicted for murder. They had tried to make a snuff film previously and had, in quotes, been "entrapped" by a female police officer.

They were then let go and then they tried again and succeeded in committing a murder and filming it.

We have information that right now snuff films are selling in the Las Vegas area—a print costs $2500 to $3000—and some places are being screened for $250 a seat.

We have information from prostitutes in one part of the country that they are being forced to watch snuff films before then being forced to engage in heavily sadomasochistic acts. They are terrified.

We have information on the survivalist from Calaveras County, the man who kept all these women as slaves and filmed his torture and his killing of them and made films of that.

We have information on something, and I hope you will excuse me but I will just simply use the language, called skull fucking, which apparently was brought back from Viet Nam, and those are films in which a woman is killed and the orifices in her head are penetrated with a man's penis, her eyes and her mouth and so on.

The information comes from women who have seen the films and escaped.

One of the problems that we have in communicating with law-enforcement people is we always get the information first, whether it's about rape or murder or anything else. We are seldom believed. We are afraid of exposing women who are already in enough jeopardy to a male legal system that will not give them either credibility or protection, so we have a great deal of evidence that would not hold up in the sphere of social policy as evidence. And I suppose until we can bring you a film, you will not believe that it exists.

MS TILTON: Along that, do you want to ask a question now?

DR DIETZ: I just want to say that the Commission is aware of cases in which offenders for their own purposes have made such things, and that it may be the case in California that they had the notion that there might be some commercial merit to what they were doing.

But so far, every example that's been offered of what was believed to be a snuff film, has been a Hollywood creation.

MS DWORKIN: No, no, there's been one Hollywood creation.

DR DIETZ: Hollywood's film *Snuff*, the George C. Scott film and, of course, many X-rated things could be considered that if anyone actually died. But Hollywood, as far as we've heard, is the source of that notion. Now, life may be beginning to imitate art and it would be very valuable if we can learn of anything that truly does exist, especially if it predated the Hollywood—

MS DWORKIN: The initial public information about snuff films was made by a policeman in 1975, before the fraudulent snuff film was distributed on the market, and he said that the films were being imported from South America. It was because of the newspaper coverage of his testimony, as I understand it—and I have done some investigating of it—that the wonderful person who made and distributed the fraudulent snuff film got the idea to do it. He simply capitalized on what he had learned about it in the newspapers and took what had been an old film and put a new ending on it that resembled the film he had read about.

But that original information was from the police, and I think that getting—I understand that nobody yet has found and has a copy. I understand that the Justice Department tried. My information comes from a journalist, whose sources I trust, that such films exist, from women who have seen them, whom I believe, whom no law-enforcement official would, that the films exist, that they have seen them. And so far, all that I could tell you is that it doesn't mean we won't be wrong, but so far we have said battery exists and the FBI has said it doesn't, and we have been right. And we've said rape exists and law-enforcement people have said, no; and we have been right. And we said incest is rife in this country and law-enforcement people first said no, and we were right. Our big secret is that we listen to the people to whom it happens. And that's what we are doing here.

MS TILTON: While we are on the subject of unprovable or proposed crimes without evidence, are you, in your work with prostitutes and victims of pornography, so to speak, finding that these women are relating stories involving more extreme types of sexual abuse as children? Do you find any evidence of their involvement in sex rings, ritualistic torture, the kinds of cases that seem to be cropping up throughout the country for which there is no evidence, in terms of the picture?

MS DWORKIN: What I found consistently, from women who have talked to me, is that there are sex rings in communities made up of people who are outstanding members of those communities. They exist not for profit. They all involve pornography and the trading of the pornography of the children as well as the trading of the children. They all involve some form of maiming of the children from cutting them up, physically injuring them very badly. They appear to be extremely sadistic. That's the information that I have on that.

MS TILTON: And that information you are receiving indicates pictures were taken in the process?

MS DWORKIN: Pictures—in every case, pictures are part of the sex. One of the things that is so interesting, even about the adult pornography that is now being produced, is that making pornography itself is presented as a sex act in the pornography that is almost the equivalent of rape. It's an act of total violation and in the course of it, the person discovers that that is part of their sexual gratification.

May I just add one more point?

MS TILTON: Sure.

MS DWORKIN: This is going back to the snuff films. That is, as I understand it, because we did a great deal of work around *Snuff* when the fraudulent film was distributed, if any of those films that you know have existed, the ones where the murderers have made them themselves, came on the commercial pornography market, they would be protected speech.

That, at least, is the position that the District Attorney of New York City took, that as long as the person who did the film was convicted of the murder, that was the crime, and the film itself would be protected speech. I think it is very important to think about that in terms of what kind of social policy recommendations you make.

306

MS TILTON: I also wanted to comment on the examples that you provide which, in the majority, are extreme cases, and would involve a crime. I am concerned about those that would be worried that victims might lose certain protections, if the obscenity laws were not enforced, but rather the responsibility for taking action would rest with the victim. Is there not a risk that we are now placing responsibility on the victims to take action, rather than the general direction of taking action on behalf of the victims because they are, in fact, victims and should not be responsible for the consequences to the victim?

MS DWORKIN: Thank you very much for that question. I think that that goes to the heart of the dilemma, which is that the state has entirely abdicated its responsibility to the people that we are talking about, and most civil rights law in fact is based on the state's abdication of responsibility for assuring human rights for discrete groups of people, based on color or based on sex.

And it seems to me that obscenity law in and of itself has the flaws that I said, and it's not going to help people who have been victimized.

But in addition, the indifference of the legal establishment to crimes of violence against women is simply too deeply in place. We are too invisible. It is always business as usual when we come before a court because of a given assault; and so what we need is some new language based on some new theory to give us real visibility and real presence inside this legal system for the things that really happen to us. But I do understand your concern and I do agree that it's a fundamental problem.

MS TILTON: Thank you.

CHAIRMAN HUDSON: The Commission is now going to stand in recess for one half an hour for lunch. I would ask that all persons please clear the courtroom, and that any witness who is on our witness list who has not as yet reported to the Commission staff, please do so during the next half an hour.

(Whereupon, at 1:45 p.m., the hearing was recessed, to reconvene at 2:15 p.m., this same day.)

307

Letter from a War Zone

1986

Written at the invitation of feminists at Emma, *Germany's premier feminist magazine,* Letter from a War Zone *has been published in German in* Emma *and in Norwegian in* Klassekampen. *It has never been published in English before.*

S ISTERS: I DON'T know who you are, or how many, but I will tell you what happened to us. We were brave and we were fools; some of us collaborated; I don't know the outcome. It is late 1986 now, and we are losing. The war is men against women; the country is the United States. Here, a woman is beaten every eighteen seconds: by her husband or the man she lives with, not by a psychotic stranger in an alley. Understand: women are also beaten by strangers in alleys but that is counted in a different category—gender-neutral assault, crime in the streets, big-city violence. Woman-beating, the intimate kind, is the most commonly committed violent crime in the country, according to the FBI, not feminists. A woman is raped every three minutes, nearly half the rapes committed by someone the woman knows. Forty-four percent of the adult women in the United States have been raped at least once. Forty-one percent (in some studies seventy-one percent) of all rapes are committed by two or more men; so the question is not how many rapes there are, but how many rapists. There are an estimated 16000 new cases of father-daughter incest each year; and in the current generation of children, thirty-eight percent of girls are sexually molested. Here, now, less than eight percent of women have not had some form of unwanted sex (from assault to obscene harassment) forced on them.

We keep calling this war normal life. Everyone's ignorant; no one

308

knows; the men don't mean it. In this war, the pimps who make pornography are the SS, an élite, sadistic, military, organized vanguard. They run an efficient and expanding system of exploitation and abuse in which women and children, as lower life forms, are brutalized. This year they will gross $10 billion.

We have been slow to understand. For fun they gag us and tie us up as if we are dead meat and hang us from trees and ceilings and door frames and meat hooks; but many say the lynched women probably like it and we don't have any right to interfere with them (the women) having a good time. For fun they rape us or have other men, or sometimes animals, rape us and film the rapes and show the rapes in movie theatres or publish them in magazines, and the normal men who are not pimps (who don't know, don't mean it) pay money to watch; and we are told that the pimps and the normal men are free citizens in a free society exercising rights and that we are prudes because this is sex and real women don't mind a little force and the. women get paid anyway so what's the big deal? The pimps and the normal men have a constitution that says the filmed rapes are "protected speech" or "free speech." Well, it doesn't actually *say* that—cameras, after all, hadn't been invented yet; but they interpret their constitution to protect their fun. They have laws and judges that call the women hanging from the trees "free speech." There are films in which women are urinated on, defecated on, cut, maimed, and scholars and politicians call them "free speech." The politicians, of course, deplore them. There are photographs in which women's breasts are slammed in sprung rat traps—in which things (including knives, guns, glass) are stuffed in our vaginas—in which we are gang-banged, beaten, tortured—and journalists and intellectuals say: Well, there is a lot of violence against women *but* ... But what, prick? But we run this country, cunt.

If you are going to hurt a woman in the United States, be sure to take a photograph. This will confirm that the injury you did to her expressed a point-of-view, sacrosanct in a free society. Hey, you have a right not to like women in a democracy, man. In the very unlikely event that the victim can nail you for committing a crime of violence against her, your photograph is still constitutionally protected, since it communicates so eloquently. The woman, her brutalization, the pain, the humiliation, her smile—because you did force her to smile, didn't you?—can be sold forever to millions of normal men (them again) who—so the happy theory goes—are having a "cathartic" experience all over her. It's the same with snuff films, by the way. You can torture and disembowel a woman, ejaculate on her dismembered uterus, and even if they do put you away someday for murder (a rather simple-minded euphemism), the film is legally *speech. Speech.*

In the early days, feminism was primitive. If something hurt women, feminists were against it, not for it. In 1970, radical feminists forcibly occupied the offices of the ostensibly radical Grove Press because Grove published pornography marketed as sexual liberation and exploited its female employees. Grove's publisher, an eminent boy-revolutionary, considered the hostile demonstration CIA-inspired. His pristine radicalism did not stop him from calling the very brutal New York City police and having the women physically dragged out and locked up for trespassing on his private property. Also in 1970, radical feminists seized *Rat*, an underground rag that devoted itself, in the name of revolution, to pornography and male chauvinism equally, the only attention gender got on the radical left. The pornographers, who think strategically and actually do know what they are doing, were quick to react. "These chicks are our natural enemy," wrote Hugh Hefner in a secret memo leaked to feminists by secretaries at *Playboy*. "It is time we do battle with them... What I want is a devastating piece that takes the militant feminists apart." What he got were huge, raucous demonstrations at Playboy Clubs in big cities.

Activism against pornography continued, organized locally, ignored by the media but an intrinsic part of the feminist resistance to rape. Groups called Women Against Violence Against Women formed independently in many cities. Pornography was understood by feminists (without any known exception) as woman-hating, violent, rapist. Robin Morgan pinpointed pornography as the theory, rape as the practice. Susan Brownmiller, later a founder of the immensely influential Women Against Pornography, saw pornography as woman-hating propaganda that promoted rape. These insights were not banal to feminists who were beginning to comprehend the gynocidal and terrorist implications of rape for all women. These were *emerging* political insights, not learned-by-rote slogans.

Sometime in 1975, newspapers in Chicago and New York City revealed the existence of snuff films. Police detectives, trying to track down distribution networks, said that prostitutes, probably in Central America, were being tortured, slowly dismembered, then killed, for the camera. Prints of the films were being sold by organized crime to private pornography collectors in the United States.

In February 1976, a day or two before Susan B. Anthony's birthday, a snazzy, first-run movie house in Times Square showed what purported to be a real snuff film. The marquee towered above the vast Times Square area, the word *Snuff* several feet high in neon, next to the title the words "made in South America where life is cheap." In the ads that blanketed the subways, a woman's body was cut in half.

We felt despair, rage, pain, grief. We picketed every night. It rained every night. We marched round and round in small circles. We watched men take women in on dates. We watched the women come out, physically sick, and still go home with the men. We leafletted. We screamed out of control on street corners. There was some vandalism: not enough to close it down. We tried to get the police to close it down. We tried to get the District Attorney to close it down. You have no idea what respect those guys have for free speech.

The pimp who distributed the film would come to watch the picket line and laugh at us. Men who went in laughed at us. Men who walked by laughed at us. Columnists in newspapers laughed at us. The American Civil Liberties Union ridiculed us through various spokesmen (in those days, they used men). The police did more than laugh at us. They formed a barricade with their bodies, guns, and nightsticks—to protect the film from women. One threw me in front of an oncoming car. Three protestors were arrested and *locked up* for using obscene language to the theatre manager. Under the United States Constitution, obscene language is not speech. Understand: it is not that obscene language is unprotected speech; it is not considered speech at all. The protestors, talking, used obscene language that was not speech; the maiming in the snuff film, the knife eviscerating the woman, was speech. All this we had to learn.

We learned a lot, of course. Life may be cheap, but knowledge never is. We learned that the police protect property and that pornography is property. We learned that the civil liberties people didn't give a damn, my dear: a woman's murder, filmed to bring on orgasm, was speech, and they didn't even *mind* (these were the days before they learned that they had to say it was bad to hurt women). The ACLU did not have a crisis of conscience. The District Attorney went so far as to find a woman he claimed was "the actress" in the film to show she was alive. He held a press conference. He said that the only law the film broke was the law against fraud. He virtually challenged us to try to get the pimps on fraud, while making clear that if the film had been real, no United States law would have been broken because the murder would have occurred elsewhere. So we learned that. During the time *Snuff* showed in New York City, the bodies of several women, hacked to pieces, were found in the East River and several prostitutes were decapitated. We also learned that.

When we started protesting *Snuff*, so-called feminist lawyers, many still leftists at heart, were on our side: no woman could sit this one out. We watched the radical boy lawyers pressure, threaten, ridicule, insult, and intimidate them; and they did abandon us. They went home. They never came back. We saw them learn to love free speech above women. Having hardened their radical little hearts to *Snuff*, what could ever make them put women first again?

There were great events. In November 1978, the first feminist conference on pornography was held in San Francisco. It culminated in the country's first Take Back the Night March: well over 3000 women shut down San Francisco's pornography district for one night. In October 1979, over 5000 women and men marched on Times Square. One documentary of the march shows a man who had come to Times Square to buy sex looking at the sea of women extending twenty city blocks and saying, bewildered and dismayed: "I can't find one fucking woman." In 1980, Linda Marchiano published *Ordeal*. World-famous as Linda Lovelace, the porn-queen extraordinaire of *Deep Throat*, Marchiano revealed that she had been forced into prostitution and pornography by brute terrorism. Gang-raped, beaten, kept in sexual slavery by her pimp/husband (who had legal rights over her as her husband), forced to have intercourse with a dog for a film, subjected to a sustained sadism rarely found by Amnesty International with regard to political prisoners, she dared to survive, escape, and expose the men who had sexually used her (including *Playboy*'s Hugh Hefner and *Screw*'s Al Goldstein). The world of normal

men (the consumers) did not believe her; they believed *Deep Throat.*
Feminists did believe her. Today Marchiano is a strong feminist
fighting pornography.

In 1980, when I read *Ordeal,* I understood from it that every civil
right protected by law in this country had been broken on Linda's
prostituted body. I began to see gang rape, marital rape and battery,
prostitution, and other forms of sexual abuse as civil rights violations
which, in pornography, were systematic and intrinsic (the pornography could not exist without them). The pornographers, it was
clear, violated the civil rights of women much as the Ku Klux Klan in
this country had violated the civil rights of blacks. The pornographers
were domestic terrorists determined to enforce, through violence, an
inferior status on people born female. The second-class status of
women itself was constructed through sexual abuse; and the name of
the whole system of female subordination was *pornography*—men's
orgasm and sexual pleasure synonymous with women's sexually
explicit inequality. Either we were human, equal, citizens, in which
case the pornographers could not do to us what they did with
impunity and, frankly, constitutional protection; or we were inferior,
not protected as equal persons by law, and so the pimps could
brutalize us, the normal men could have a good time, the pimps and
their lawyers and the normal men could call it free speech, and we
could live in hell. Either the pornographers and the pornography did
violate the civil rights of women, or women had no rights of equality.

I asked Catharine A. MacKinnon, who had pioneered sexual
harassment litigation, if we could mount a civil rights suit in Linda's
behalf. Kitty worked with me, Gloria Steinem (an early and brave
champion of Linda), and several lawyers for well over a year to
construct a civil rights suit. It could not, finally, be brought, because
the statute of limitations on every atrocity committed against Linda
had expired; and there was no law against showing or profiting from
the films she was coerced into making. Kitty and I were despondent;
Gloria said our day would come. It did—in Minneapolis on December
30, 1983, when the City Council passed the first human rights
legislation ever to recognize pornography as a violation of the civil
rights of all women. In Minneapolis, a politically progressive city,
pornography had been attacked as a *class* issue for many years.
Politicians cynically zoned adult bookstores into poor and black areas

of the city. Violence against the already disenfranchised women and children increased massively; and the neighborhoods experienced economic devastation as legitimate businesses moved elsewhere. The civil rights legislation was passed in Minneapolis because poor people, people of color (especially Native Americans and blacks), and feminists demanded justice.

But first, understand this. Since 1970, but especially after *Snuff*, feminist confrontations with pornographers had been head-on: militant, aggressive, dangerous, defiant. We had thousands of demonstrations. Some were inside theatres where, for instance, feminists in the audience would scream like hell when a woman was being hurt on the screen. Feminists were physically dragged from the theatres by police who found the celluloid screams to be *speech* and the feminist screams to be *disturbing the peace*. Banners were unfurled in front of ongoing films. Blood was poured on magazines and sex paraphernalia designed to hurt women. Civil disobedience, sit-ins, destruction of magazines and property, photographing consumers, as well as picketing, leafletting, letter-writing, and debating in public forums, have all been engaged in over all these years without respite. Women have been arrested repeatedly: the police protecting, always, the pornographers. In one jury trial, three women, charged with two felonies and one misdemeanor for pouring blood over pornography, said that they were acting to prevent a greater harm—rape; they also said that the blood was already there, they were just making it visible. They were acquitted when the jury heard testimony about the actual use of pornography in rape and incest *from the victims:* a raped woman; an incestuously abused teenager.

So understand this too: *feminism works;* at least primitive feminism works. We used militant activism to defy and to try to destroy the men who exist to hurt women, that is, the pimps who make pornography. We wanted to destroy—not just put some polite limits on but *destroy*—their power to hurt us; and millions of women, each alone at first, one at a time, began to remember, or understand, or find words for how she herself had been hurt by pornography, what had happened to her because of it. Before feminists took on the pornographers, each woman, as always, had thought that only she had been abused in, with, or because of pornography. Each woman lived in isolation, fear, shame. Terror creates silence. Each woman had lived in unbreachable silence. Each woman had been deeply hurt by the rape, the incest, the battery; but something more had happened too, and there was no name for it and no description of it. Once the role of pornography in *creating* sexual abuse was exposed—rape by rape, beating by beating, victim by victim—our understanding of the nature of sexual abuse itself changed. To talk about rape alone, or battery alone, or incest alone, was not to talk about the totality of how the women had been violated. Rape or wife-beating or prostitution or incest were not discrete or free-standing phenomena. We had thought: some men rape; some men batter; some men fuck little girls. We had accepted an inert model of male sexuality: men have fetishes; the women must always be blond, for instance; the act that brings on orgasm must always be the same. But abuse created by pornography was different: the abuse was multifaceted, complex; the violations of each individual woman were many and interconnected; the sadism was exceptionally dynamic. We found that when pornography created sexual abuse, men learned any new tricks the pornographers had to teach. We learned that anything that hurt or humiliated women could be sex for men who used pornography; and male sexual practice would change dramatically to accommodate violations and degradations promoted by the pornography. We found that sexual abuses in a woman's life were intricately and complexly connected when pornography was a factor: pornography was used to accomplish incest and then the child would be used to make pornography; the pornography-consuming husband would not just beat his wife but would tie her, hang her, torture her, force her into prostitution, and film her for pornography; pornography used in gang rape meant that the gang rape was enacted according to an already existing script, the sadism of the gang rape enhanced by the contributions of the pornographers. The forced filming of forced sex became a new sexual violation of women. In sexual terms, pornography created for women and children concentration camp conditions. This is not hyperbole.

One psychologist told the Minneapolis City Council about three cases involving pornography used as "recipe books": "Presently or recently I have worked with clients who have been sodomized by broom handles, forced to have sex with over 20 dogs in the back seat of their car, tied up and then electrocuted on their genitals. These are children [all] in the ages of 14 to 18 ... where the perpetrator has read the manuals and manuscripts at night and used these as recipe books by day or had the pornography present at the time of the sexual violence."

A social worker who works exclusively with adolescent female prostitutes testified: "I can say almost categorically never have I had a client who has not been exposed to prostitution through pornography... For some young women that means that they are shown pornography, either films, videotapes, or pictures as this is how you do it, almost as a training manual in how to perform acts of prostitution. ... In addition, out on the street when a young woman is [working], many of her tricks or customers will come up to her with little pieces of paper, pictures that were torn from a magazine and say, I want this.... it is like a mail order catalogue of sex acts, and that is what she is expected to perform.... Another aspect that plays a big part in my work ... is that on many occasions my clients are multi, many rape victims. These rapes are often either taped or have photographs taken of the event. The young woman when she tries to escape [is blackmailed]."

A former prostitute, testifying on behalf of a group of former prostitutes afraid of exposure, confirmed: "[W]e were all introduced to prostitution through pornography, there were no exceptions in our group, and we were all under 18." Everything done to women in pornography was done to these young prostitutes by the normal men. To them the prostitutes were synonymous with the pornography but so were all women, including wives and daughters. The abuses of prostitutes were not qualitatively different from the abuses of other women. Out of a compendium of pain, this is one incident: "[A] woman met a man in a hotel room in the 5th Ward. When she got there she was tied up while sitting on a chair nude. She was gagged and left alone in the dark for what she believed to be an hour. The man returned with two other men. They burned her with cigarettes and attached nipple clips to her breasts. They had many S and M magazines with them and showed her many pictures of women appearing to consent, enjoy, and encourage this abuse. She was held for 12 hours, continuously raped and beaten. She was paid $50 or about $2.33 per hour."

Racist violation is actively promoted in pornography; and the abuse has pornography's distinctive dynamic—an annihilating sadism, the brutality and contempt taken wholesale from the pornography itself. The pornographic video game "Custer's Revenge" generated many gang rapes of Native American women. In the game, men try to capture a "squaw," tie her to a tree, and rape her. In the sexually explicit game, the penis goes in and out, in and out. One victim of the "game" said: "When I was first asked to testify I resisted some because the memories are so painful and so recent. I am here because of my four-year-old daughter and other Indian children.... I was attacked by two white men and from the beginning they let me know they hated my people ... And they let me know that the rape of a 'squaw' by white men was practically honored by white society. In fact, it had been made into a video game called 'Custer's Last Stand' [sic]. They held me down and as one was running the tip of his knife across my face and throat he said, 'Do you want to play Custer's Last Stand? It's great, you lose but you don't care, do you? You like a little pain, don't you, squaw?' They both laughed and then he said, 'There is a lot of cock in Custer's Last Stand. You should be grateful, squaw, that All-American boys like us want you. Maybe we will tie you to a tree and start a fire around you.'"

The same sadistic intensity and arrogance is evident in this pornography-generated gang rape of a thirteen-year-old girl. Three deer hunters, in the woods, looking at pornography magazines, looked up and saw the blond child. "There's a live one," one said. The three hunters chased the child, gang-raped her, pistol-whipped her breasts, all the while calling her names from the pornography magazines scattered at their campsite—Golden Girl, Little Godiva, and so on. "All three of them had hunting rifles. They, two men held their guns at my head and the first man hit my breast with his rifle and they continued to laugh. And then the first man raped me and when he was finished they started making jokes about how I was a virgin ... The second man then raped me ... The third man forced his penis into my mouth and told me to do it and I didn't know how to do it. I did not know what I was supposed to be doing.... one of the men pulled the trigger on his gun so I tried harder. Then when he had an erection, he raped me. They continued to make jokes about how lucky they were to have found me when they did and they made jokes about being a virgin. They started ... kicking me and told me that if I wanted more, I could come back the next day ... I didn't tell anyone that I was raped until I was 20 years old." These men, like the men who gang-raped the Native American woman, had fun; they were playing a game.

I am quoting from some representative but still relatively *simple* cases. Once the role of pornography in the abuse is exposed, we no longer have just rape or gang rape or child abuse or prostitution. We have, instead, sustained and intricate sadism with no inherent or predictable limits on the kinds or degrees of brutality that will be used on women or girls. We have torture; we have killer-hostility.

Pornography-saturated abuse is specific and recognizable because it is Nazism on women's bodies: the hostility and sadism it generates are carnivorous. Interviewing 200 working prostitutes in San Francisco, Mimi H. Silbert and Ayala M. Pines discovered astonishing patterns of hostility related to pornography. No questions were asked about pornography. But so much information was given casually by the women about the role of pornography in assaults on them that Silbert and Pines published the data they had stumbled on. Of the 200 women, 193 had been raped as adults and 178 had been sexually assaulted as children. That is 371 cases of sexual assault on a population of 200 women. Twenty-four percent of those who had been raped mentioned that the rapist made specific references to pornography during the rape: "the assailant referred to pornographic materials he had seen or read and then insisted that the victims not only enjoyed the rape but also the extreme violence." When a victim, in some cases, told the rapist that she was a prostitute and would perform whatever sex act he wanted (to dissuade him from using violence), *in all cases* the rapists responded in these ways: "(1) their language became more abusive, (2) they became significantly more violent, beating and punching the women excessively, often using weapons they had shown the women, (3) they mentioned having seen prostitutes in pornographic films, the majority of them mentioning specific pornographic literature, and (4) after completing the forced vaginal penetration, they continued to assault the women sexually in ways they claimed they had seen prostitutes enjoy in the pornographic literature they cited." Examples include forced anal penetration with a gun, beatings all over the body with a gun, breaking bones, holding a loaded pistol at the woman's vagina "insisting this was the way she had died in the film he had seen."

Studies show that between sixty-five and seventy-five percent of women in pornography were sexually abused as children, often incestuously, many put into pornography as children. One woman, for instance, endured this: "I'm an incest survivor, ex-pornography model and ex-prostitute. My incest story begins before pre-school and ends many years later—this was with my father. I was also molested by an uncle and a minister... my father forced me to perform sexual acts with men at a stag party when I was a teenager. I am from a 'nice' middle-class family... My father is an $80000 a year corporate executive, lay minister, and alcoholic... My father was my pimp in pornography. There were 3 occasions from ages 9–16 when he forced me to be a pornography model... in Nebraska, so, yes, it does happen here." This woman is now a feminist fighting pornography. She listens to men mostly debate whether or not there is any social harm connected to pornography. People want experts. We have experts. Society says we have to prove harm. We have proved harm. What we have to prove is that women are human enough for harm to matter. As one liberal so-called feminist said recently: "What's the harm of pornography? A paper cut?" This woman was a Commissioner on the so-called Meese Commission.* She had spent a year of her life looking at the brutalization of women in pornography and hearing the life-stories of pornography-abused women. Women were not very human to her.

In pain and in privacy, women began to face, then to tell, the truth, first to themselves, then to others. Now, women have testified before governmental bodies, in public meetings, on radio, on television, in workshops at conventions of liberal feminists who find all this so messy, so declassé, *so unfortunate*. Especially, the liberal feminists hate it that this mess of pornography—having to do something about these abuses of women—might interfere with their quite comfortable political alliances with all those normal men, the consumers— who also happen to be, well, friends. They don't want the stink of this kind of sexual abuse—the down-and-dirty kind for fun and profit—to

* Named by the pornographers and their friends after the very right-wing Edwin Meese, the Commission was actually set up by the moderate former Attorney General, William French Smith.

rub off on them. Feminism to them means getting success, not fighting oppression.

Here we are: weep for us. Society, with the acquiescence of too many liberal-left feminists, says that pornographers must *not* be stopped because the freedom of everyone depends on the freedom of the pornographers to exercise speech. The woman gagged and hanging remains the speech they exercise. In liberal-left lingo, stopping them is called *censorship*.

The civil rights law—a modest approach, since it is not the barrel of a gun—was passed twice in Minneapolis, vetoed twice there by the mayor. In Indianapolis, a more conservative city (where even liberal feminists are registered Republicans), a narrower version was adopted: *narrower* means that only very violent pornography was covered by the law. In Indianapolis, pornography was defined as the graphic, sexually explicit subordination of women in pictures and/or words that also included rape, pain, humiliation, penetration by objects or animals, or dismemberment. Men, children, and trans-sexuals used in these ways could also use this law. The law made pornographers legally and economically responsible for the harm they did to women. Makers of pornography, exhibitors, sellers, and distributors could be sued for trafficking in pornography. Anyone coerced into pornography could hold the makers, sellers, distributors, or exhibitors liable for profiting from the coercion and could have the coerced product removed from the marketplace. Anyone forced to watch pornography in their home, place of work or education, or in public, could sue whoever forces them and any institution that sanctions the force (for instance, a university or an employer). Anyone physically assaulted or injured because of a specific piece of pornography could sue the pornographer for money damages and get the pornography off the shelves. Under this law, pornography is correctly understood and recognized as a practice of sex discrimination. Pornography's impact on the status of women is to keep all women second-class: targets of aggression and civilly inferior.

The United States courts have declared the Indianapolis civil rights law unconstitutional. A Federal Appeals Court said that pornography did all the harm to women we said it did—causing us both physical injury and civil inferiority— but its success in hurting us only proved its power as speech. Therefore, it is protected speech. Compared with the pimps, women have no rights.

The good news is that the pornographers are in real trouble, and that we made the trouble. *Playboy* and *Penthouse* are both in deep financial trouble. *Playboy* has been losing subscribers, and thus its advertising base, for years; both *Playboy* and *Penthouse* have lost thousands of retail outlets for their wares in the last few years. We have cost them their legitimacy.

The bad news is that we are in trouble. There is much violence against us, pornography-inspired. They make us, our bodies, pornography in their magazines, and tell the normal men to get us good. We are followed, attacked, threatened. Bullets were shot into one feminist antipornography center. Feminists have been harassed out of their homes, forced to move. And the pornographers have found a bunch of girls (as the women call themselves) to work for them: not the chickenshit liberals, but real collaborators who have organized specifically to oppose the civil rights legislation and to protect the pornographers from our political activism—pornography should not be a feminist issue, these so-called feminists say. They say: Pornography is misogynist *but*... The *but* in this case is that it derepresses us. The victims of pornography can testify, and have, that when men get derepressed, women get hurt. These women say they are feminists. Some have worked for the defeated Equal Rights Amendment or for abortion rights or for equal pay or for lesbian and gay rights. But these days, they organize to stop us from stopping the pornographers.

Most of the women who say they are feminists but work to protect pornography are lawyers or academics: lawyers like the ones who walked away from *Snuff*; academics who think prostitution is romantic, an unrepressed female sexuality. But whoever they are, whatever they think they are doing, the outstanding fact about them is that they are ignoring the women who have been hurt in order to help the pimps who do the hurting. They are collaborators, not feminists.

The pornographers may well destroy us. The violence against us—in the pornography, in the general media, among men—is escalating rapidly and dangerously. Sometimes our despair is horrible. We haven't given in yet. There is a resistance here, a real one. I can't tell you how brave and brilliant the resisters are. Or how powerless and hurt. Surely it is clear: the most powerless women, the most exploited women, are the women fighting the pornographers. Our more privileged sisters prefer not to take sides. It's a nasty fight, all right. Feminism is dying here because so many women who say they are feminists are collaborators or cowards. Feminism is magnificent and militant here because the most powerless women are putting their lives on the line to confront the most powerful men for the sake of all women. Be proud of us for fighting. Be proud of us for getting so far. Help us if you can. The pornographers will have to stop us. We will not give in. They know that and now so do you.

Love,
Andrea Dworkin

EPILOGUE

In the seventies, rebellion died away and
criticism fell silent. Feminism was an
exception, but this movement began much
earlier and will surely continue for several
decades more. It is a process that belongs to
the realm of the "long count." Although it
has lost some of its impetus in the last few
years, it is a phenomenon destined to endure
and to change history.

Octavio Paz, *One Earth, Four or Five Worlds*

EPILOGUE

Feminism Now

1987

The Sunday Times in London wanted my views on the current state of feminism. Here they are. The newspaper on its own decided to print about one-third of what I wrote. There were a bunch of thoughts from other feminists published too, also cut off at the knees I assume. No one else mentioned sexual violence—or was it edited out? I would like to know. This is my full text, all three paragraphs. This has never been published in the United States in any form.

FEMINISM IS IN crisis. Choices must be made. Will the Women's Movement be an authentic liberation movement for women, a force for the egalitarian redistribution of power, resources, and opportunity; or will feminism be a polite nudge toward superficial reform, mostly of manners, sometimes of social or legal codes or practices? Will feminism be a political movement that confronts the power of men over women in order to dismantle that power; or will feminism be a "lifestyle" choice, a post-modernist fad, a cyclically noted fashion?

Will feminism devote itself to the *elimination*, not the containment, of rape, battery, incest, prostitution, and pornography, the most egregious violations of women's human rights; or will feminists settle for nearly everyone saying how much they deplore the violence as the violence continues unabated? Will feminism continue the difficult and costly politics of confrontation—rebellion against the power of men in public and in private, resistance to a status quo that takes the civil inferiority of women to be natural, sexy, and a piece of political trivia; or will an élite of women, annointed to influence (not power) by the media, keep demonstrating (so that the rest of us will learn) how to talk nice and pretty to men, how to ask them politely and in a feminine tone to stop exploiting us?

In the United States, there is a feminist establishment, twenty years in the making, media-created and media-controlled, that is fairly corrupt, bought out by the privilege of its own prominence. There is also a grassroots feminism in every nook and cranny of this vast and diverse country with its complex physical and ethnic geography. This grassroots feminism is strong, brave, militant, enduring, creative, economically impoverished, and socially dispossessed. At this point in time, this is the feminism of moral and political significance out of which comes action, truth, and hope. I don't know if this grassroots feminism will be crushed or if it will prevail. Right now, it is an honest resistance movement. Here we have neither a revolutionary nor a reform movement; we have an organized resistance, sometimes above ground, sometimes underground, to male dominance. I think we will last a long time, at great cost. In a time of political resistance, endurance is everything.

AFTERWORD

Still harping on the same subject, you will
exclaim—How can I avoid it, when most of
the struggles of an eventful life have been
occasioned by the oppressed state of my sex:
we reason deeply, when we forcibly feel.

> Mary Wollstonecraft, *Letters
> Written During a Short Residence
> in Sweden, Norway, and Denmark*
> (Letter XIX)

In the long months of confinement, I often
thought of how to transmit the pain that a
tortured person undergoes. And always I
concluded that it was impossible.

It is a pain without points of reference,
revelatory symbols, or clues to serve as
indicators.

> Jacobo Timerman, *Prisoner
> Without a Name, Cell Without a
> Number*

What Battery
Really Is

1989

On November 1, 1987, Joel Steinberg, a criminal defense lawyer, beat his illegally adopted daughter, Lisa, 6, into a coma. She died on November 5. Hedda Nussbaum, who had lived with Steinberg since 1976, was also in the apartment. She had a gangrenous leg from his beatings; her face and body were deformed from his assaults on her. With Lisa lying on the bathroom floor, Steinberg went out for dinner and drinks. Nussbaum remained in the apartment. When Steinberg came home, he and Nussbaum freebased cocaine. Early the next morning, Lisa stopped breathing, and Nussbaum called 911. She was arrested with Steinberg. She was given immunity for testifying against him. Steinberg had started beating Nussbaum in 1978; in that year alone, according to Newsday, she suffered at least ten black eyes. In 1981, he ruptured her spleen. During this time, she worked as a children's book editor at Random House. She was fired in 1982 for missing too much work. Socially speaking, she was disappeared; she got buried alive in torture.

Susan Brownmiller, author of Against Our Will: Men, Women and Rape and a founder of Women Against Pornography, began a media crusade against Nussbaum. She blamed Nussbaum not only for Lisa's death but also for being battered herself. Hearing Susan take this stand had a devastating impact on me. I began to have flashbacks to when I was battered: to when it was impossible for me to make anyone believe me or help me. Susan was denying the reality of battery just as my friends, neighbors, and acquaintances had done, just as doctors had done, just as police had done, when I was trying to escape from being physically and mentally tortured. Flashbacks are different from memories. They take over the conscious mind.

They are like seizures—involuntary, outside time, vivid, almost three-dimensional; you can't stop one once it starts. You relive an event, a trauma, a piece of your own history, with a precision of detail almost beyond belief—the air is the same—you are there and it is happening. I wrote this piece to try to stop the flashbacks.

Newsweek *accepted this piece for publication. Then* Newsweek's *lawyer halted its publication. The lawyer said I had to prove it. I had to have medical records, police records, a written statement from a doctor who had seen the injuries I describe here. I had to corroborate my story. Or I had to publish this anonymously to protect the identity of the batterer; or I couldn't say I had been married—to protect the identity of the batterer; and I had to take out any references to specific injuries unless I could document them, prove them. Outside evidence. Objective proof. I asked* Newsweek *when the freedom of speech I kept hearing about was going to apply to me; I asked* Newsweek *when the batterer was going to stop having control over my life—over what I can say, what I can do.*

The Los Angeles Times *published this article on March 12, 1989. The same week, I read about the murder of Lisa Bianco. Ms. Bianco was twenty-nine. She was killed by a batterer, her ex-husband, who was on an eight-hour prison furlough. Prison authorities were supposed to tell her if he was ever let out because she knew he would kill her. They didn't. Guess they didn't believe her. "Indeed,"* The New York Times *reported, "prison officials said that on paper Mr. Matheney did not look as dangerous as Ms. Bianco said he was." She had been preparing to change her identity, go underground, on his release from prison, which was a year off. Lisa Bianco escaped. She hid, wore disguises, got protection orders, had security guards escort her to classes at Indiana University. After her divorce, the batterer still showed up to beat her savagely (my own experience as well). Once he kidnapped and raped her. She prosecuted him. He plea-bargained so that the rape and assault charges were dropped to a single count of battery. Largely because he had also kidnapped their children, he was sentenced to eight years in prison, three of them suspended. She did things right; she was exceptionally brave; she could have proven everything to* Newsweek's *lawyer; she's dead. Escaped or captive, you are his prey. Most of us who have been hurt by these men need to hide more than we need proof. We learn fast that the system won't protect us—it only endangers us more—so we hide from the man and from the system—the hospitals, the police, the courts—the places where you get the proof. I still hide. It's not easy*

*for a public person, but I do it. I'm a master of it. I don't have any proof,
but I'm still alive—for now.*

*Now, about being a writer: are there other writers in the United States
whose freedom is constantly threatened by murder or beatings; whose lives
are threatened day in, day out; who risk their lives in publishing a piece
like this one? There are: women hurt by men, especially husbands or fathers.
What is Newsweek or PEN or the ACLU doing for writers like us?
Following is the piece that was accepted, then declined, by Newsweek; it
was subsequently published in The Los Angeles Times in a slightly
different form.*

My FRIEND AND colleague Susan Brownmiller does not want
Hedda Nussbaum to be "exonerated"—something no battered woman ever is, even if a child has not died. Gangsters are
given new identities, houses, bank accounts, and professions when
they testify against criminals meaner, bigger, and badder than they
are. Rapists and murderers plea-bargain. Drug dealers get immunity. Batterers rarely spend a night in jail; the same goes for pimps.
But Susan feels that Nussbaum should have been prosecuted, and
a perception is growing that Nussbaum is responsible legally and
morally for the death of Lisa Steinberg.

I don't think Hedda Nussbaum is "innocent." I don't know any
innocent adult women; life is harder than that for everyone. But
adult women who have been battered are especially not innocent.
Battery is a forced descent into hell and you don't get by in hell by
moral goodness. You disintegrate. You don't survive as a discrete
personality with a sense of right and wrong. You live in a world of
pure pain, in isolation, on the verge of death, in terror; and when
you get numb enough not to care whether you live or die you are
experiencing the only grace God is going to send your way. Drugs
help.

I was battered when I was married, and there are some things I
wish people would understand. I thought things had changed, but
it is clear from the story of Hedda Nussbaum that nothing much
has changed at all.

Your neighbors hear you screaming. They do nothing. The next day they look right through you. If you scream for years they will look right through you for years. Your neighbors, friends, and family see the bruises and injuries and they do nothing. They will not intercede. They send you back. They say it's your fault or that you like it or they deny that it is happening at all. Your family believes you belong with your husband.

If you scream and no one helps and no one acknowledges it and people look right through you, you begin to feel that you don't exist. If you existed and you screamed, someone would help you. If you existed and you were visibly injured, someone would help you. If you existed and you asked for help in escaping, someone would help you.

When you go to the doctor or to the hospital because you are badly injured and they won't listen or help you or they give you tranquilizers or threaten to commit you because they say you are disoriented, paranoid, fantasizing, you begin to believe that he can hurt you as much as he wants and no one will help you. When the police refuse to help you, you begin to believe that he can hurt or kill you and it will not matter because you do not exist.

You become unable to use language because it stops meaning anything. If you use regular words and say you have been hurt and by whom and you point to visible injuries and you are treated as if you made it up or as if it doesn't matter or as if it is your fault or as if you are stupid and worthless, you become afraid to try to say anything. You cannot talk to anyone because they will not help you and if you talk to them, the man who is battering you will hurt you more. Once you lose language, your isolation is absolute.

Eventually I waited to die. I wanted to die. I hoped the next beating would kill me, or the one after that. When I would come to after being beaten unconscious, the first feeling I would have was an overwhelming sorrow that I was alive. I would ask God please to let me die now. My breasts were burned with lit cigarettes. He beat my legs with a heavy wood beam so that I couldn't walk. I was present when he did immoral things to other people; I was present when he hurt other people. I didn't help them. Judge me, Susan.

A junkie said he would give me a ticket to far away and $1,000 if I would carry a briefcase through customs. I said I would. I knew it had heroin in it, and I kept hoping I would be caught and sent to jail because in jail he couldn't beat me. I had been sexually abused in The Women's House of Detention in New York City (arrested for an anti–Vietnam War demonstration) so I didn't have the idea that jail was a friendly place. I just hoped I would get five years and for five years I could sit in a jail cell and not be hit by him. In the end the junkie didn't give me the briefcase to carry, so I didn't get the $1,000. He did kindly give me the ticket. I stole the money I needed. Escape is heroic, isn't it?

I've been living with a kind and gentle man I love for the last fifteen years. For eight of those years, I would wake up screaming in blind terror in the night, not knowing who I was, where I was, who he was; cowering and shaking. I'm more at peace now, but I've refused until recently to have my books published in the country where my former husband lives, and I've refused invitations to go there—important professional invitations. Once I went there in secret for four days to try to face it down. I couldn't stop trembling and sweating in fear; I could barely breathe. There isn't a day when I don't feel fear that I will see him and he will hurt me.

Death looks different to a woman who has been battered; it seems not nearly so cruel as life. I'm upset by what I regard as the phony, false mourning for Lisa Steinberg—the sentimental and hypocritical mourning of a society that would not really mind her being beaten to death once she was an adult woman. If Lisa hadn't died, she would be on West Tenth Street being tortured—now. Why was it that we wanted her to live? So that when the child became a woman and she was raped or beaten or prostituted we could look right through her? It's bad to hit a girl before she's of age. It's bad to torture a girl before she's of age. Then she's of age and, well, it isn't so bad. By then, she wants it, she likes it, she chose it. Why are adult women hated so much and why is it all right to hurt us? Those who love children but don't think adult women deserve much precisely because we are not innocent—we are used and compromised and culpable—should try to remember this: the only way to have helped Lisa Steinberg was to have helped Hedda Nussbaum. But to do it, you would have had to care that an adult woman was being hurt: care enough to rescue her. And there was a little boy there too, remember him, all tied up and covered in feces. The only way to have spared him was to rescue Hedda. Now he has been tortured and he did not die. He will grow up to be some kind of a man: which kind? I wish there was a way to take the hurt from him. There isn't. Is there a way to stop him from becoming a batterer? Is there?

Copyright Information

"The Lie," first published in *New Women's Times*, Vol. 5, No. 21, November 9–22, 1979. Copyright © 1979 by Andrea Dworkin. "The Night and Danger," copyright © 1979 by Andrea Dworkin. "Pornography and Grief," first published in *New Women's Times*, Vol. 4, No. 11, December 1978. Copyright © 1978 by Andrea Dworkin. "The Power of Words," first published in *Massachusetts Daily Occupied Collegian*, Vol. 1, No. 1, May 8, 1978. Copyright © 1978 by Andrea Dworkin. "A Woman Writer and Pornography," first published in *San Francisco Review of Books*, Vol. VI, No. 5, March-April 1981. Copyright © 1980 by Andrea Dworkin. "Whose Press? Whose Freedom?" first published in *The Women's Review of Books*, Vol. 1, No. 4, January 1984. Copyright © 1983 by Andrea Dworkin. Preface to *Our Blood*, in *Our Blood: Prophecies and Discourses on Sexual Politics* (New York: Perigee Books, 1981). Copyright © 1981 by Andrea Dworkin. "Nervous Interview," first published in *Chrysalis*, No. 10, May 1980. Copyright © 1978 by Andrea Dworkin. "Loving Books: Male/Female/Feminist," first published in *Hot Wire*, Vol. 1, No. 3, July 1985. Copyright © 1985 by Andrea Dworkin. "Mourning Tennessee Williams," first published in slightly changed form under the title, "Tennessee Williams' Legacy," in *Ms.*, Vol. XI, No. 12, June 1983. Copyright © 1983 by Andrea Dworkin. "*Wuthering Heights*," copyright © 1987 by Andrea Dworkin. "*Voyage in the Dark*: Hers and Ours," copyright © 1987 by Andrea Dworkin. "A Feminist Looks at Saudi Arabia," copyright © 1978 by Andrea Dworkin. "A Battered Wife Survives," first published under the title, "The Bruise That Doesn't Heal," in *Mother Jones*, Vol. III, No. VI, July 1978. Copyright © 1978 by Andrea Dworkin. "A True and Commonplace Story," copyright © 1978 by Andrea Dworkin. "Biological Superi-